Post-Pandemic Leadership

This book shows readers how to rethink and reimagine leadership and charts a course towards a new vision of leadership. It outlines lessons to be learned for leadership – not only after the COVID pandemic but also in light of other ongoing crises around issues such as climate change and global inequality.

The pandemic has shone a harsh spotlight not just on the leaders of organisations but on the concept of leadership itself and the way we lead. Many of those who were in positions of power before the crisis have been found wanting; too often, our idols have turned out to have feet of clay. But does the problem lie with the leaders themselves, or do the roots of the problem lie deeper? Do we need to start rethinking and reimagining the kind of leadership we will need in a post–COVID world? *Post-Pandemic Leadership* brings voices from every sector to demonstrate what changes we can make in order to make leadership fit for purpose in the twenty-first century.

Illustrating a need for a radical change in leadership, with leaders focusing much more on human relationships, kindness, fairness, well-being and a general sense of responsibility, this book will be of interest to both established leaders and the next generation of leaders in education and in practice.

Morgen Witzel is a lecturer and Fellow of the Exeter Centre for Leadership at The University of Exeter Business School, UK. His recent publications include *Management: The Basics, 2nd edition* (Routledge 2022) and *A History of Leadership* (Routledge 2019).

Post-Pandemic Leadership

Exploring Solutions to a Crisis

Edited by Morgen Witzel

Routledge
Taylor & Francis Group

LONDON AND NEW YORK

Cover image: © Getty Images

First published 2022
by Routledge
4 Park Square, Milton Park, Abingdon, Oxon OX14 4RN

and by Routledge
605 Third Avenue, New York, NY 10158

Routledge is an imprint of the Taylor & Francis Group, an informa business

British Library Cataloguing-in-Publication Data
A catalogue record for this book is available from the British Library

Library of Congress Cataloging-in-Publication Data
A catalog record for this book has been requested

ISBN: 978-0-367-77515-5 (hbk)
ISBN: 978-0-367-77514-8 (pbk)
ISBN: 978-1-003-17173-7 (ebk)

DOI: 10.4324/9781003171737

Typeset in Times New Roman
by Apex CoVantage, LLC

Contents

Contributors

Anthony Bash is an honorary professor of theology at Durham University, where he teaches biblical studies at undergraduate and postgraduate level. His specialism is reconciliation, forgiveness and remorse. He has published six books and a number of articles and is a (non-practising) solicitor. He has also taught business law at Durham University.

Richard Bolden is Professor of Leadership and Management at Bristol Business School, University of the West of England. His teaching and research explore the interface between individual and collective approaches to leadership and leadership development. He has published on topics including distributed, shared and systems leadership; leadership paradoxes and complexity; cross-cultural leadership; and leadership and change in healthcare and higher education. He is director of Bristol Leadership and Change Centre and associate editor of the journal *Leadership*.

Mike Cladingbowl has been a senior leader in education for over 25 years. After success as a secondary school headteacher, he was appointed one of Her Majesty's Inspectors of schools, children's services and skills in 2002. After specialising in school improvement, he worked in senior executive roles for Ofsted. His latter roles included leading inspection reform in England. He returned to school leadership in a small multi-academy trust in early 2015.

Ciara Eastell OBE was the founding Chief Executive of Libraries Unlimited and has a long track record in the library sector. She now works as professor of practice in the Exeter Centre for Leadership and has been working for the past year as interim director of people and culture at the Tate in London. Ciara is a Fellow of the Clore Leadership Programme and sits on the National Council of Arts Council England.

Justin Featherstone MC is a leadership consultant, expedition leader and both a Leadership Fellow at the University of Exeter Business School and a Fellow of the Royal Geographical Society. A former major in The Princess of Wales's Royal Regiment, he was awarded the Military Cross for gallantry while commanding a company in Iraq in 2004. Justin has led and participated in over thirty overseas expeditions to the mountains, rivers and rainforests of the world.

Tanmoy Goswami writes about the global mental health movement and his own journey through mental illness as the sanity correspondent at *The Correspondent*. Earlier, he was Associate Editor at *Economic Times Prime*, and head of desk at *Fortune* magazine's Indian edition. Tanmoy is a winner of IE Business School's Asian Journalism Prize. He lives in New Delhi.

Keith Grint is Professor Emeritus at Warwick University, where he was Professor of Public Leadership until 2018. He spent ten years working in various positions across a number of industry sectors before switching to an academic career. He has held chairs at Cranfield University and Lancaster University, and was Director of the Lancaster Leadership Centre. He spent twelve years at Oxford University and was Director of Research at the Saïd Business School. His latest book, *Mutiny and Leadership*, is due out in late 2020.

Liam Hartley is a data engineer working for Sainsbury plc, and has previously worked with excellent leaders in data departments at Schroders. He has a master's degree in physics from a Russell Group University and is passionate about finding signals amongst the noise.

Lucie Hartley has worked in the health and social care sector for over thirty years. For eleven of those years, she was chief executive of a Devon-based drug and alcohol charity, which grew during her tenure from a small charity to one of the largest charities in the southwest of England. A Fellow the Exeter Centre for Leadership, Lucie is particularly interested in system-based and collaborative leadership models.

William S. Harvey is Professor of Leadership at the University of Bristol. He is an International Research Fellow at the Oxford Centre for Corporate Reputation and Chair of the Board of Libraries Unlimited. Will advises leaders on reputation, talent management and leadership. His work has appeared in *Harvard Business Review*, *Journal of Management Studies*, *Human Relations* and the *British Journal of Management*, and has been featured in the *Financial Times*, Institute of Directors, Bloomberg and *Wired*. He received a first-class degree from the University of Durham, an MPhil with distinction and PhD from the University of Cambridge.

Gay Haskins is an associate fellow of the Said Business School, University of Oxford. She was formerly Dean of Executive Education at Said Business School and also at London Business School and the Indian School of Business in Hyderabad.

Alison Hogan is a systemic coach and facilitator to senior leaders and teams seeking to lead wisely and collaboratively and be a force for good through a time of radical uncertainty. She was formerly head of global media and PR at Unilever; a director with Brunswick, a strategic advisory firm focused on critical issues; and a business journalist with the *Daily Mail* and the *Financial Times*. She is a Fellow of the Exeter Centre for Leadership.

Simon Hollington's first career was in the Royal Marines, where he saw service in Northern Ireland, worked with both the UN and NATO, was part of the central planning staff for the First Gulf War (experiencing the workings of the Ministry of Defence during a national crisis), and played a key role in the headquarters that supported British Forces during the Balkans conflict. For the last twenty-five years, he has worked closely with a variety of UK and global businesses from FTSE 100 companies to SMEs, helping them tackle the complex challenge of leadership.

Clare Holt worked in Air Traffic Services with NATS Ltd (formerly National Air Traffic Services) as an operational air traffic controller before obtaining her PhD from Warwick Business School. Her main area of interest, research and writing is around the subject of relational leadership. This includes blame versus just culture, the importance of constructive dissent and difficult/effective conversations, complex problems and engaging individuals to work more effectively together. Advisory roles include supporting the Doctors

Association UK (DAUK) and the General Medical Council in the areas of just culture, effective communication and professional behaviours.

Alan Hooper is a former senior Royal Marines officer and founder of the Centre for Leadership Studies at Exeter University, where he remains a fellow. He served in the Ministry of Defence in 1982 and was at the centre for the plans to retake the Falkland Islands. He was also formerly a member of the faculty of the Institute of General Practice at Exeter University.

Alison Hooper's career spans thirty years, starting in Moss Side, Manchester, where her interest in development education began. She moved to Cheshire as a deputy headteacher at a large primary school. In 2005, she took up post as headteacher of a primary school in Cheshire. She is a Founding Fellow of the Chartered College of Teaching and her commitment to shared leadership and desire for excellence has resulted in her school being formally recognised by the British Council as a school of excellence for global learning. She has an MA in Development Education and is a British Council Ambassador.

Lauren Kirigin is a recent graduate of McGill University's BCom program with distinction in honours in investment management. She is an analyst with the Investment Banking Division at Credit Suisse Securities in Toronto.

Ian MacQueen opened his first grocery store at the age of 18 and spent much of the rest of his career in retailing, beginning with British Home Stores. He held directorships in a number of well-known UK companies and retired from mainstream corporate life as Group Managing Director of Fiskars UK. He currently runs an online retail company, which has since expanded several times. Ian is also a trustee and chair of a number of charities, including St John Ambulance in East Devon, as well as a governor of a large academy trust, and chairman of his local chamber of commerce.

Tawanda Mhindurwa is a multimedia journalist with a master's degree from the University of Westminster. He is one of the founders of the Precious Innovations Ubuntu Global Charitable Trust Zimbabwe, focusing on community outreach programs in health, education with social services focusing on women and the girl child. As the marketing and transmissions officer, he was in the inaugural team that launched the first commercial talk radio station in Harare, Capitalk FM, in 2017. Tawanda also worked as an account executive at DDH&M and Dicomm Mcann. One of his career highlights was being part of a team that interviewed The Elders on BBC News Global in 2015. He has produced and presented documentaries on men's mental health and colorism in the black community and women in entertainment.

Karl Moore is an associate professor at McGill University in Montreal. He was a Fellow/ Associate Fellow at Green Templeton College for over 20 years. His next book, *It's OK, Boomer: How to Effectively Work With Millennials/Generation Z*, will be published by the McGill Queen's Press, Autumn 2021.

Eve Poole is the Third Church Estates Commissioner for England, Chairman of the Board of Governors at Gordonstoun and Ashridge Adjunct Faculty at Hult International Business School. She has a BA from Durham, an MBA from Edinburgh, and a PhD in theology and capitalism from Cambridge. Her recent books are *Leadersmithing, Capitalism's Toxic Assumptions* and *Buying God*.

Stefan Stern is a former *Financial Times* columnist and now visiting professor in management practice at Cass Business School, City, University of London. He is the author (with

Prof Cary Cooper) of *Myths of Management: What People Get Wrong About Being the Boss* (Kogan Page 2017) and *How To Be a Better Leader* (2019).

Mike Thomas is Chair of the Morecambe Bay NHS Foundation and a visiting professor at the University of Chester. Formerly, he was Vice-Chancellor of the University of Central Lancashire.

Graham Wilson works in financial services for a FTSE 100 company. He studied history at the University of Glasgow, looking at past leaders in the modern and medieval periods, and enjoys finding out lessons that can be learnt from history.

Morgen Witzel is an internationally known writer on management and leadership. His most recent books are *The Ethical Leader* (2018) and *A History of Leadership* (Routledge 2019). He is a Fellow of the Exeter Centre for Leadership and lectures at the University of Exeter Business School, and also at the University of Edinburgh and Audencia Nantes.

Illustrations

Figures

Tables

1 Introduction

Morgen Witzel

*

We are in the middle of a perfect storm. Global pandemic, the onrushing environmental disaster, rampant inequality and the rise of authoritarianism loom over us. Old certainties and old faiths about society, community, organisations and leadership are being challenged. Emotionally, it feels like the future is probably more uncertain than it has been at any point in our lifetimes. Rationally, that is probably not true – for one thing, how do you measure uncertainty? – but there is a feeling of existential threat nonetheless.

In times of crisis, we look to our leaders. We ask questions of them: what are they going to do about the problems? How are they going to help us? Where are they going to lead us? But increasingly, it seems our leaders are just as much in the dark as the rest of us. Alarmingly few of them seem to have any plan for dealing with the crisis, or if they do have one, they aren't communicating with the rest of us. Do our leaders actually know how to lead in the modern world, or are they still clinging to outdated models like command and control in hopes that if they shout loudly enough, someone will listen and obey their orders?

It is relatively easy to lead when times are good, the economy is stable, society is functioning more or less as normal and we can predict the short-term future, at least, with a moderate amount of certainty. But crisis is the true test of a leader. To borrow a metaphor from Warren Buffett, when the tide goes out, that's when you find out who has been swimming naked. The pandemic and the other crises have exposed the weaknesses of many people in positions of leadership.

Blaming individuals for failures of leadership is easy; too easy. The problem lies much deeper than just the leaders themselves. It lies in our own expectations of leadership, how we define it, what we expect leaders to do. It lies in how we train, develop and select leaders, and the qualities we mistakenly look for in a leader, like authority and decisiveness and charisma. It lies in what we all – leaders included – think makes the ideal leader. Above all, it lies in the long-standing view that leadership is something that is inherent in leaders, a quality that radiates out from them. Leadership is something we do *to* people, not *with* them.

And that view of leadership is not longer good enough, if it ever was. The title of this book, *Post-Pandemic Leadership: Exploring Solutions to a Crisis*, has two meanings. We talk here about leadership lessons from the crisis, but we also believe that leadership itself is in crisis. We need to fundamentally rethink the nature of how we lead, and how we teach and train others to lead. That is what this book is about. It discusses concepts like kindness, humility, fairness, trust and service, and argues that these are the fundamental platform on which leadership is built. If we are to get through the crisis and build a better, fairer world, we need a new kind of leadership and a new kind of leader.

DOI: 10.4324/9781003171737-1

Origins

The idea for this book arose during an online meeting of the Fellows of the Exeter Centre for Leadership during the early days of the COVID pandemic in 2020. The Fellows are a network of professionals from many different backgrounds who support the Centre and the University of Exeter Business School more generally, and one of the purposes of the meeting was to see what, if anything, we could do to respond to the crisis.

These were particularly dark times; hospitalisation rates and death tolls were rising sharply, the UK and most of the rest of the world was under severe lockdown, little was understood about the nature and spread of the disease, and vaccination looked a very long way off. The group was determined, however, to find a silver lining and to do something positive. What lessons could be learned from the crisis? What could we do to make a positive contribution?

Comparing notes from our various perspectives, one of the things we all noticed was how the 'official' recognised leaders in a wide range of organisations were struggling to cope with the demands of the crisis. But there was something else. When these leaders failed, others stepped in to fill the void. Community volunteers, doctors and nurses on COVID wards, teachers in beleaguered schools, workers adapting to working from home – all found that when their official leaders failed them, the only thing left was to step up and take the reins oneself.

Other books will hopefully tell the story of these tens of thousand of unsung heroes who got us through the initial stages of the crisis. Our purpose is not to write a history of leadership during the pandemic, but to look at the lessons for leadership and think about some ways of re-imagining leadership in the future. When commissioning this book, we went out to look for people with very different perspectives on leadership, who could suggest different directions going forward. The brief we gave them was simple: we want to see something different, new ways of thinking about and doing leadership.

The contributors come from many different backgrounds: academia, business, journalism, the education and arts sectors, charities, the armed forces. Some were on the front line during the pandemic, or had access to front-line sources; others don't mention it at all. Some of the chapters are academic and scholarly; others are commentaries or are based on personal experience. Some of the authors are household names in their fields, thought leaders and respected authorities; others are young, first-time writers who write from the perspective of the future of leadership, not its past. Some of the people we originally approached and who were full of enthusiasm for the project were not in the end able to contribute; writing chapters for a book like this was never going to be easy, but writing during a pandemic brought its own special pressures. As a result, some subjects which were dear to our hearts have been left out of the book. To everyone who supported this project in whatever way, we say a heartfelt thank you.

Structure of the book

We have divided the chapters into two parts, although there is considerable overlap between the parts in terms of chapter content. Part I, 'Reflections on Leadership in Crisis', is a mix of personal accounts and commentaries on the nature of the crisis and how 'traditional' leadership is failing us.

In Chapter 2, Justin Featherstone recounts his experiences among the Konyak people of Nagaland. The history of the Konyaks is one of near continuous warfare and raiding, and danger was ever-present; the sort of society where we would assume that authoritarian leadership was necessary for survival. That assumption would be wrong. What Justin found instead was a form of leadership based on kindness and respect for others. 'Kindness is so important in a good leader', one of the Konyak elders tells him. 'Leaders who lack the quality of kindness cannot build the true relationships that ensure the success of a community.' The lesson is that in a time of crisis, good leaders concentrate on building communities that can survive the test.

Another quality essential to good leadership is fairness and equity. According to Gay Haskins and Mike Thomas in Chapter 3, fairness is essential to creating trust, which in turn leads to greater engagement and a share sense of purpose. All too often, fairness is a casualty of leadership; leaders who try to be fair to everyone are seen as being weak. But in a world where inequality is rampant, be in terms of educational opportunities, chance for job advancement or access to vaccines, fairness has become something to be prized. Fair leaders tend also to be trusted leaders.

The arguments made by Justin, Gay and Mike would seem to be unassailable; so why, ask Keith Grint and Clare Holt, do we continue to respect leaders who aren't up to the job? Why do we support the charismatic narcissists who make promises they cannot keep? There is a tendency, they say in Chapter 4, to put our faith in individuals rather than systems, and despite the lessons of history, we keep repeating the same mistake. Their dissection of global failures in the response to COVID is strong evidence for the argument that not only do we pick the wrong leaders, but we also need to think again about what we expect of our leaders and what leadership actually is.

Alan Hooper also questions in Chapter 5 whether we are right to place our hopes in individuals. In his comparative study of two crises, the COVID pandemic and the Falklands War in 1982, Alan suggests that the response to crisis depends on things such as thorough advance planning – even if the plan later has to be substantially adapted – and rapid response when the crisis strikes. Some leaders are capable of responding to crisis, others are not. Systems, rather than individuals, are what often make the difference. Systems are resilient; many people are not.

Building on this, Ian MacQueen argues in Chapter 6 that in times of crisis, compassion, empathy and integrity are among the most valuable attributes a leader can possess. Like Keith and Clare, Ian is sharply critical of 'messianic' leaders who promise to lead us to a shining future; very seldom are those promises kept. Instead, he points approvingly to local initiatives and leaders who step into the breach and build strong communities. 'What has been conceived as effective leadership practices in the past may not work in the future', Ian warns, calling for leaders to be people of character and judgement rather than charisma.

This argument is reinforced by Stefan Stern, who calls in Chapter 7 for the dismantling of 'leadership myths' and a new vision of leadership to embrace the radical uncertainty of our times. Among the myths Stefan dismantles are: 1) the people want a heroic figure out front; 2) the big picture is most important; 3) 'boosterism' will carry people along; and 4) men make the most successful, assertive leaders. None of these things is remotely true, says Stefan, and the pandemic has shown all four to be myths. Will these old beliefs about leadership disappear in the aftermath of the epidemic? Human nature being what it is, there is no way of knowing for certain, but there is an opportunity for us to re-invent leadership – should we care to take it.

The counterpunch to Stefan's article comes from Tawanda Mhindurwa, who issues in Chapter 8 a clarion call for leadership in Africa to become more responsive to the needs of the people. 'How do we begin creating the continent that will not leave anyone behind, and serve its peoples' aspirations before selfish needs?' he asks. 'What is standing in the way of

Africa being great?' The answer, he argues, is Africa's leaders who are not only failing to lead progress but in some cases are actively hindering it. Many of the arguments Tawanda makes about Africa can be applied to other parts of the world, as well – including, I submit, the developed West. We have all suffered under leaders who hold us back. It is time for change.

Part II of the book, 'Future Directions', discusses some of the future directions for that change. We begin with Alison Hogan's discussion in Chapter 9 of lessons to be learned from philosophical anarchism. We often think of anarchism as being an absence of leadership, but as Alison points out, leadership actually plays an important role in anarchism. Unlike conventional leadership, in anarchism power is heavily distributed and is exercised through networks rather than individuals. Community leadership has real power, but often that power is latent, buried beneath the weight of bureaucracy and top-down command and control. Clearing away these weighty and inefficient structures can allow leadership to flourish.

Taking a different angle, Eve Poole and Anthony Bash argue in Chapter 10 that leadership should be treated like a craft rather than profession, and focus on what leaders need to do rather than conceptual views of what leadership is. Among a number of key leadership tasks, they identify issues such as taking responsibility and managing ambiguity, but they also point out that leaders need to accept they will not get it right every time. Conventional wisdom suggests that failure is unacceptable in a leader, but the reality is that all leaders fail at some point, and what really matters is how they handle failure. Candour and the swift making of amends are important to rebuild relationships and refashion trust, and one of the ultimate tests of a leader is how well they live and embody their values.

Picking up on some of the points made in earlier chapters, Lucie Hartley and Richard Bolden in Chapter 11 look at why we default towards toxic types of leadership and compare this to the drivers behind drug and alcohol addiction. Changing our mental models of leadership, they argue, is akin to the process of recovery. They describe how the behaviours of toxic leaders create dependence on the part of followers and show how some of the techniques of recovery can be used to reduce that dependence and show us the limitations of so-called 'heroic' leadership. One of the conclusions we can draw from this chapter is that toxic leadership is bad for us in many ways, not least for our mental health.

Leaders themselves can become addicted to power, but power comes in different forms. In my own contribution, I argue in Chapter 12 that traditional leadership models concentrate on legal authority and the power to reward and punish. However, these forms of power are often inflexible, and as we saw during the pandemic, and thus are not well suited to leading through a crisis. I argue that other, softer forms of power based on personal skills and experience, and the ability to communicate the trust we engender in other people, are more reflexive and more adaptable, and it is these forms of power that leaders need to cultivate.

Tanmoy Goswami in Chapter 13 gives a practical case study of this in his study of psychotherapists during the pandemic and how they coped with the stresses of working in a time of fear and danger. One of the lessons is that therapists can't control everything and cannot make everything better. Tanmoy urges leaders to learn from this and to '[give] up the fantasy of omnipotence'. This is hard, because – harking back to Lucie and Richard's chapter – people often expect leaders to be omnipotent, and so leaders believe this is what they must do. But crisis offers us a chance to challenge our beliefs, and in the words of one of the therapists Tanmoy spoke to, 'learn that many of the so-called rules we tie ourselves to exist only in our mind.'

William S. Harvey looks next in Chapter 14 at issues around credibility. Leaders, he says, need to build relationships with multiple stakeholders, and he strongly links leaders to their organisations; leaders do not exist in a vacuum. Among other things, Will argues that trust and credibility are vital to establishing reputation, and also that leaders and organisations are judged on the basis of what they do, not just what they say. Boosterism and rhetoric will work against the leader unless words are backed up with actions. The need for trust and relationships has never been stronger, and all leaders need to put these at the centre of their thinking.

Those themes come through in the next group of chapters which focus on the experience of particular sectors. In her analysis of leadership in the arts sector, Ciara Eastell in Chapter 15 picks out the importance of transparency and honesty and also recounts experiences of the power of shared leadership and networks, and the importance of mental health. Ciara also suggests that leaders in this sector are increasingly embracing the most challenging issues of our time, including inequality and climate change. In the education sector, Mike Cladingbowl and Alison Hooper emphasise in Chapter 16 the importance of certainty and clarity. Crises breed uncertainty, which again can be dangerous in terms of trust relationships; for Mike and Alison, the key priority in a crisis was to create certainty and give reassurance to pupils and parents. Leaders need to be good communicators.

In the first of his two chapters, Simon Hollington looks in Chapter 17 at how the National Health Service in the UK responded to the crisis. He concludes that while many of the NHS's systems were inadequate to the task, the dedication and persistence of staff, especially frontline staff, allowed the service to cope with huge levels of demand. One of the key lessons he draws out are that leadership styles need to flex; there is no one-size-fits-all model. Rather than trying to find their own particular style, leaders need to be responsive to the demands of the situation. In his second chapter on the social enterprise sector, Simon argues in Chapter 18 for a more conscious approach to leadership with an emphasis on building a strong, resilient culture.

In the penultimate Chapter 19, Liam Hartley and Graham Wilson discuss how wellbeing and mental health became so important during the pandemic, and argue that wellbeing needs to be a priority for leaders. Evidence suggests that organisations that prioritise wellbeing perform better, and leaders who pay attention to employee wellbeing have a positive impact on their organisations. Leaders need to do more than just the bare minimum to ensure wellbeing; they need to make this a central part of their thinking.

Finally, Karl Moore and Lauren Kirigin in Chapter 20 explore changing expectations of leadership on the part of younger generations. Younger people are more comfortable with uncertainty and ambiguity, but they also demand more freedom. The pandemic, they say, offers us an opportunity to 'a chance to explore what we want out of life and re-evaluate the directions we are taking to create the future we want to see'. The older generation needs to recognise these changes, and at the same time be available as a source of wisdom to younger generations and help them to keep from re-inventing the wheel.

Taken together these chapters, we hope, offer some understanding of how and why leadership needs to change. We do not pretend to have all the answers. But we have, we hope, identified some of the important questions that need to be asked.

Part I

Reflections on Leadership in Crisis

2 Don't Lose Your Head

Resilience Through Kindness With the Konyaks of Nagaland

Justin Featherstone

***

Kindness is so important in a good leader, as I must speak softly with everyone to make a connection and making connections with people is what being a leader is all about. Leaders who lack the quality of kindness cannot build the true relationships that ensure the success of a community.

I listen intently to Tonpah as he quietly responds to my questions while making tea in bamboo cups over his open fire. The fire casts a gentle light that softens the glow of the three bare bulbs hanging from the rafters of the lofty longhouse. There are no windows, so the brilliant sunlight is shut outside but the indirect light available catches on the rows of animal skulls and weapons hanging from the soot-blackened walls of this old warrior's home. Perhaps little would seem remarkable about this conversation between this 101-year-old man, myself and my interpreter, except for the faded intricate green-blue tattoos that adorn most of Tonpah's face, leaving only the skin around his eye sockets bare. These distinct markings identify him as a Konyak warrior who has been part of a successful headhunting raid, and he is one of the last few surviving men who can talk to me about this long discontinued practice.

I had come to Nagaland in order to interview the last living Konyak headhunters to find out what the concept of leadership meant to them. This mountainous state in the northeast of India has a population of 2.4 million people and is home to the sixteen officially recognised Naga tribes.[1] My village home for three weeks was Sheanhagh Chingnyu, which is situated in Mon District, the northernmost district in the state and only a few hours' drive by road and rough track from the eponymous district capital. The village sits at 968 metres, dominating the surrounding land and echoing its martial history, with a clear view to the border with Myanmar only 8 kilometres away. The surrounding landscape is a series of forested hills and interlocking ridges, which rise to 2,700 metres at the summit of the highest peak in the state. Distant villages perch on top of their respective hilltops, with a patchwork of terraces and fields clearly visible around them; it is a truly beautiful and remote environment. I had deliberately chosen to spend my time here in the Lower Konyak region because of its distinct angh system and that fact its communities were among the very last to cease headhunting, at some point between the late 1950s and early 1960s. Throughout my stay, I lived with the family of my interpreter, Anyam Konyak, and his family, headed by his father, Nowang, and step-mother, Toingam, along with his grandmother and six younger siblings. Their welcome placed me at the heart of their family, and their clan status allowed me to an accelerated acceptance into the daily activities of the village and its kingdom.

DOI: 10.4324/9781003171737-3

For centuries, the villages within the seven principal competing Konyak kingdoms had conducted headhunting raids against each other. Even where there was no clear territorial or military advantage, attacks were made to take heads in the belief that powerful forces are contained within the skull and their ritual capture can bring fertility and prosperity (Von Fürer-Haimendorf, 1969, pp. 95–96; Hutton, 1928, p. 403). In addition, successful headhunting parties brought status to the individual warriors and their respective communities. These territories fell outside of the administered areas of the British colonial administration, which banned headhunting in 1935 and had long tried to forcibly impose negotiated peace between warring factions within its jurisdiction. As a result, headhunting in the Lower Konyak continued well into the twentieth century and decades after other Nagas had stopped the practice. I therefore wanted to understand how the Konyaks maintained both individual and communal resilience during prolonged hostilities across multiple generations, with a view to seeing whether this might inform my own views on leading in crises.

Sheanhagh Chingnyu is the centre of one of the seven kingdoms and was traditionally ruled with absolute power by the angh, or king, along with his anghya, or queen. The angh's appointment is established through a patrilineal system, which gives sovereignty to over 9,000 subjects, 4,000 of whom reside in his own village, while the other four constituent villages are ruled by appointed deputy-anghs, also belonging to the royal bloodline (Von Fürer-Haimendorf, 1938). The angh system is unique, amplified by the years of conflict-induced isolation leading to all major villages having their own very

Figure 2.1 Ngampe, Sheanhagh Chingnyu

distinct dialect, some being almost unintelligible to each other. The angh was seen as the embodiment of the community's power and spirit, or "life principle" (Hutton, 1965, p. 23), and this concept is seen in the common representation of anghs' spirit animals as supernaturally powerful tigers or lions. Today, official administrative authority lies with the democratically elected village chairman and the village council, of which the angh is a member in Sheanhagh Chingnyu. The council itself is an all-male assembly, although women are present through leadership roles in the church, Women's Self Help Group and Student Council.

As I settled into my first few of days in the village, it was easy to wonder what the place of strength, autocracy and physical presence had in the leadership culture of this martial patriarchy in which traditionally every man had been both warrior and farmer. I was hoping that my planned conversations with thirteen surviving face-tattooed warriors and any women who also remembered these times would help me find this understanding. I would then contrast this with the contemporary views of their children and grandchildren to see whether views on leadership had changed across the generations, as the initial novelty of peace endured. One of the first significant insights into the critical components of Konyak leadership came from Anyam's father in my first few days. Toingam was preparing a breakfast of rice and soya beans with chilli pickle on the cooking fire, when Nowang said to me, "Kindness is so important in a leader, but kindness should not be confused with taking the easy path. Leaders must take responsibility for doing the right thing." Just like Tonpah, Nowang saw kindness as an essential strength in any leader, angh or otherwise. He had also added a second component, showing moral courage. It became apparent that these two themes of gentleness and truth are central to the Konyak culture.

The brutal practice of headhunting was so integral to Konyak life that although there were times of peace and trade with enemy villages through brokered deals and occasional intermarriage, it was rare for there to be no hostilities with any other group at all. This was largely due to headhunting being an act of reciprocal violence, perhaps more akin to a feud, which often led to a form of balance. Remarkably, it was possible to be feuding with individual morungs (village wards) within other villages (Von Fürer-Haimendorf, 1969, p. 45; Jacobs, 2012, p. 139) while being on a peaceful accord with the rest of that same community. The compulsion to take heads for the success of the village ensured an almost constant war footing for hundreds of years. Villages were structured as military organisations and often found themselves in periods of constant operational readiness. Systems of watchtowers provided early warning and protection, both around the village and in the fields, and a number of warriors might be placed on permanent standby for at least part of the day. Some men even remembered a network of 2-metre-deep bunkers constructed to provide cover during attacks. Houses were locked from the inside at night and one of the reasons that homes traditionally had few, if any, windows was for protection during enemy raids. No one was safe as men, women and children were all considered legitimate targets. Although weeks or sometimes months might go by without an attack, the threat was always there. Casualties to raids conducted only for the purpose of taking heads were relatively low but when attacks were made for territorial expansion, the results could be horrific, albeit seemingly very rare. The British observer W.G Archer recorded two instances when whole villages had been wiped out in 1939 and 1948 respectively, leaving around 400 dead in each case (Jacobs, 2012, p. 142).

I considered what it would be like to live in such circumstances as I listened intently to Akhao recounting her experiences as a young woman. Her narration seemed incongruous within the domestic setting of her hut, a serene scene in which her son wove a bamboo basket

Figure 2.2 Akhao (Anyam's Grandmother)

and a puppy lay sprawled next to the embers of the slowly burning fire which was heating water for black tea.

> I remember we were always scared of enemy attack. Some times were worse than others, especially when we had just taken some heads. Attacks would not come every day, even though we might be worried about them all the time but we might be attacked three or four times in a month, particularly if we were at war with a village that was close to us . . . In a bad year, we may lose over thirty or forty people to headhunting, mostly warriors. Sometimes our raids would go wrong and the enemy would surprise and surround our headhunting party and twenty of our warriors would be killed.

Figure 2.3 Ngamphong

This environment shared many, if not all, of the VUCA (volatile, uncertain, complex and ambiguous) characteristics used to define our contemporary asymmetric operational coun-terparts. What intrigued me was the Konyak leadership response to them. Superficially, there was little of surprise when viewing Konyak culture through its morung system upon which Konyak society was built. The village was primarily a framework with political influence, based on a defined territory and the rule of a single chief or deputy angh. Operating within this framework were the morungs, the primary social units within the village (Von Fürer-Haimendorf, 1969, p. 40) and this system endures today. The physical morung is a ceremo-nial barn which traditionally served as the leadership and social hub for each ward within the village, as well as the dormitory and training academy for its unmarried men. Morungs have replaced this preparation role with that of cultural custodians, while retaining their local leadership function. This social unit continues to have great autonomy, with its lead-ers having delegated power over many aspects of justice and disputes, as well as decisions over most principal activities outside of the few that are mandated as collective endeavours, such as field burning and major festivals. One role which remains as important today as any-time time in history is providing a system to facilitate romantic relationships, as marriage is exogamous to Konyak clans. The morungs also served as the network for the Konyak animist belief system, which incorporated a central spiritual figure called Hahgang Jungang ('Earth-Sky'). Much knowledge of these beliefs has been lost during the conversion of the popula-tion of Sheanhagh Chingnyu to Baptist Christianity, which began in the 1950s and 1960s in parallel with the relinquishment of the headhunting practice. Each morung has different clans within its membership and has representation at the village council. Villages are divided even today into several morungs, with around ten in Sheanhagh Chingnyu. Headhunting raids were usually planned and mounted by morungs, with village-wide coordinated operations being very rare and reserved for military actions with primary political and territorial intent. Such operations would be led by the angh, who otherwise would only go on sorties from his own royal morung.

During the headhunting times, boys normally entered the morung somewhere between the ages of 10 and their early teens. Although they would spend much of their time working in their families' fields, they would always return to the morung to sleep and it was at the morung that they received their preparation to become an active member and economic contributor to the community. It was a disciplined and arduous routine, whereby the older men taught and mentored the boys through a process that might take anything from 3–5 years to complete. Bhoowang, the deputy angh of Hong Phoi village, explained how harsh the environment could be, saying, "we taught them to obey their elders by treating them like slaves. We made them collect water and firewood, and if one made a mistake, all were beaten." The curriculum was broad, encompassing subjects as diverse as basket weaving, a task only conducted by men, conducting spiritual rituals and hunting. The boys practised using spears, guns and the ubiquitous dao, the distinctive Naga machete and axe hybrid used for both general and fighting purposes. The regime was loose and might include running, wrestling and high jump competitions, often organised by the apprentice warriors themselves on an ad hoc basis. Graduation was followed by the tattooing of the young men's chests by the anghya and usually confirmed by participation in a headhunting raid (Von Fürer-Haimendorf, 1938, p. 361). Because of this, it would be easy to assume that the focus of the morung's teaching was about resilience and functional skills, but Ngamphong explained that the most important things he came to understand were "about caring and feeling strongly about my community.

Figure 2.4 Penjum and His Granddaughter

The elders were always talking about working together. We were always told 'whatever you do, ensure you work together and never alone.'" This togetherness was also remembered fondly by Penjum from Longwa village.

> We always woke up so early. At the first rooster crow, which is around two-thirty, maybe three o'clock in the morning, we would slowly open our eyes and nudge each other to check everyone was stirring. The first murmuring of waking and quiet conversations would begin but we would remain lying in our beds. Then when the second rooster crows came at around four o'clock, we would rouse properly and start singing and getting ready for the day.

I sat outside the hut of Penglung, an 85-year-old warrior, as he stripped bamboo canes for weaving as his wife, Gangem, prepared freshly picked gooseberries. His high cheek bones accentuated the arching lines of tattooing across his face, the ink framed by the silver grey hair that covered the top of his head above the sides of his customarily shaved skull. He talked fondly of his time as a young man in his morung:

> Headhunting was part of everyday life when I was a child. It was just normal, so every day. I remember wanting to see heads come in to the village as it would mean we would have our victory rituals, which were exciting to me. I entered the morung when I was about ten and joined my first headhunting party when I was still young, maybe 16, perhaps even younger. I felt so strong and proud to enter the morung, as it meant I was now a responsible boy thought capable of serving my society.

The considered cultural and practical preparation of the morung had two testing grounds: each warriors performance as an economic provider through farming and hunting, and ultimately in a headhunting party. When the warriors spoke of their participation in these attacks, their tone was often of humility and measured pride, yet tinged with uncertainty. The latter an uncertainty about the legitimacy of speaking so openly about a practice considered taboo by so many outside of this village for so long – so taboo that a few villages had gone so far to have destroyed all associated artefacts from these times, largely erasing the physical embodiment of their past. They visibly relaxed when I spoke of my own combat experiences as a veteran and related my interest as the desire of one warrior wanting to understand the traditions of another.

Shengang's description of the warriors he admired seemed unsurprising but it was only a small part of the story:

> a great warrior has lots of heads and is always hungry to take more. A great warrior is very attractive and outwardly kind to all but underneath he will always have a hunger to take more heads . . . A true warrior did not show fear and everyone would believe they were truly fearless. Great warriors are born and it is in their blood that is why they never appeared scared. They are different to common men and that is how they inspired other men to fight . . . you could feel their presence.

This depiction of heroic and charismatic leadership uses almost mythological language, and it represents one side of the apparent tension so clear within the environment of the morung; the tension between toughness and kindness. However, as my time in Sheanhagh Chingnyu continued, I came to understand that there was little or no tension. In fact, I came to believe

Figure 2.5 Penglum and Gangem

that the Konyaks developed toughness *through* kindness. Kindness and connectedness were evident in the everyday conversations and actions that I witnessed throughout my stay, and they were also considered essential qualities for any leader, from angh and village council member to mother and teacher.

An organisational crisis is often defined as rapidly developing and often unforeseen events that pose a substantial and potentially existential risk. In short, it is the result of low-probability but high-impact situations. Crisis leadership is seen as the response that secures resilience in both the organisation and its people, enabling both to bounce back when the crisis is overcome or subsides. Some of the types of crises identified as risks for modern organisations

(Pearson & Clair, 1998) are as historically apposite for Konyak communities and, with this in mind, the Konyak idea of placing kindness at the centre of leadership becomes more intriguing. There are three distinct strands to Konyak community effectiveness: kindness, connectedness and matkapu, each of which appears to have the potential to enhance leadership influence in challenging operational settings and even more when considered together.

Kindness is not a common word within the contemporary leadership lexicon, although its use in this context has notably increased during the COVID pandemic. For Konyak leaders, kindness is about example, sense of service and building the levels of trust required for the community to function. It is their responsibility to identify those who need help and to support them with compassion and care. As a deputy anghya for the village, Likhao believes it is this mindset that cements the relationship between leader and follower: "A good leader never hurts others, but only comforts them. This quality makes others want to follow their footsteps." The Konyak experience of kindness is not restricted to practical assistance and resource sharing; it goes far deeper than that. At its core, it seems to be about an emotional open-ness and a willingness to selectively show and to share vulnerability. This is often formalised in song, as Panglem, the Village Guard commander and songwriter, explains: "songs are the only way for Konyaks to truly express emotions. Composing and singing songs are part of my ancestry." Village songwriters compose songs for all sorts of events, from celebration to romantic serenades through to loss. I was sitting at the edge of the village one night, looking out across the moonlit forested hills when I heard the plaintive calling of gongs which accompanied impassioned songs of grief, as the community mourned the death of an old woman. I was deeply moved as I listened to this emotional outpouring. When I commented how affected I was, a woman told me "we cry from our bones" and this simple and stark phrase summed up for me the strength of the Konyak's engagement with their emotions, which allows them to see crying as perfectly natural and not a sign of weakness. As exemplars of this culture, leaders are expected to be empathic and attuned to the needs of others in order to build trust, two of the four qualities identified by Goffee and Jones in their study of what people want from their leaders (2000). Regularly engaging in small acts of kindness has been shown to improve wellbeing (Lyubomirsky, 2007, pp. 23, 129) and it might be possible that its central placement within Konyak culture is as much to do with this as to meeting any clear practical needs addressed by the individual acts.

Kindness is supported by a Konyak societal structure that enables people to connect in a manner that meets their needs for intimacy and access, while optimising both autonomy and operational agility. These formal connections start with the closeness of family groups, to the formation of platoon sized headhunting parties through to the communities represented by each morung. The size of each of these respective groups corresponds directly to those described circles of social need, from intimacy and sympathy through to functional and ending with the morung, whose affiliated populations roughly correspond to Dunbar's Number (2010, p. 32). More specifically, Konyak societal structure is optimised to create opportunities to build and maintain trust with various-sized groups, each of which is capable of different levels of operational independence. Daily work is decided and allocated within these structures, with village-wide activity very infrequent and restricted to events such as field burning – which occurs on a single day each year, as directed by the village council. The Konyaks also understand that serendipitous meetings are essential for a successful community, and they therefore create nolaks all around the village's fields and hunting territory, sometimes as frequent as every 500 metres. A nolak is a meeting place and each has a tree for shade and fruit, seating made from rocks or logs and, where possible, a water source. These small pools of calm water encourage people meeting in the fields or on the trail to stop, talk and reflect together. This creates bonds beyond regular family and working groups, while allowing for information to be exchanged and for the maintenance of a cohesive identity. Research also suggests that these chance encounters support wellbeing and enhance happiness for days after (Epley & Schroeder, 2014). All nolaks are named and some are centuries old, silent witnesses to generations of shared kindness, insights and the beginning of new relationships.

The final strand partially defies description and it is the underpinning concept for all of Konyak culture. Matkapu roughly translates as "standing for the truth of things." Acting with integrity is at the heart of Konyak identity, and it remains as important today as it has across the centuries. It requires people to deeply reflect upon the potential consequence of any given action and to make decisions based on the undeniable truth of things. It is a powerful concept that focuses on the long-term benefit of the community and the avoidance of enmity or unnecessary conflict within the village. Its strength lies in an acceptance that every action was overseen by Hahgang Jungang, a role now assumed by the Christian deity, following conversion in the latter half of the twentieth century. Tonpah's words show the power held in this sense of purpose:

> As a leader, people may dislike you, talk badly about you, they might attack you or even want to kill you. Just remember, if you stand for truth, forget about them as they simply don't matter.

A traditional education ensured every Konyak was taught to do matkap before considering any significant situation or challenge, as Konyaks see a specific relationship between moral courage and taking the right path, resilience and survival. This is expressed in their saying "a long road leads to a long life and a short road leads to a short life." It is unsurprising that to a Konyak, the relationship between leaders and modelling being matkapu is absolute, as Toingam unequivocally pointed out: "A leader is a person who only speaks the truth. That's it."

There is one additional element that flows through the other three, and that is the notion of attentiveness. An attentiveness drawn from listening and presence. Listening is seen as the first step towards building and maintaining trust, and it is considered essential by anghs and more junior leaders alike. Face-tattooed warriors and young people alike all agreed that listening lay at the heart of effective relationships, and effective relationships in turn lay at the heart of effective leadership. There was a consistent view that leaders must take the time to listen to the voices of their followers and more unexpectedly, and that they must ensure they give space to views contrary or in opposition to their own. Anyam's grandmother had this to say:

> Leaders . . . take the time to speak to everyone in order to understand their needs, wishes and ideas. All good leaders, just like a good queen, will always make time to work, walk and talk with their followers; this is the time when they can really listen to those around them and good leaders must spend so much time listening. A good leader cannot always be right and they must ensure he understands the views of others, takes good counsel and always understands the circumstances of others.

I journeyed to Nagaland to conduct a smash-and-grab ethnography in order to understand what leadership meant to the last surviving face-tattooed warriors of Sheanhagh Ching-nyu. I had no idea of what to expect but I left the village with so much more than a clear understanding of Konyak leadership; I had also reached a deeper understanding of my leadership and its roots in my military past. This simplicity of form allowed no room for ambiguity, which in turn led to the pillars of kindness, connection and matkapu being lived authentically wherever I looked. For people without a long history of the written word, I saw why. These intrinsically human qualities have sustained this tribe through centuries of hostilities, followed by the dramatic changes brought about by the arrival of the modern world in the last seventy years, and they appear aligned with Joanne Ciulla's view of leadership as something that is "not a person or a position. It is a complex moral relationship between people, based on trust, obligation, commitment and a shared vision of the good" (2004, p. xv). These same three things resonate with new collaborative and more fluid ideas of leadership such as Western's ecoleadership and in particular his concept of leadership spirit; a quality drawn from identity, a sense of community and the relationship between people and the natural world (2019); all elements that are at the heart of Konyak culture. The foundations of purpose, belonging and kindness are seen by many as intrinsic to eudaimonic wellbeing, and looking even further, it is possible to identify evidence of every one of the New Economics Foundation's five ways to wellbeing (Aked & Thompson, 2011) being fully integrated into Konyak life. It would seem that while this literature may be relatively recent, these concepts have been lived for longer than might be imagined in a setting that could not be more different to the organisations more usually targeted in such research.

At first glance, the differences in culture, history and operating environments between Konyak society and contemporary organisations might suggest there is little to learn from the leadership practice of these former headhunters, but looking deeper, I came to a very different realisation. Lessons from the pandemic have highlighted the crucial role that compassionate leadership plays in time of crisis, for both strategic and operational leaders alike. The characteristics of such leadership include sharing the hardships, reading the emotional cues of others and listening attentively (Maak et al., 2021). This responsible leadership refocuses on relational elements and makes space for "the human moments" (Frost, 2003, p. 22), in which a leader gives their full attention to individuals to acknowledge their emotional needs in times of difficulty. These same tenets are clearly observable in the leadership of kindness that Konyaks have practised for generations, enabling them to flourish culturally through sustained periods of conflict and uncertainty. For a people with no written language before the arrival of English through formal education, leadership is a felt connection, intrinsic and beyond words, and it requires purposeful attention. Leaders attend to the wellbeing of those around them and make time to listen and to build trust. This relationship is the same between Angh and Anghya and their 10,000 subjects, a senior warrior and his thirty-strong headhunting party and a mother showing her children how to plant crops. It is not about process, but about meeting complexity with the simplicity of kindness and presence, and it requires intentional nurturing.

The time set aside by Konyak leaders to sustain this kindness-based dyadic leader–follower relationship creates high levels of mutual trust, respect and sense of obligation (Graen & Uhl-Bien, 1995). This mutuality supports an inclusive environment in which every voice is not just heard but actively encouraged, whether at the village council, within the morungs or within extended families. It should be noted that one of the most significant factors that led to peace and the cessation of headhunting in Sheanhagh Chingnyu was the pressure applied by the Student's Union, the organisation that represents school children and students within the village. To this day, the president of the Students' Union has a permanent seat on the village council. Even during the times when absolute power resided in the angh, successful anghs were seen to actively seek challenging counsel and to make time to listen to their subjects. This attention showed by leader to follower leads to very high levels of mutual trust and corresponding autonomy within morungs and their constituent families, supported by a structure based on dispersed authority and distributed decision making on most matters from disputes to hunting. The angh and village council maintain a focus on strategic matters and act as the final arbiters in situations when an individual morung is unable to come to a decision. This is possible because of the shared sense of common purpose and the strength of the relationships across the community. This culture is very familiar to me from my service in the Army, and it ensures a genuine agility and sense of contribution; I would call it mission command. It is perhaps no surprise that this same ethos has evolved in another martial culture to meet the need for responsive decision making in order to generate initiative in dynamic situations. It is also the same distributed decision-making structure suggested as a response to times of crisis (Levinson & McLaughlin, 2020). As discussions about future working environments and structures continue, I find myself irritated by use of terms such as 'the new normal.' For me, they lack ambition and imply a desire to return to the status quo. It is important that we actively embrace the opportunities that advances in the digitised environment, and artificial intelligence in particular, offer us. However, processes and digital infrastructures must not crowd out the time required to actively develop and nurture the meaningful relationships at the heart of cohesive organisations. As we consider what new working structures will look like, we must ensure we explore how to optimise the ability of people to connect in order to find intimacy and share purpose in these reshaped spaces, whether virtual or face to face.

So, what does this mean for us? There is a Konyak expression that says "not everyone can be an angh but everyone can be a wise elder." For a Konyak, leadership is a mindset, not a position or title. If you want to ensure that you and those around you keep your heads during crises, you might consider thinking like a goipa (leader). As a leader, do you make time for those human moments? Are kindness and a willingness to show vulnerability central to your leadership? Is your organisation structured to best support the levels of intimacy and trust your people need, and how do you create opportunities to unexpectedly expand networks and understanding? Finally, how central is your sense of purpose and standing for the truth of things to you and your organisational ethos? Kindness, nolaks and matkapu. Three small words, each with a powerful potential to deepen your relationship with the people you lead and to enhance the trust and wellbeing so essential to successfully navigating crises. This is not about competing choices, but about understanding that kindness in leadership is essential in developing the sustainable individual and organisational toughness required to negotiate challenging operational environments. After all, these very same words represent an ethos that gave courage to warriors, carrying them into battle with the belief that they would not lose their heads but that they would instead take those of their enemies and secure success for their village. As you reflect, I leave you with a final question. Have you changed your relationship with the word kindness, and will you integrate it into your everyday discussions about leadership?

Before I left, I was sitting with Anyam by the fireside, drinking black tea. The longhouse was filled with the laughter of his siblings as they played with his grandmother, and I could just make out the gentle breathing of the two dogs dozing next to us. On the wall, a collection of daos, spears, crossbows and guns spoke proudly of a history that only ended with Anyam's grandfather, the last face-tattooed warrior in his family and the person who had taught him how to be a Konyak leader. I reflected that I had come looking for leadership but would leave having found kindness, an even more precious idea. At that moment Anyam turned to me and said:

> (Leadership) means having a good and clear vision, perhaps out to ten or even twenty years. It means setting a good example and having a positive mind. It means having the courage to do what is right and not to hesitate to make the right decision. Leadership is about taking the hard decisions for the benefit of the people. It is not about taking the easy path.

Note

1 'Tribe' is used to describe this ethnic group throughout this account, as the term has a distinct legal status within India.

References

Aked, J., & Thompson, S. (2011). *Five ways to wellbeing: New applications, new ways of thinking.* New Economics Foundation.

Ciulla, J. (2004). *Ethics, the heart of leadership* (2nd ed.). Praeger, XV.

Dunbar, R. (2010). *How many friends does one person need? Dunbar's number and other evolutionary quirks.* Faber & Faber.

Epley, N., & Schroeder, J. (2014). Mistakenly seeking solitude. *Journal of Experimental Psychology: General, 143*(5), 1980–1999.

Frost, P. J. (2003). *Toxic emotions at work: How compassionate managers handle pain and conflict.* Harvard Business School Press.

Goffee, R., & Jones, G. (2000). Why should anyone be led by you? *Harvard Business Review, 68*(5), 63–70.

Graen, G.B., & Uhl-Bien, M. (1995). Relationship-based approach to leadership: Development of leader-member exchange (LMX) theory of leadership over 25 years: Applying a multi-level multi-domain perspective. *Leadership Quarterly, 6*(2), 219–247.

Hutton, J.H. (1928). The significance of head-hunting in Assam. *The Journal of the Royal Anthropological Institute of Great Britain and Ireland, 58*(July–December), 399–408.

Hutton, J.H. (1965). The mixed culture of the Naga tribes. *The Journal of the Royal Anthropological Institute of Great Britain and Ireland, 95*(1), 16–43.

Jacobs, J. (2012). *The Nagas: Hill peoples of Northeast India, society, culture and the colonial encounter* (2nd ed.). Thames & Hudson.

Levinson, A., & McLaughlin, P. (2020, June 4). New challenges for the virtual world of work. *MIT Sloan Management Review.* https://sloanreview.mit.edu/article/new-leadership-challenges-for-the-virtual-world-of-work/

Lyubomirsky, S. (2007). *The how of happiness: A practical guide to getting the life you want.* Sphere.

Maak, T., Pless, N.M., & Wohlgezogen, F. (2021). The fault lines of leadership: Lessons from the global Covid-19 crisis. *Journal of Change Management, 21*(1), 66–86.

Pearson, C.M., & Clair, J.A. (1998). Reframing crisis management. *Academy of Management Review, 23*(1), 59–76.

Von Fürer-Haimendorf, C. (1938). The Morung system of the Konyak Nagas, Assam. *The Journal of the Royal Anthropological Institute of Great Britain and Ireland, 68*(July–December), 349–378.

Von Fürer-Haimendorf, C. (1969). *The Konyak Nagas: An Indian frontier tribe.* Holt, Rinehart & Winston.

3   In Search of Fairness in Leadership

Gay Haskins and Mike Thomas

Introduction: Towards a Fairer World

In the midst of the World Financial Crisis between 2007 and 2009, the International Labour Organisation (ILO) made an important declaration on social justice and fair globalisation, calling us all to commit to creating a fairer world. The declaration states:

> achieving an improved and fair outcome for all has become even more necessary . . . to meet the universal aspiration for social justice, reach full employment, ensure the sustainability of open societies and the global economy, to achieve social cohesion and combat poverty and rising inequalities.
>
> (ILO, 2008, p. 6)

Is this aspirational goal achievable? Some would say not. We do not have much choice about where we come into this world, how we are born and brought up, the gender we were born with and our race. Also, if we look back on our childhood and our shouts of, "It's not fair," to our parents or at school, we can see that we very often look at fairness in terms of fairness to ourselves, rather than fairness to others. However, the Confucian Golden Rule of "Do unto others as you would have them do unto you" has inspired many faiths and its adoption as a guideline for our lives leads to an aspiration to be fair, kind, caring and humane.

A dozen years after 2008, another crisis – arguably with even more visible economic and social consequences – hit the world: the COVID pandemic. This worldwide crisis has drawn attention to unfairness. It has shown how the front-line workers in many countries are the lower paid people. It has raised awareness of gender and racial unfairness and social exclusion.

Mark Carney is currently the UN Special Envoy for Climate Action and Finance and Former Governor of the Bank of England and the Bank of Canada. His path-breaking book *Value(s): Building a Better World for All* calls for boards and senior managers of businesses to

> Define the purpose of their organisations, channelling the dynamism of the company to improve some aspect of the world. They must promote a culture of fairness and responsibility within their organisations. Employees must be grounded in strong connections to their clients and their communities.
>
> (Carney, 2021, pp. 481, 482)

Our chapter delves into a complex topic: fairness in organisations and particularly in businesses (whether public or private, for profit or not for profit). The more we focussed on

DOI: 10.4324/9781003171737-4

fairness, the more we realised the challenges of a commitment to trying to be fair. To these ends, we have:

• Briefly examined what we can learn about fairness from religious teaching and philosophy;
• Sought feedback from present and future leaders from a range of backgrounds as to their perceptions of fairness in the organisational context;
• Described some of the traits and attributes of fair leaders;
• Drawn some tentative conclusions as to what fairness in organisations is and of the key underpinnings of fairness and fair leadership in organisations today and in the future.

Fairness: The Impact of Philosophical and Religious Teaching

Can fairness be conceptualised in a way that provides general agreement about it? The answer appears to be "yes, it can, in many ways," and there is a long history in this area. However, as this section indicates, there are a number of nuances to its meaning, and its key ingredients shift and develop.

• **Classical Philosophy: Fairness and Justice and to Each According to Their Need**
  It is difficult to differentiate between what people see as "fair" and what is considered "just." They are intertwined and cannot be put into practice without affecting each other. Perhaps the best way of defining fairness and justice is to think of being just as the intellectual aspect of fairness, and fairness as the equally important emotional aspect of being just. Aristotle, in his Nicomachean Ethics, also equated justice with morality, and provided the phrase "to each according to their need."
• **Roman Law and Christianity: A Moral Life, Harm No-one and Give Others Their Due**
  These early philosophical views were assimilated into Roman law and captured in the three principles of justice: live a moral life, do harm to no-one and render to each what is their own or due. Since the Middle Ages, these three concepts have been accepted as the basis for Western jurisprudence. They are also deeply embedded in the Christian view of justice and in the principle of giving others their due and acting in accordance with their rights. To be just is not only an intellectual exercise in deciding what is the truth of a matter or otherwise, but also an emotional discipline.
• **Confucianism: Humane and Familial Love and a Focus on the "Ordinary Man"**
  In Chinese Confucian philosophy, there is less differentiation between the intellect and emotion and a more integrated view that humane or familial love sustains fairness and justice. Mencius (Mengzi, 372–289 BC), for example, proposed that status, fame and power were denied to the dispossessed – yet within the context of societal justice, the ordinary individual was more valuable than rulers because the individual's interpersonal relationships and familial groups sustained the powerful and the monarchy, not the other way round. Mencius believed in the need for society to have agreed laws but not if they unfairly placed a burden on families or intimate relationships. In moral terms, Mencius held the idea of right and wrong as innate and feelings such as empathy, sympathy and a sense of fairness should be prioritised in any body of legal knowledge or the application of justice.

Islamic Teaching: Incorporating Emotions, the Intellect and Behaviours

The Qur'an is explicit in its view of fairness and justice and encompasses the emotional, intellectual and behavioural aspects of morality. For example, when judgements are applied in whatever situation those who judge should be guided by fairness (Qur'an, 4:57). A fair system of justice is important in the Islamic faith because of its scriptural guidance for experiencing a good moral life. Islamic scripture leaves no ambiguity regarding moral choices, both individually and for those in power, and the scales of justice should always guide individuals to conduct themselves with fairness, (Qur'an, 57:25).

Food for Thought

• Which of these teachings most influence your own leadership?

Fair Organisations 2021: The Underpinnings

When we spoke with people from several different countries and a variety of age groups in the preparation of this chapter, we found a number of shared responses about the underpinnings of a fair organisation. As shown in Figure 3.1, these can be divided into three areas: Purpose and Values, The Way We Work, and Policies and Practices. We will consider each of these in turn.

Purpose and Values

• **A Strong Sense of Purpose:** "Your Purpose is your why," writes Darin Fox, Principal Consultant, HFL Australia, in a 2020 Australian best seller *What the Hell do We Do Now?*: "Purpose is your reason for being . . . it is the positive difference your product or service will make in the world and it is the criterion you use to decide what products and services you will produce" (Fox, 2020, p. 86*)*. Fair organisations are purposeful. As Mohammad Nazim, education management consultant, Pakistan said to us, "If leaders compromise on purpose, they compromise on fairness" (Nazim, 2021).

  Many charities have a strongly motivational sense of purpose: UNICEF, for instance, is mandated to "advocate for the protection of children's rights, to help meet their basic needs and to expand their opportunities to reach their full potential" (http://unicef.org).

• **Living by Values and Ethical Behaviour:** values can be described as, "A small set of guiding principles" (Collins and Porras, 1996). They strongly complement the purpose of an organisation, endure over time and can be described in behavioural terms (Ibid.).

  Mark Carney has called for fairness to be a core value underpinning institutional activities (Carney, 2021, p. 472). John Mackey, co-CEO of Whole Foods Market (United States), goes further: "It is essential that the ethic of fairness apply to all key organizational processes, such as hiring, promotion, compensation, discipline, and termination" (Mackey and Sisodia, 2014, p. 225). A fair organisation should be known for ethical behaviour towards all its stakeholders. When we read that online retail giant Amazon paid only £293 million in tax in the UK last year, whilst its sales surged to £13.73 billion, we cannot help feeling that this might be ethically unfair, whatever the explanation (BBC, 2020).

• **Profit, People and Planet:** in 1970, Professor Milton Friedman famously wrote, "The social responsibility of business is to increase its profits" (Friedman, 1970). These words had a profound impact on business in the capitalist world, leading over time to profit and shareholder dominance, a growing short-termism and an obsession with quarterly

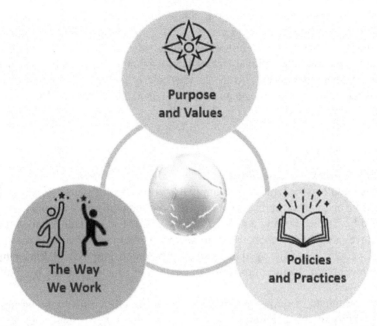

A strong sense of purpose
Living by values and ethical behaviour
Profit, people and planet
Serving all stakeholders

**Purpose
and Values**

**The Way
We Work**

**Policies
and Practices**

Putting people to the fore
All feel valued
Inclusive and diverse
Inspiring trust and trusting others
Transparency, consistency and
openness
Kind and empathic, firm and just
A commitment to training and
development
Strongly customer focused

Clear policy and process guidelines
Equity of opportunity
Less hierarchy more networks
Teamwork
Equitable employee pay & rewards
Fair rewards to owners
& investors
Fiscal responsibility; we pay our taxes
Health & safety a priority

Figure 3.1 The Underpinnings of a Fair Organisation

results. But a decade or so later, other eminent professors began to call for an alternative approach:

Society expects from business not only high economic performance, but also an equally high responsibility in the social field . . . firms have to find . . . purposeful roles . . . acceptable not only to managers and shareholders but also to internal and external stakeholders.

(Ansoff et al., 1982, p. 7)

This view has increasingly taken hold. (Interestingly, China's state-owned enterprises [SOEs] have long had a dual purpose: to deliver value and to move society forward. This echoes the Confucian underpinning of China throughout its history.) In 1987, the Brundtland Report (Brundtland Report, 1987) added sustainable development and meeting the needs of the world's poor to the agenda. Profit, people and planet became the rallying cry.

- **Serving All Stakeholders:** accepting a threefold purpose of profit, people and planet, requires that companies should serve all their stakeholders fairly: founders, owners, investors and shareholders; employees at all levels; local, regional and global customers; governments (international, national, regional and local); the regions in which they are located; and the planet as a whole, particularly in view of the environmental challenges facing the world. Balancing conflicting demands of stakeholders is a key requirement of fairness.

The Way We Work

- **Putting Employees to the Fore**
  Putting people to the fore is not to imply that profits do not matter. Businesses (whether for profit or not for profit), must have sound budgeting and financial performance, reward both investors and employees fairly, price products and services at an acceptable level and show responsibility to society. But organisations are essentially made up of people, working together to serve a common purpose. Making employees at all levels central to the purpose of organisations was mentioned by many that we interviewed.

  Marion Oliver, a former senior manager at The Open University, wrote: "Fairness is the ability to enable all individuals to contribute to their organisation to the best of their skills and abilities" (Oliver, 2021). Dr Vivian Iwar, executive director, Regional Animal Health Centre, ECOWAS, Nigeria, emphasised the positive impact of fairness: "Humans generally recognise when they are treated fairly and if organisations operate on the principles of fairness, this is likely to have a positive effect on staff performance and therefore on the organisation overall" (Iwar, 2021).

- **All Feel Valued**
  In 2014–2015, Professor Caroline Rowland carried out a study on fairness and equity in Western organisations (Rowland, 2015). A key finding was that for individuals in organisations, the most important personal incentive to becoming more engaged was feeling valued. Such a small duo of words, *"feeling valued"*; yet Julie Claxton, an expert on employee engagement, carried out an analysis of several organisations which demonstrated support for this view. Emotional awareness drives increased productivity, engagement, better management, positive co-operation and increased health and well-being (Claxton, 2015).

  WAVE for Change (www.wave-for-change.org.uk) is an inspirational charity set up by Bernice Hardie and Celia Webster, parents with experience of integrating a child with learning disabilities into their community (WAVE stands for "We're All Valued Equally"). They realised that the barriers to integration can't be overcome by legislation or policy. Within organisations, being valued equally means working together to create an inclusive culture: of disability, race, national origin, gender, sexual orientation, ethnicity, age, socio-economic status, religion. It involves searching out the contribution that each employee can make.

- **Inclusive and Diverse**

  Inclusion was viewed as of critical importance to organisational fairness. Paul Coyle, founder of the Entrepreneurial Mindset Network, defines inclusion as follows: "It's about a culture of belonging. If you are made to feel comfortable and to share your whole self at work, you can be your best self. That is good for you and . . . for the company too" (Coyle, 2021a). "Fairness and inclusiveness go hand in hand," wrote Belgian lawyer Eve Vlemincx. "You need to prevent personal feelings and unconscious biases getting in the way" (Vlemincx, 2021).

  Appreciation of the value of diversity sits alongside inclusion. Fifty years ago, when we were both growing up in the UK, there was far less diversity in organisations than there is now. Nandu Nandkishore started his career at Nestlé in 1989, and in 2010 became the first Asian to be appointed to the Executive Board. As a member of a minority group in successively more senior positions, he felt that he always had to work harder than others: "We all need to understand how context shapes behaviour" (Nandkishore, 2021). In 2017, Boston Consulting Group identified diversity as a key driver of innovation, finding that diverse teams produce 19% more revenue (BCG, 2017).

- **Inspiring Trust and Trusting Others**

  A fair organisation has to inspire trust. Research has suggested that no other aspect of leader behaviour has such a large impact on profits (Frei and Morriss, 2020). Sydney-based communications coach Paul Matthews wrote of a personal experience.

  I once had to sack a senior manager . . . I included them in the entire process and ensured that they were informed and aware at every turn. . . . I wanted them to trust that even though the outcome might FEEL unfair, it had been achieved with dignity, honesty and consideration. . . . They left trusting me with dignity intact.

  (Matthews, 2021)

  Both inspiring trust in others *and* trusting in others are important. In *What Philosophy Can Teach You About Being A Better Leader*, you will find an innovative chapter 'A Question of Example and Fairness.' The authors describe the ethos of the Laboratory of Molecular Biology at Cambridge University, set up in 1949 by Nobel Prize winner Max Perutz. Perutz's operating assumption was "that those with whom he worked were just as trustworthy as he was" (Reynolds et al., 2020, p. 87).

- **Transparency, Consistency and Openness**

  The young people with whom we spoke particularly emphasised transparency. Whether positive, negative or neutral, organisational transparency means sharing and keeping people in the loop. The more employees know, the more they feel part of what the organisation is doing. Tiger Whiteley has been regularly employed by the fast-growing file-sharing company WeTransfer during his university years. He has developed a strong commitment to the company and its culture. "There are regular weekly chats with the whole company in which everyone feels empowered to speak up," he said to us. "I feel part of the family" (Whiteley, 2021). Beth Kellie has been named in Management Today's "35 Women Under 35." Like Tiger, she looks for transparency:

  For me, fairness, transparency and consistency are intrinsically linked. The teams I have worked in that I would consider most fair are the ones where there is complete transparency around everything . . . role responsibilities, deliverables, performance measurement, pay (within bands), training and development . . . it is consistently applied or can be accessed, no matter the person and with no room for bias.

(Kellie, 2021)

- **Kind and Empathic, Firm and Just**
  In researching our book, *Kindness in Leadership* (Haskins et al., 2018), we found that kindness and fairness were closely linked. In her chapter on "Kindness in Sports Performance," Olympic rower Alison Gill concluded:

  Kindness was a word that struck a chord with many of my interviewees. . . . (They) spoke of the need for discipline within a framework and fairness, not favouritism. . . . My reflection on this is that perhaps without the foundations of firmness and fairness, kindness somehow cannot flourish.

  (p. 144)

  A fair organisation marries kindness and fairness. Organisations that encourage both a culture of kindness and daily acts of kindness will motivate their members. Being just also means no tolerance for bullying, a practice condemned but carried out in organisations around the world. Fair organisations should be empathetic, searching to understand individual needs, but underpinning empathy to individuals with a lack of favouritism and justice to all. It's a balancing act: kindness, care and empathy *and* fairness, firmness and justice.
- **A Commitment to Training and Development**
  Fair organisations make a strong commitment to training at all levels. "They should support opportunities for training with no discrimination in opportunity," wrote Ruba Innab, a senior manager at the Water Authority in Jordan (Innab, 2021). Two priorities mentioned that link to fairness were training in fair process and unconscious bias training. The latter is strongly related to growing demands for inclusion. Recurring training and a commitment to diversity and inclusion on the part of leadership is essential (see Coyle, 2021b).
- **Strongly Customer Focussed**
  Fair organisations are strongly customer focussed. They seek to offer their products and services at a fair price and focus on quality and honesty to their clients. McKinsey & Company, long regarded as one of the world's leading consultancies, has recently been embroiled in a number of scandals: for instance, for misleading doctors and regulators about the risk of the drug OxyContin. Whether guilty or not, such allegations cause huge damage to an organisation's reputation. Talking to us from Pakistan, educator Mohammad Nazim stressed, "Developing countries are inundated with sub-standard pharmaceutical products. Fair organisations don't compromise on quality" (Nazim, 2021).

Policies and Practices

- **Clear Policy and Process Guidelines**
  Written policies and processes are an underpinning of organisational fairness and justice: for recruitment, remuneration, holidays, training, performance measurement, disciplinary action, redundancy and retirement, for instance. They can also offer useful ethical guidance and information on the organisation's social responsibility practices. But many of us have experiences when joining an organisation when we were given

a large folder, neatly named "Human Resource Policies and Procedures," which we never reviewed comprehensively. Policies and procedures need to be explained to new recruits, and to be reviewed on a regular basis in order for an up-to-date basis of fairness and justice to be maintained. In parallel, there needs to be an organisational culture in which policy issues can be openly discussed with management. Avoid creating organisations where, in the words of international consultant and coach, Bernadette Conraths, "Fair practices are exemplified in terms of existing rules and regulations – but not lived as part of the corporate culture" (Conraths, 2021).

- **Equity of Opportunity**

Many of those with whom we spoke underlined the importance of equity of opportunity. This has to be part both of the policies and processes of organisations and of the way in which these are implemented. For instance, many of us have experiences of feeling that these were done at the end of the year in order to tick off a box. As Coventry University Provost Ian Dunn wrote to us: "Fairness in an organisation means equity of opportunity to think creatively and express those views and to progress through that organisation. I do also have an expectation that I have to act in the same way to others in the organisation" (Dunn, 2021).

- **Less Management and Fewer Rules**

"We need policies yes," said Nick Ellerby, founder of The Oasis School of Human Relations. "But don't oversimplify them into rules" (Ellerby, 2021). In the UK, the preponderance of rules over professional decision making has been evident in the health care sector. Health specialists Jill McCarthy, Pauline Alexander, Moyra Baldwin and Jan Woodhouse have examined the impact of managerialism and the growth in external auditing and inspections on professional decision making in health care (McCarthy et al., 2010). They argue that professional judgements and decisions are neither intuitive nor free of context. Professionals may like to think they apply professional judgements with a degree of individuality, but in many cases, the professional practitioner makes decisions based on group expectations, externally applied rules and processes, and management directives. Ironically, the decrease in trust of professional integrity has given free rein to an explosion in "evidence-based" approaches with a myriad of auditors, inspectors, professional groups, consultancies and politically driven interventions in the name of public safety, quality, efficiency and effectiveness. Such managerialism and political approaches have had a negative effect by decreasing trust and confidence in care providers (Thomas, 2016).

- **Flatten the Hierarchies**

Carolyn Dare, Director of Empowered Achiever Ltd., wrote:

Fairness for me is a flat hierarchy, people work across different networks both within and outside the company with open minds, opportunities to learn and to make a difference. The foundation of the culture is built on good and supporting relationships between people who . . . . have deep mutual respect and are curious to explore inclusive solutions that are best for the greater whole (stakeholders, community, ecosystem).

(Dare, 2021)

Max Perutz, founder of the Laboratory of Molecular Biology at Cambridge University (see section on "Inspiring Trust and Inspiring Other" earlier in this chapter), "kept the administration of the lab to a bare minimum. . . . No politics, no committees, no reports, no referees. . . . Everyone was treated with the utmost respect, humanity and affection"

(Reynolds et al., 2020, pp. 85, 86). You may argue that this was a very special organisational context. But when we asked for examples of fair organisations, interviewees often talked about consultancies, research centres and creative and professional services organisations – organisations in which the levels of hierarchy are not high.

- **Teamwork and Networking**
  In her research on fairness and equity, Professor Caroline Rowland found teamwork to be a highly valued concept related to self-esteem and purposefulness because colleagues, rather than management, were the strongest re-enforcers of hard work, quality and discipline in the workplace (Rowland, 2015). Perceptions of fairness and justice were reviewed and appraised by the workforce, not just in terms of reward or recognition. Fairness and justice were also evaluated with reference to how leaders and management dealt with poor performance or identified poor effort. This was particularly sensitive if employees perceived inequalities when colleagues were not disciplined and sometimes even rewarded for poor work practices, or if management placed more stress on financial remuneration over value-based rewards.

- **Equitable Employee Pay and Rewards**
  Bernie Sanders, who has twice made bids to become the US Democratic Party candidate for president, has stated that income and wealth inequality are both the moral and political issues of our time (Sanders, 2017). In 2018, the United States topped the list of a pay gap survey between CEOs and average workers in ten countries. For every US dollar that an average worker received, the average CEO earned US $265. India followed with $229, the UK with $201 and South Africa with $180 (Statista, 2021). These ratios are very high in all cases. Emphasis needs to be paid worldwide to narrowing differentials, both in pay and annual bonuses. "In my experience," wrote seasoned executive Ross Rennie, "The rewards that leaders hand out are far more likely to have people question your fairness than any policy or practice" (Rennie, 2021).

- **Fair Rewards to Owners and Investors**
  The author, philosopher and thinker Charles Handy examined societal perceptions of fairness and the financial return for investors and executives against perceptions of their contributions to corporate success. He gives the example that the 1% of society that holds the most wealth would argue that they deserved the rewards because they worked very hard; the wealth they hold is fair and just. They would say that those who invest their hard-earned money in companies take all the risks and responsibilities for its success or failure. The other 99% would argue that wealth is unequally shared and that whilst the rich get richer, the poor get poorer. Perceptions of fairness depend on your position in society (Handy, 2015). Charles Handy also argued that the shared understanding of fairness and justice has broken down with too many different views, each in conflict with the understanding of another and that political and other leaders need to "restore proper justice to the creation and distribution of wealth. Wealth has to be spread more widely without destroying the motivation to create it" (p.152).

- **Fiscal Responsibility: We Pay Our Taxes**
  Taxation is widely viewed as an irritant, but reflects societal fairness. Legally required direct taxation of the individual, whereby each pays irrespective of personal circumstances, contributes to the common good. Indirect taxation, often on goods, has a different effect on society as it more often affects on the individual (what you buy, for example). Government sets taxation rules, and the disparity between low and high earners being directly taxed is often reflected in the percentage earned before taxation and therefore judged on fairness. High earners typically pay more tax after a certain threshold, but

there remains a constant tension within all governments as to the level considered fair. There is also the issue of how the government spends the income received from taxation, with many voices proposing more funding for one area than another. In addition to personal taxation is the vexed problem of business taxation. This has the same principles as personal taxation and contributes towards the greater good of society, so generally the more profitable an organisation is, the more tax it pays. Whilst many companies fulfil their responsibilities, others find ways of avoiding contributing their full tax payment (by registering out of country, tax benefit schemes and so on).

- **Strongly Focussed on Health and Safety**
Following the pandemic, health and safety will need to become an organisational priority. Organisations will be judged on how they go beyond basic needs. Hygiene will become even more important. With the hugely increased number of virtual meetings, psychological safety has also become an increasing priority. Writing in the *Harvard Business Review*, Amy Edmondson and Gene Daley point out how virtual meetings can undermine psychological safety making people more reluctant to raise questions or share their ideas:

There are good reasons to worry. Detecting social cues or non-verbal agreement is nearly impossible. Team members may feel isolated without the natural support of an ally nodding from across the table. And distractions (emails, texts, doorbells, children, pets) are everywhere . . . virtual meetings are inherently difficult . . . the current environment – the health and economic threats, the overwork, and the social unrest – makes them even more so.

(Edmondson and Daley, 2020)

Food for Thought: The Underpinnings of Fair Organisations

- Think of an organisation that you consider to be fair. Which of these features does it exemplify? Are there others to add?
- Is paying tax an ethical responsibility of citizens and companies for the common good?

Fair Leaders: Ten Attributes

Let us now turn to the attributes and behaviours required of the leaders or organisations that aspire to be fair. Figure 3.2 shows ten that we have identified.

- **Set an Example**
In a conference run by *The Economist* in June 1989, the management guru Peter Drucker asked participants to share their thoughts as to the most important leadership attribute. Twenty or so ideas came up before he shook his head and said that everyone had given the wrong answer. In his view, the greatest leadership attribute was to "be a role model and set an example to others" (Drucker, 1989). A fair leader should be an exemplar of fairness.

Fair Leaders: 10 Attributes

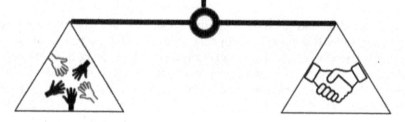

Set an example
Live the organisation's purpose and values
Make fair and balanced judgements
Engage, communicate and include
Listen, dialogue and trust

Give time to all: No favoritism
Appreciate diversity and difference
Are kind, respectful and decent
Combine fairness with firmness
Value profit, people and planet equally

Figure 3.2 Fair Leaders: Ten Attributes

- **Live the Organisation's Purpose and Values**
  There is no point in having a stated purpose and a list of core values for an organisation unless those in leadership roles at all levels commit to them. That means ensuring that the organisation lives by its purpose and that its leaders discuss them with employees, demonstrate them and ensure that they become valued beliefs and part of the fabric of the organisation: known, understood and lived by. It has been suggested that "Perhaps fairness should be regarded as the first virtue of a well-led organisation" (Reynolds et al. (2020, p. 90).
- **Make Fair and Balanced Judgements**
  Fair leaders need to see both sides of a situation and arrive at a balanced judgement. This is not easy, and fair leaders will be considered unfair at times. Rob Bell led the London Emergencies Trust between 2017 and 2018, distributing £9 million to the victims of London's Grenfell Tower disaster. He recounted that despite clear policies for the distribution of donations, "It was incredibly difficult to always be seen as distributing the money fairly" (Bell, 2021). Pete Stubbs, Chair, AgeUK Mid Mersey, wrote, "Learn to be wrong. Just because you are the leader doesn't mean that you have all the answers and are always right" (Stubbs, 2021). But, as Jordanian chemical engineer Ruba Annab stressed, "What is important is to try to be fair, consistent, credible and reliable" (Annab, 2021).

- **Engage, Communicate and Include**
  Being fair is an inter-relational attribute just as much as an intellectual one. The previous section of this chapter illustrated how important it is for a fair organisation to be one where all feel valued. Arthur Shartsis founded Shartsis Friese LLP in 1975. Since then, the firm has grown to be one of the most successful mid-sized legal practices in the United States. Growth has deliberately been careful: the purpose of the firm being to provide premium legal work but with more personal service, lower billing rates and more efficient staffing than larger firms. "All in the firm are valued," said Art. "Turnover at all levels is very low; we try to be inclusive. As Founding Partner, I make sure that I know and communicate with every member of the firm" (Shartsis, 2021).

- **Listen, Dialogue and Trust**
  "Fair leadership involves listening more, and talking less," wrote leadership expert Michael Pitfield on LinkedIn (Pitfield, 2021). Canadian Ross Rennie, who has extensive executive experience in Canada and the United States, gave a concrete suggestion:

  The cost to be fair is five minutes a day. Dialogue with one or more of your team each day to see how the organization can improve fairness to them individually, to other employees, to customers, and to suppliers. That's a reasonable price to pay for the benefits you will get: increased morale, productivity, loyalty, and job satisfaction for employees. For both customers and suppliers, you build loyalty, reduce costs and improve relationships.
  (Rennie, 2021)

- **Give Time to All: No Favouritism**
  When leading a team of people, it can be very easy to spend more time with those you like the most or those who tend to agree with you! Alternatively, we can find ourselves spending more time with those who are having difficulty with their work and neglecting the high performers. This can be perceived as favouritism – an unfairness. The fair leader aims to give equal time to all.

- **Appreciate Diversity and Difference**
  It is all too easy to create an organisation in which everyone looks the same and comes from similar backgrounds. But we live in a global world and should learn to appreciate the value that diversity and difference can bring. Fair leaders celebrate diversity: they celebrate special days in all religious faiths, they encourage opportunities to share different world views, and they make efforts to develop multicultural awareness across the organisation. They understand the negative impact of discrimination and unconscious bias. They seek to respect everyone.

- **Are Kind, Respectful and Decent**
  In his book, *The Art of Fairness*, David Bodanis writes: "The path to greatness doesn't require crushing displays of power or tyrannical ego. Simple fair decency can prevail" (Bodanis, 2020, pg. 6). Fair leaders are humane; they recognise that living a good moral life underpins fairness. Fair leaders show respect to the rights and contributions of others, are kind and empathetic (putting the focus on others), and are honest and decent, showing behaviour that conforms to accepted standards of morality and respectability.

- **Combine Fairness with Firmness**
  In 2009, early in Nandu Nishkishore's career with Nestlé, Nandu was serving as CEO in the Philippines. This involved working closely with their principal customer, the supermarket SM. When Nandu left the Philippines, Herbert Sy, the top manager of SM, praised him, "You were 'firm but fair' and I respect that," he said (Nandkishore, 2021).

It takes strength for a leader to be fair and firm. Fair leaders have to show that they make decisions as fairly as they can, involving others, but being firm in the delivery of the decision once made.

- **Value Profit, People and Planet Equally**

  Carney wrote: "To bring climate risks and resilience into the heart of financial decision making, climate disclosure must become comprehensive, climate risk management must be transformed and sustainable investment must go mainstream" (Carney, 2021). The fair leader embraces these challenges seeking to ensure that the organisation meets all environmental regulations, demonstrates a deep commitment to environmental protection and looks for business opportunities that will help us all to meet the goals of the Paris Agreement. As Carbon Literacy Project coach Carolyn Dare wrote:

Whatever we do affects many others and we need to consider, be fair and be connected with our natural environment, to other species and to all that surrounds us. We can no longer act as if we are totally detached from nature: we are part of the bigger system. We need to rethink, ensure fairness across our businesses and place it firmly at the centre of our profit, people and planet considerations.

(Dare, 2021)

Food for Thought: Fair Leaders

- Can you think of leaders – either on the world stage or personally known to you – who exemplify these attributes?
- Which attribute do you feel you need to work on? How will you go about it?

In Search of Fairness: Some Tentative Conclusions

As the ILO Declaration on Social Justice has stated, "Achieving an improved and fair outcome for all" is critically important (ILO, 2008). Contributing to a fairer globalisation is a challenge for us all. Leaders need to take account of its importance: for themselves as individuals, for their organisation and its members, for their clients and customers, and for society. Greater fairness is a critical global need, especially in the areas of poverty and income distribution, equity and equality, inclusion and diversity, and the worldwide environmental crisis.

Can we define fairness? Philosophers have shown that fairness and justice are intertwined, with justice as the intellectual aspect of fairness and fairness the emotional aspect of justice. Fairness is also linked to being a good citizen, and exemplifying a principled, purposeful and values-driven approach to leadership; to the qualities of honesty, humanity, decency, respectfulness, empathy and kindness; and to giving others their due and showing equity in our treatment of others, trying to reach balanced unbiased judgements and not favouring one individual over another. Arguably, fairness is best without a dictionary-type of definition. Rather, "As with trust, we intuitively know what it means. We recognise its presence – and particularly its absence" (Reynolds et al., 2020, p. 90).

In recognising the presence of fairness, our interviewees agreed on a number of underpinnings to fair organisations. These fell into the following three core areas.

- Purpose and values: a strong sense of purpose; living by values and ethical behaviour; equally valuing profit, people and planet; and serving all stakeholders;
- The way we work: putting people to the fore; valuing all; being inclusive and diverse; inspiring trust and trusting others; being transparent, consistent and open; demonstrating kindness, empathy, firmness and justice; committing to training and development at all organisational levels; and being strongly customer focussed;
- Policies and practices: clear policy and process guidelines; equity of opportunity; less hierarchy and more networks; teamwork; equitable pay and rewards; fair rewards to owners and investors; fiscal responsibility and a commitment to health and safety.

Being considered fair in the application of leadership is an attribute which appears to have huge benefits. Being judged as a fair leader encourages and consolidates trust, engagement and a shared sense of purpose. For many people, particularly the post-millennial generation, the perception of fairness is closely aligned to their sense of commitment and belonging. Believing that they work for organisations in which transparency and openness are valued and are engaged in activities that are purposeful provides a sense of vocation.

But we also have to recognise that even if we aspire to behave in a very balanced way, impartially and without favouritism, we all have unconscious biases: self-awareness is important. What is a fair judgement in one person's view may be considered unfair to another. What is needed in an organisational context is for leaders at all levels to seek to develop a shared sense of fairness through dialogue, open and transparent communication, and trust.

This chapter is our first step in a "search for fairness" in organisations and leadership. Fairness, we have found, is complex, but fundamental to creating a better world. We all need to work at fairness if we are to play a role – however large or small – in putting profit, people and planet on an equal footing. We would welcome your ideas and perspectives on this vitally important topic.

References

Annab, R. (March 2021) Questionnaire response to Gay Haskins.

Ansoff, I. et al. (1982) *Facing Realities: The European Societal Strategy Project: Summary Report*. Foreword, European Institute for Advanced Studies in Management/European Foundation for Management Development

BBC. (2020) "Amazon Pays £290 Million in UK Tax as Sales Surge to £14 Billion." September 9, 2020. www.bbc.co.uk.news.business

Bell, R. (2021) Telephone interview with Gay Haskins, March 31, 2021

Bodanis, A. (2020) *The Art of Fairness: The Power of Decency in a World Turned Mean*. The Bridge Street Press

Boston Consulting Group (BCG) (2017) "The Mix that Matters: Innovation through Diversity." April 4, 2017. www.bcg.com>publications

Brundtland, Report (1987) *Our Common Future*. World Commission for Economic Development, UN Documents

Carney, M. (2021) *Value(s): Building a Better World for All*. Williams Collins

Claxton, J. (2015) "Understanding Being Valued: A Key Driver for Engagement." Chapter 2, pp. 29–55 In *Innovative Management Perspectives on Confronting Contemporary Challenges*, Vrontis, D., Tsoukatos, E. and Maizza, A. (Eds.). Cambridge Scholars Publishing

Collins, J. and Porras, J. (1996) "Building Your Company's Vision." *Harvard Business Review*, September/October

Conraths, B. (2021) Questionnaire Response to Gay Haskins, March 8, 2021

Coyle, P. (2021a) "Diversity Alone is Not Enough (Interview)." https://web.skype.com/share?url=https%3A%2Farticle%2Fwww.meritsummit.com%2Fblog%2F article%2Fdiversity-alone-is-not-enough-interview&lang=en=us

Coyle, P. (2021b) "Does Unconscious Bias Training Work? It Depends." August 4, 2021. www.merit summit.com/blog/article/does-unconscious-bias-training-work-it-depends

Dare, C. (2021) Email to Gay Haskins, April 30, 2021

Drucker, P. (1989) "Statement made at The Economist Conference, Honouring the Business Experts, Peter Drucker, June 1989." *The Role of the Role Model*, December 8, 2013. www.drucker.institute

Dunn, I. (2021) Questionnaire Response to Mike Thomas, March 2021

Edmondson, A. and Daley, G. (2020) "How to Foster Psychological Safety in Virtual Meetings." *Harvard Business Review*, August 25, 2020

Ellerby, N. (2021) Interview with Gay Haskins, March

Fox, D. (2020) *What the Hell do We Do Now?: An Enterprise Guide to Covid-19 and Beyond*. Kienco Piety

Frei, F. and Morriss, A. (2020) "Everything Starts with Trust." *Harvard Business Review*, (online), May–June 2020

Friedman, M. (1970) "The Social Responsibility of Business is to increase its Profits." *The New York Times Magazine*, September, 13

Handy, C. (2015) *The Second Curve: Thoughts on Re-Inventing Society*. Penguin Random House

Haskins, G. Thomas, M. and Johri, L. (2018) *Kindness in Leadership*. Routledge

Innab, R. (2021) Questionnaire Response to Gay Haskins, March 2021

International Labour Organisation. (2008). International Labour Organisation Declaration on Social Justice for a Fair Globalisation, Resolution adopted by the International Labour Conference, Geneva, 10 June 2008 and UN General Assembly, December 19, 2008 and published by ILO 2008, page 6

Iwar, V. (2021) Questionnaire Response to Gay Haskins, March 2021

Kellie, B. (2021) LinkedIn Conversation, March 2021

Mackey, J. and Sisodia, R. (2014) *Conscious Capitalism*. Harvard Business Review Press

Matthews, P. (2021) Questionnaire Response to Gay Haskins, March 2021

McCarthy, J., Alexander, P., Bladwin, M. and Woodhouse, J. (2010) "Valuing Professional Judgement." Chapter Five, pp. 97–121 In *Value-Based Health and Social Care: Evidence-based Practice*, McCarthy, J. and Rose, P. (Eds.). Sage Publishing

Nandkishore, N. (2021) Telephone Interview with Gay Haskins, March 22, 2021

Nazim, M. (2021) Telephone Interview with Gay Haskins, March 18, 2021

Oliver, M. (2021) Questionnaire Response to Gay Haskins, March 2021

Pitfield, M. (2021) LinkedIn Comment to Gay Haskins, March 2021

The Qur'an (2014) Editor al-Mehri, A.B. The Qur'an Project, Birmingham

Rennie, R. (2021) Email to Gay Haskins, March 5, 2021

Reynolds, A., Houlder, C., Goddard, G. and Lewis, D. (2020) *What Philosophy Can Teach You About Being a Better Leader*. Kogan Page

Rowland, C. (2015) "Rethinking the Management of Team Performance: No Longer Disingenuous or Stupid." Chapter 9, pp. 197–220 In *Innovative Management Perspectives on Confronting Contemporary Challenges*, Vrontis, D. Tsoukatos, E. and Maizza, A. (Eds.). Cambridge Scholars Publishing

Sanders, B. quoted in Roberts, D. (2017) "Ridiculed Reviled, Resurgent . . . Is Corbyn's Campaign Beginning to #feeltheBern?" *The Guardian*, May 31, 2017 g2 9. www.theguardian.com/poli tics/2017/may/30/ridiculed-reviled-resurgent-jermey -corbyn-bernie-saunders-campaign

Shartsis, A. (2021) Telephone Interview with Gay Haskins, March 25, 2021

Statista (2021) "Ratio between CEO and Average Worker Pay in 2018, by Country." eu.support@statista.com

Stubbs, P. (2021) Questionnaire Response to Mike Thomas, April 2021

Thomas, M. (2016) "An Historical View of Mental Health Care." Chapter 1, pp. 1–20 In *Mental Health, Across the Lifespan*, Steen, M. and Thomas, M. (Eds.). Routledge

Vlemincx, E. (2021) Questionnaire Response to Gay Haskins, March 2021

Whiteley, T. (2021) Telephone Interview with Gay Haskins, March 24, 2021

4 The boy who cried Flow

Unicorns and fabulist leadership in times of COVID-19

Keith Grint and Clare Holt

Introduction

In Aesop's fable of 'The Boy Who Cried Wolf,' the shepherd boy repeatedly tries to frighten the villagers by pretending that a wolf is approaching so that when a real wolf arrives, the boy's cries are ignored and the sheep are eaten. In this COVID–updated palindrome of the tale, the political leaders of the countries with the greatest number of COVID deaths – and they are all boys – spent so much energy proclaiming fabulist days are approaching ('Make American Great' [US President Donald Trump], 'Take back control' [UK Prime Minister Boris Johnson], and 'Make Brazil Great Again!' [Brazil President Jair Bolsonaro]) that they claimed the imminent arrival of the opposite of a Wolf – the golden age of Flow. Not for these leaders, then, the difficult task of telling followers bad news, or what Enzensberger (1997) calls 'leading the retreat.'

What follows is primarily focused on the 'serial fabulist' Boris Johnson (Bennett, 2021: 43), who paints a Pollyanna future of such uninterrupted post-Brexit benefits and grandiose schemes (garden bridges, bridges across the Irish sea, a 'match-ready' military, [unused] Nightingale hospitals, no form filling, and a socially levelled up country) that many of 'the villagers' are entranced by the imaginary approach of unicorns and forget about the approaching Wolf. But when the age of rhetorical Flow is inverted into the COVID Wolf, the village is unprepared for bad times, the villagers are distracted by Brexit unicorns, the boys have no coherent plan, and are first in denial; then, when the Wolf starts eating the villagers, they start displacing blame anywhere but themselves. Meanwhile, the Wolf continues to consume the villagers.

In all kinds of ways, the COVID Wolf has exposed and exacerbated some inequalities, whether they are between or within countries: the poor are usually the most likely to succumb to the disease rather than the wealthy, the lower skilled are more likely to lose their jobs permanently, the children of poor parents are more likely to fall behind in education than their richer compatriots, and so on. Yet these issues are compounded by a phenomenon that is much easier to change and wholly preventable: inadequate political leadership. This is not a general criticism of all political leaders, because COVID is likely to test all nations and even the best political leadership is constrained by the situation, but there is a growing divide between those nations that remain resilient – and those that are not. Indeed, some political leaders have enhanced their reputation, such as Jacinda Ardern in New Zealand and Mark McGowan in Western Australia. But others have generally done badly, and the latter are not randomly assigned by the virus but directly reflect those allegedly 'in charge,' and they are all led by a particular group of leaders: narcissistic men – such as Trump, Johnson and Bolsonaro – who operate as 'Prozac leaders' (Collinson, 2012) whereby only good news

DOI: 10.4324/9781003171737-5

is tolerated. This over-positivity leads to wildly exaggerated assumptions of optimism or downright lies in the face of realistic – but negative – news, and the development of a blame culture whereby responsibility for errors, mistakes and failures are laid at the sharp end where the operators work, not the blunt end, where the leadership and regulators live. As Jenkins (2021) suggests in considering Johnson's 'shenanigans' over Brexit and Northern Ireland, such individuals are often (in Arnold's, 1867 phrase) 'averse to the despotism of facts' and much prefer to live in a world of vanity projects than the mundane world inhabited by the rest of us. In fact, at the time of writing (May 2021), Johnson is riding relatively high in the British polls, but this reflects the single success of his time in office – the vaccine roll-out – rather than all the other failures, a refraction of the relatively short term memory of most voters (Achen and Bartell, 2016).

So the question might be: why do we consistently fall for such charismatic and narcissistic leaders? As Max Weber (1922/1978) argued, we are attracted to charismatics in times of distress when someone appears to be brimming with positivity and self-confidence, and offers a radical solution to our collective woes. Alas, it is also the case that we consistently confuse confidence with competence. And this fatal attraction starts early, as Brummelman et al.'s (2015, 2021) research suggests: children consistently pick the most narcissistic child to be leader, despite the fact that these same apparently gifted leaders are no better at facilitating the group in achieving its goal than any other child. Indeed, the penchant for putting faith in individuals rather than collectives or systems is manifest, for example, in Boris Johnson's (2014) own hagiography of Churchill as the individual hero turning the wheel of history – rather similar, no doubt, to what he assumes his own destiny to be. Yet, as Brown (2014) insists, most political leaders make relatively little difference to the overall wheel of history, even if some do.

It is tempting to argue that gender is *the* differentiating factor that distinguishes the disaster facing the United States, the UK and Brazil from the significantly better approach taken by Angela Merkel (Germany), Jacinda Ardern (New Zealand), Katrín Jakobsdóttir (Iceland), Tsai Ing-wen (Taiwan) and Erna Solberg (Norway). But, as Lewis (2020) points out, since only 15 of the UN's 193 countries are led by women, the sample size is small. However, an early assessment by Garikipati and Kambhampati (2020: 8) suggests that this is no coincidence, and even when controlling for GDP per capita, population, health infrastructure, tourism, size of urban concentration and proportion of elderly people, female leaders have done better than male leaders. Indeed, even when the numbers infected are relatively similar, women-led countries experience fewer deaths because the policies are different. They relate this first to the more risk-averse behaviour in women. For instance, on 3 March 2020 – after being briefed by aides that if a journalist asked about shaking hands, he should advise against it (Kuenssberg, 2021) – Johnson insisted that he was going to continue shaking hands with people in a hospital with COVID patients: 'I can tell you I am shaking hands continually . . . I was at a hospital the other night when I think there were actually a few coronavirus patients and I shook hands with everybody, you'll be pleased to know.' Ten days later, Johnson told the country it was facing the worse health crisis in a generation, and on 16 March Johnson told everyone to stay at home and avoid unnecessary social contact because the data suggested the NHS couldn't cope if that didn't happen.

Johnson was taken into hospital on 6 April, leaving the government bereft of a formal leader and chief unicornist. Towards the end of July, the British Chancellor, Rishi Sunak, introduced the 'Eat out to help out' scheme subsidising restaurants, leading to yet another spike in infections. On 17 September, the data clearly showed the beginning of rapid increases and Professor Chris Whitty, the UK's Chief Medical Officer, and Sir Patrick Vallance, the

Chief Scientific Advisor, were arguing for another lockdown or even a short 'circuit-breaker,' but Johnson remained unpersuaded and made only marginal changes to the restrictions on 22 September. This was followed by a set of regional variations, on top of the pre-existing national regulations, that would have made Kafka blanch. Fortunately for the government and the country, Sir Patrick Vallance and the Deputy Chief Medical Officer, Professor Jonathan Van-Tam, persuaded the treasury to risk huge sums on supporting an as yet untested vaccination programme. Nevertheless, the UK ranks fourth in the number of deaths per million (behind Czechia, Belgium and Slovenia) and at the time of writing (12 March 2021), the number of COVID–related deaths in the United States were 540,000, in Brazil they were 270,000, and in the UK they were over 125,000.[1] As a whole, the UK saw deaths rise by 7 per cent in 2020 (England's rise was 8 per cent), though 2021 looks like we will see the UK fall back down the list as the faster British vaccination programme takes effect (BBC News, 2021a).

Of course, it may be that risk-taking is a necessary aspect of those seeking political power, but perhaps the issue is less how differently risk-averse the genders are and more how these risks can be amplified when fed through a culture rooted in the narcissistic displays of some alpha males; in effect, men are more overconfident of their own skill. As Trump was wont to remind everyone, he was 'a very stable genius' (*Global News*, 2 October 2019). Moreover, as Garikipati and Kambhampati (2020: 12) note, the risk appetite is different in focus rather than in scale, so that women leaders are actually more willing to risk damage to their economies for the sake of preserving lives.

It could also be that women leaders are a symptom of better governance systems, rather than a cause of them. Moreover, the United States, the UK and Brazil have produced less toxic leaders in the past – and that might be the clue: it is not just that contemporary women leaders are generally better than their equivalent male political leaders, but that the decision-making style of Trump, Johnson and Bolsonaro is totally ill-suited to the situation and that all three are out of their depth when facing a viral opponent that is uninterested in fabulist diversions, popularity, or stock market numbers – and doesn't have a Twitter account.

We can particularly contrast the leadership of Trump and Johnson with that of Merkel, who has managed to keep German death rates relatively low. Might one reason be that Merkel is a scientist by training (she has a PhD in chemistry), whereas Trump was a TV show host and Johnson is an archetypal Conservative leader – that is, the product of Eton school and a classics degree at Oxford? Unlike the Prozac-infused leaders (or previous leader) of the United States and the UK, both of whom are more interested in polling figures and good news stories than facing up to bad news, Merkel is notable for her understanding that science generates hypotheses rather than facts, for the latter, as Popper (1959) explained, can always be disproved. Thus, ironically, Merkel the scientist is much more tentative in her leadership because she knows just how complex life is. As Miller (2020) insists, 'Her ability to admit what she doesn't know, and delegate decisions, has been a particularly good fit for post-war Germany's federalized political structure.' But it also the case that some countries have come through relatively unscathed but led by men. For example, the Ghanaian President, Nana Addo Dankwa Akufo-Addo, has adopted an approach that embodies taking responsibility, telling the truth and demonstrating empathy (Lilleker, 2021).

In what follows, we look at the level of preparedness in the UK before considering in more detail Johnson's responses to COVID. First we start with the importance of the context and consider the preparedness of the country in terms of depleted resources, distracted politicians and default strategy, before moving on to consider the role of the leadership in terms of denial and displacement.

The context

Harold Macmillan, the British Prime Minister between 1957 and 1963, allegedly responded to a question about what might blow him off course, with the response, 'Events, dear boy; events.' No-one seems to know whether he actually said it, but this perfectly captures an enquiry into leadership and COVID because this single event has indeed blown the whole world out of alignment, and where it will end, no-one seems to know. It is worth starting with the events that swirled around the beginning of the pandemic for the UK in January 2020 and three events seemed to have the eye of British politicians when the Wolf was approaching.

First, the UK had suffered severe flooding between November 2019 and February 2020, mainly in the north and midlands of England and in Wales. All told, England and Wales had the wettest February since records began in 1766. After ten years of austerity, imposed by first a coalition Conservative/Liberal government and then Conservative governments, front-line flood response budgets had been cut by 20 per cent and fire and rescue budgets cut by 25 per cent (BBC News, 2019). Second, the Labour Party – the official opposition that should have been holding the government to account – was embroiled in a lengthy re-election process to replace Jeremy Corbyn after he led Labour into its worst electoral defeat since 1935 on 12 December 2019. Corbyn announced his intention to resign in due course, once his successor had been chosen, and by the time Sir Keir Starmer was elected, it was 4 April and too late. The third event that persuaded Boris Johnson's new government itself to look inwards at the Flow, not outwards at the Wolf, was Brexit. Three and a half years after the referendum to leave the European Union (EU) in June 2016, since when almost everyone had been focused on the intricacies of getting an agreement through Parliament, Johnson signed the Withdrawal Agreement on 31 January 2020 and the government began to congratulate itself on its achievement, even as the Wolf pawed at the door. This was also the day the first two people with COVID were admitted to hospital in the UK. A week later, Johnson waved away fears over shutting down economies to contain the virus in a speech at the Old Royal Naval College in Greenwich – symbol of British imperial rule (Calvert and Arbuthnott, 2021: 5).

The first of the relevant emergency COBR (Cabinet Office Briefing Room) meetings of the UK government was on 24 January 2020. Matt Hancock (the Secretary of State for Health and Social Care) chaired the meeting in the absence of the Prime Minister, and announced that the risk to the UK was 'low,' even though an article in the *Lancet* of the same date by Chinese medics suggested that COVID was likely to be as dangerous as Spanish flu – which killed 50 million people in 1919. A *Sunday Times* investigation subsequently discovered that Johnson had missed five COBR meetings dealing with the pandemic, and though British Prime Ministers do not always chair such meetings, it seems that Johnson was not dealing with other important issues but actually spent the whole period relaxing at his country retreat, Chequers, leaving the Labour opposition to accuse him of being MIA (missing in action). As the *Sunday Times* suggested, quoting an unnamed senior advisor, 'Johnson didn't do weekends . . . he didn't do urgent crisis planning' (quoted in Walker, 2020). Indeed, Johnson was overheard saying 'The best thing would be to ignore it,' on the grounds that an overreaction would do more harm than good (Kuenssberg, 2021). Anyway, as a spokesperson for Johnson announced when questioned about the virus, the UK was 'well prepared for any new diseases' (quoted in Calvert et al., 2020). Johnson did not attend another COBR meeting until 2 March – five weeks later. So, if Brexit had not happened, there had been no floods, and the Labour Party had a stable leadership, would the British state have been in a better place to withstand the COVID Wolf?

Not necessarily, because by then, it was already too late. As an unnamed source explained:

> Contrary to the official line, Britain was in a poor state of readiness for a pandemic. Emergency stockpiles of PPE [personal protective equipment] had severely dwindled and gone out of date after becoming a low priority in the years of austerity cuts. The training to prepare key workers for a pandemic had been put on hold for two years while contingency planning was diverted to deal with a possible no-deal Brexit.
>
> (quoted in Calvert et al., 2020)

So when COVID arrived in the UK, after a decade of austerity, the budget had been cut and nursing shortages in 2019 were at 40,000. Severin Schwan, CEO of Roche, told BBC Newsnight:

> the real issue here is that the UK has probably not invested enough into healthcare, both in absolute terms and in relative terms over many years. That was a problem to start with, but it really shows up in such a crisis when the system is more stressed . . . The cooperation and the partnership with the government is excellent, but you can't fix the infrastructure in a couple of weeks.
>
> (quoted in Thomas, 2020)

The first warning to the World Health Organization (WHO) from China came on 31 December 2019, and it noted that Wuhan city had experienced several cases of an unusual pneumonia, but the warning suggested the virus could not be passed between people. However, Devi Sridhar, Professor of Global Public Health at Edinburgh University, had already predicted the possibility of a virus jumping species – and turning into a pandemic – two years earlier. And on 16 January 2020, she tweeted 'Take it seriously because of cross-border spread (planes means bugs travel far and fast), likely human-to-human transmission and previous outbreaks have taught overresponding is better than delaying action' (quoted in Calvert et al., 2020).

One of those learning sessions occurred in October 2016, at Imperial College London, through "Exercise Cygnus." It was a drill involving government departments, the NHS and local authorities to establish the preparedness of the country in the face of a pandemic generated by an H2N2 influenza virus. This is different from COVID, but the results have been alarmingly similar: in both 2016 and in 2020, there was a clear recognition that the UK was woefully underprepared for any such eventuality: there was not enough personal protective equipment (PPE) or ventilators or critical care beds and the morgues were unable to cope with the increasing number of bodies arriving on a daily basis. In fact, Toynbee (2020) suggest that it was deliberate government policy to run down the stock of PPE by 40 per cent during the decade of austerity.

The report on "Exercise Cygnus" was never published, perhaps because the government did not want to alarm the public and perhaps because the government did not want to fund the extra resources necessary to cope with a real pandemic. After all, both Jeremy Hunt, the then Health Secretary, and Simon Stevens, Chief Executive of NHS England, were reducing NHS bed numbers then in line with the government's austerity programme. Moreover, the two previous alarms, the 2009 H1N1 (swine flu) pandemic, and the 2013–2016 West African Ebola case, had proved to be nothing like the dangers first envisaged. But by the time the real Wolf arrived, the shepherd had fallen asleep on duty.

As one source told Calvert et al. (2020),

> the plans to protect the UK in a pandemic had once been a priority and had been well funded for the decade following the 9/11 terrorist attacks in 2001. But then austerity cuts struck. We were the envy of the world, but pandemic planning became a casualty of the austerity years, when there were more pressing needs.

The NHS has been chronically underfunded for years (Levi, 2021),[2] partly because it spends so much on the PFI (Private Finance Initiative) loans with which many hospitals were built or updated in previous administration.[3] In fact, the claim that the government had already provided 'a billion items of PPE' by late April turns out to hinge on how items were counted. Thus, it appears to include counting pieces of cleaning equipment, waste bags and even counting gloves as two items, which might explain why so many front-line NHS workers appear in a variety of garb, including domestic swimming goggles, and home-made visors and gowns. This was probably helped by the government downgrading the status of COVID from 'a high consequence infectious disease' and removing it from the list which included a legal requirement for the government to provide the requisite PPE; that is, a respiratory face mask, a full face visor, gowns and gloves. The effect of the downgrading was to reduce the legal requirements to 'apron, alcohol hand rub and gloves' – and, as John Ashton, former president of the Faculty of Public Health noted, 'This must have been done because they [the government] realised they weren't going to have enough equipment and they needed to somehow have a story that stacked up with being caught out on supplies' (quoted on BBC1, 2020). As Ashton concluded, 'There's no excuse for not having adequate stockpiles. You need everything to protect against this kind of virus. It's heart-breaking that there were no gowns at all in stock; breath-taking' (quoted on BBC1, 2020).

Moreover, the whole month of February 2020 seemed to have been wasted, and that was after the European Centre for Disease Control warned the government in early February that COVID was going to result in need for a huge supply of respirator masks, gowns, eye protectors and gloves. But Johnson's party of libertarian Brexiteers were looking inwards and celebrating their efforts, and almost certainly not going to pay any attention to any European institution, having just abandoned the EU. As Ashton contends,

> The government failed to understand what was coming our way at the end of January. They failed to get a grip. And when things started to get out of control, they started to spin a story to make out that they had been following the science and that everything made perfect sense. I think it's disgraceful.
>
> (quoted on BBC1, 2020)

In fact, infections accelerated from 200,000 to 1.5 million in the nine days before lockdown and Southampton University estimated that 190,000 people had flown from Wuhan and other high-risk Chinese cities to the UK between January and March, all unmonitored (Calvert and Arbuthnott, 2021: 9, 64).

Why were these warnings also ignored? One reason is because the Conservative Party has historically been rooted in running the smallest possible state, leaving proactive decisions to the market; and only if the market fails, then, and only then, should the state step in and create the necessary infrastructure. In effect, the Conservative government is ideologically primed for being reactive not proactive – and is thus usually chasing public or national problems, rather than preventing them.

> As one source with knowledge of the Cabinet Office document said, the UK had not properly focused on the pandemic threat, and had been caught flat-footed. . . . The really frustrating thing is that there were plans. But over the last few years emergency planning has been focused on political drivers, like Brexit and flooding. . . . There was a national plan for dealing with a pandemic that should have been implemented. But who took control of that? And who was responsible for making sure that plans were being made at a local level? The truth is, I am not sure anyone was doing this.
>
> (quoted in Hopkins, 2020)

Sridhar (2020a) has argued that actually the UK government got it wrong from the start by misunderstanding the nature of the threat. If COVID had been a conventional influenza virus, then two of the three standard responses would have been viable: (1) allow the virus to spread, knowing that its effects were dangerous but not deadly and eventually immunity would resolve the problem – this would have suited the neo-liberal playbook since the state need not intervene; or (2) lock down the country so that the level of illness was kept within the existing capacity of the NHS. The UK seemed to have 'mutated' from (1) to (2) over the first few weeks of the outbreak, by which time the virus was running free in the community and the UK has spent every moment thereafter catching up. Option (3), which was taken by South Korea and subsequently New Zealand, was to assume the virus was unlike influenza and was deadly – if allowed to spread. The response, therefore, was much more proactive than the reactive responses embodied in (1) and (2), and involved seeking out and isolating the virus through a widespread and rapid test, trace and isolate strategy – which effectively meant the entire population did not have to be locked in, only those who had the virus, including those checked at the border. The result has been that South Korea has 50 times fewer deaths than the UK (BBC Panorama, 2021). But the UK government never had enough PPE for (3), and at the time of writing (March 2021) still doesn't have what Johnson called a 'World beating' infrastructure for track, trace and isolate despite spending £37 billion (Triggle, 2021).[4] The UK only addressed its open borders a year after the pandemic was announced by the WHO – and the alleged reason it didn't close the borders a year earlier was because the Foreign Office needed to allow time for the Brits abroad to get home. Twelve months later, it is little wonder that the UK has some of the highest rates of infection and death (Calvert and Arbuthnott, 2021).

We can contrast the British response with that of South Korea, which had its first COVID patient just eleven days before the UK. According to Dr Lee Hyuk Min, director of infection control affairs at the Korean Society for Laboratory Medicine, by the time the country had its fourth positive test, the government was already holding emergency meetings and had devised the three-fold strategy that has seen the country escape the worst of the COVID pandemic: mass testing, real-time tracking and self-isolation. Within a fortnight, the country was producing 100,000 self-testing kits. In contrast, the UK has played constant catch-up – and never caught up because they both missed the critical 'golden time' very early on in the pandemic (Moon, 2020). It is not as if there were no plans – but the plans were not implemented, partly because planning smacked of the 'Nanny State' and Johnson's government was ideologically disinterested in public planning. According to Martin Hibberd, who advised Singapore about the dangers, Singapore prepared instantly for the first infections from China – using UK planning procedures which the UK itself failed to implement.

Beyond the poor state of preparation that the UK was in as the pandemic broke, what is the role of decision-makers in all this? In the next section, we consider this question, focusing particularly on the role of denial, delusion and displacement.

The Wolf arrives

When we search for explanations for failure, we need to consider whether the investigation seeks out the systemic problems or the personal failings of individual leaders. As Durkheim argued (1973), when we focus on leaders, we expect them to be god-like in their ability to solve all our problems, and then – the other side of the same coin – we scapegoat them when they inevitably fail us (the followers), because not only are they not gods but they are merely cogs, albeit large cogs, in a system that has also failed. We should keep that in mind when considering the COVID outbreak and recognise that the leadership cadre of the NHS had responsibilities, too – demanding better from the government, speaking truth to power, accepting responsibilities and learning from them. Indeed, as the testimony of Dominic Cummings to the British Parliament Select Committee on 26 May 2021 suggests, the failures at the top were not just those of Boris Johnson (BBC News, 2021b). Yet, the history of scapegoating suggests that searching out the systematic causes of failure is often too painful because the mirror reflects badly upon all; better then, for the majority, to seek out and cast out a few scapegoats so that the body-politic can continue.

The displacement also involved reconstructing 'Durkheim's coin': the opposite of a scapegoat this time – the hero. In order for the public not to concentrate their ire on the villain of the piece, there is also a need to generate a hero or heroes to distract attention. In the COVID example, the heroes are groups like all front-line health workers for whom a weekly public clapping event was organised, supported by the government, combined with calls for the NHS to receive the George Cross, as did the island of Malta during the Second World War. This displacement has clearly not enthralled everyone: as one NHS nurse suggested, 'Calling us heroes just makes it OK when we die' (quoted in BBC1, 2020). Or the heroes are individuals, like Captain Moore and his remarkable fundraising walks around his garden which have led to all kinds of honours, from having a postal frank in his honour to securing a Knighthood and an RAF (Royal Air Force) flypast. But the point about these phenomena is not that they are binary choices: *either* genuine displays of public support *or* events open to cynical political manipulation, but rather that they are complex ensembles that embody both extremes and every point in between. For the Conservative government, with its preference for market-based policies (the Conservatives voted against setting up the NHS 22 times before 1948), recognising that the NHS is, as Nigel Lawson (Conservative MP at the time) once admitted, 'the closest thing the English people have to a religion' (quoted in Timmins, 2012: 12), is itself a dilemma, solved by the double strategy of denuding it of resources across time and pushing the merits of private health, while simultaneously lauding the NHS front-line staff (though not its management) as heroes.

The displacement from failure to heroism is mirrored by the displacement from politics to science. The UK government trotted out the 'guided by science' mantra on a regular basis – even when those scientific experts often disagreed – and ultimately, the decision was not about scientific data but political acumen, because each decision will have positive and deleterious effects on different parts of the community; in other words, there isn't a win-win solution – there are just trade-offs because this is a Wicked Problem (Grint, 2005). Moreover, since the previous Conservative government spent a lot of effort decrying the value of experts, it has been difficult to suddenly claim conversion to the cause. As Michael Gove (then the Secretary of State for Justice) said on 3 June 2016 on Sky News, 'I think the people in this country have had enough of experts from organisations with acronyms saying that they know what is best and getting it consistently wrong.' To shift from this statement to claiming that we have to listen to the experts from SAGE is an interesting, but all too common, intellectual U-turn.

Conclusion

This chapter has suggested that the poverty of the British response to COVID – with the single exception of the vaccine programme – can be lain at the door of both individual political leaders like Johnson and those before him who denuded the NHS of resources for a decade, compounded by the consequence of the distraction generated by Brexit. But it is also a result of the ideological preferences of the government that has consistently promoted the market over the state as the best way to deal with the pandemic. It also important to highlight the fabulist nature of populist leaders like Johnson: in the land of unicorns, it seems it is best to deal with wolves simply by denying their existence. On 8 November 2019, Johnson was touring Northern Ireland to assure business people that Brexit would offer nothing but bountiful largesse, and certainly not the mountain of paperwork that has actually swamped many businesses there. Thus when asked by Irwin Armstrong, owner of CIGA Healthcare, whether he could 'go back to my company in the morning and tell my staff we will not be filling in any customs declarations for good leaving Northern Ireland to go to GB?', Johnson replied, 'You can [and] if somebody asks you to do that, tell them to ring up the Prime Minister and I will direct them to throw that form in the bin' (quoted in Daily and Baines, 2019). But the real question is why do people still follow such leaders? From a psychoanalytic perspective, followers appear to identify with these kinds of charismatics or even regress as they substitute their own ego-ideal for that of their leaders, and perhaps this is why their support base remains so robust (Maccoby and Cortina, 2021). Whatever the reason, the assumptions of rational debate and logical reasoning do not play much part in this. And the moral of the tale? If a leader promises something that is too good to be true, it probably isn't true.

Notes

1 (www.statista.com/statistics/1104709/coronavirus-deaths-worldwide-per-million-inhabitants/) accessed 12 March 2021.
2 Germany spent proportionately more on health than the UK: €4,271 (£3,744) per person (11.1 per cent of gross domestic product) in 2016, when the UK spent €3,566 per person on healthcare (9.7 per cent of GDP) (Morris, 2020). Germany also has four times the number of intensive care beds and 50 per cent more doctors than the UK (BBC Panorama, 2021).
3 Using PFI enables the government to adopt an accounting sleight of hand and not to add the loan to the accumulated national debt.
4 That's more than the UK spends on primary and pre-primary education in a year, three times the cost of the highly effective vaccination programme; it would provide every working adult with £1,000, and was described by Nick Macpherson (ex-leading Treasury civil servant) as the 'most wasteful and inept public spending programme of all time' (quoted in Rawnsley, 2021: 41).

References

Achen, C. H. and Bartell, L. M. (2016) *Democracy for Realists*. Princeton: Princeton University Press.
Arnold, M. (1867/1932) *The Study of Celtic Literature*. London: Dent.
BBC1 (2020) 'Has the government failed the NHS?' *Panorama*, 27 April.

BBC News (2019) 'Have fire and flood services been cut?' 12 November.

BBC News (2021a) 'UK's death rate 7% above normal in 2020', 19 March.

BBC News (2021b) www.bbc.co.uk/news/blogs-the-papers-57263551.

BBC Panorama (2021) 'Covid: Who got it right?' *Broadcast*, 22 March.

Bennett, C. (2021) 'Boris Johnson a feminist? Well, apart from his policies, his antics and his jokes. . .' *The Guardian*, 14 March.

Brown, A. (2014) *The Myth of the Strong Leader: Political Leadership in the Modern Age*. London: Bodley Head.

Brummelmen, E., Nevicka, B. and O'Brienet, J.M. (2021) 'Narcissism and Leadership in Children', *Psychological Science*. https://doi.org/10.1177/0956797620965536

Brummelman, E., Sander, T., Nelemans, S.A., Orobio de Castro, B., Overbeek, G. and J. Bushman, B.J. (2015) 'Origins of narcissism in children', *Proceedings of the National Academy of Sciences* 112(12), 1–4.

Calvert, J. and Arbuthnott, G. (2021) *Failures of State: The Inside Story of Britain's Battle with Coronavirus*. London: Mudlark.

Calvert, J., Arbuthnott, G. and Leake, J. (2020) 'Coronavirus: 38 days when Britain sleepwalked into disaster', *Sunday Times*, 19 April.

Collinson, D. (2012) 'Prozac leadership and the limits of positive thinking', *Leadership* 8(2), 87–107.

Daily, P. and Baines, M. (2019) 'Johnson tells Northern Ireland businesses to "bin" customs forms', *Belfast Telegraph*, 8 November. www.belfasttelegraph.co.uk/news/northern-ireland/johnson-tells-northern-ireland-businesses-to-bin-customs-forms-38674258.html, accessed 17 March.

Durkheim, E. (1973/1883) 'Address to the Lycéen of Sans', in Bellah, R.N. (ed.) *Emile Durkheim on Morality and Society*. Chicago: University of Chicago Press.

Enzensberger, M. (1997) 'The hero as demolition man', in *Zig Zag: The Politics of Culture*. New York: The New Press.

Garikipati, S. and Kambhampati, U. (2020) 'Leading the fight against the pandemic: Does gender really matter?' https://ssrn.com/abdstract=3617953, accessed 11 September.

Grint, K (2005) 'Problems, problems, problems: The social construction of leadership', *Human Relations* 58(11), 1467–1494.

Hopkins, N. (2020) 'Revealed: UK ministers were warned last year of risks of coronavirus pandemic', *Guardian*, 24 April.

Jenkins, S. (2021) 'Boris Johnson's Brexit shenanigans have met their reckoning in Northern Ireland', *The Guardian*, 8 March.

Johnson, B. (2014) *The Churchill Factor: How One Man made History*. London: Hodder & Stoughton.

Kuenssberg, L. (2021) 'Covid: The inside story of the government's battle against the virus', *BBC News*, 16 March.

Levi, M. (2021) 'Underfunded but "fabulously well organised": A hospital trust chief on the NHS', *The Guardian*, 19 March.

Lewis, H. (2020) 'The Pandemic had revealed the weakness of strongmen', *The Atlantic*, 6 May.

Lilleker, D. (2021) 'Coronavirus one year on: Two countries that got it right, and three that got it wrong', *The Conversation*, 10 March.

Maccoby, M. and Cortina, M. (eds.) (2021) *Leadership, Psychoanalysis, and Society*. London: Routledge.

Miller, S. (2020) 'The secret to Germany's COVID-19 success: Angela Merkel is a scientist', *The Atlantic,* 20 April. www.theatlantic.com/international/archive/2020/04/angela-merkel-germany-coronavirus-pandemic/610225/, accessed 30 April.

Moon, G. (2020) 'What the UK can learn from South Korea's success with flattening the curve?' *Independent*, 9 April.

Morris, C. (2020) 'Coronavirus: What can the UK learn from Germany on testing?' *BBC News*, 11 April. www.bbc.co.uk/news/health-52234061, accessed 28 April.

Popper, K. (1959) *The Logic of Scientific Discovery*. London: Routledge.

Rawnsley, A. (2021) 'The record-beating cost to the taxpayer of this shockingly wasteful government', *The Observer*, 14 March.

Sridhar, D. (2020a) 'Interview on BBC Radio 4', *Today*, 1 May.

Thomas, H. (2020) 'UK underinvested in healthcare, says pharma boss', BBC *Newsnight*. www.bbc.co.uk/news/business-52387605, accessed 30 April.

Timmins, N. (2012) *Never Again? The Story of the Health and Social Care Act 2012*. London: The Kings Fund and the Institute for Government.

Toynbee, P. (2020) 'Boris Johnson is the wrong man in the wrong job at the wrong time', *The Guardian*, 20 April.

Triggle, N. (2021) 'Covid-19: NHS test and trace "no clear impact" despite £37bn budget', *BBC News*, 11 March.

Walker, P. (2020) 'Boris Johnson missed five coronavirus Cobra meetings, Michael Gove says', *The Guardian*, 19 April.

Weber, M. (1922/1978) *Economy and Society*. Berkeley: University of California Press.

5   Leadership in a National Crisis

Alan Hooper

Every leader of any organisation, be it large or small, knows that they will face a number of crises during their tenure and that these invariably arrive when least expected. They are also aware that their reputations are likely to be lost or made on how they respond, especially at the beginning. This is even more pronounced for those who lead their nations. This chapter explores how the UK national leadership responded at the beginning of two crises: the Falklands War in 1982 and the COVID pandemic in 2020. Both events were unexpected and resulted in the UK having to respond very quickly to numerous and varied challenges which stretched the capabilities of the country to its limit. After the two case studies have been addressed, the chapter will conclude with an analysis comparing the reaction of the government and the lessons learnt in these two very different scenarios.

The criteria for leadership in crisis will have been addressed elsewhere in this book; this chapter is focussed on *national leadership*, especially the requirements at the beginning of a crisis. There are four key requirements at that level. The first is for the government to recognise that it is facing a real crisis. Sometimes this is relatively easy (such as the threat of war), but at other times, it can be complicated because it is difficult to identify what is actually happening. Indeed, some argue that there is no such thing as a crisis (Spector, 2019). In the chaos of the first hours and days, with a multitude of conflicting information swamping the systems, the behaviour of the national leader is crucial. Their attitude at the beginning of the crisis will set the tone for the duration. Although personally they may be uncertain what to do, a calm and authoritative presence will provide a confidence to those around them which will steady the nerves. There is also the need to identify early the important information required to take crucial decisions subsequently at the appropriate time. Decisiveness and clear direction at the beginning of the crisis is essential for the planning to commence. It is the planning process which enables all the government agencies to collaborate together to address the key issues.

The second ingredient is credibility, both with their close team and the wider public. Inevitably, there will be anxiety within the nation which is likely to increase as events unfold. Winning peoples' trust from the outset and sustaining it throughout is crucial and difficult, especially in a democratic society. This becomes particularly important when the public are asked to accept restrictions which impact on their daily lives. Regular press briefings, reinforcement of key messages, being open about failures, countering false information, and never over-promising and under-delivering are all accepted standard public relations principles (Hooper, 1982). It is a tricky role for a Prime Minister to fulfil; on the one hand, people look to them for inspiration, but on the other hand, they also expect their leader to level with them when things look bleak. Without the latter, trust is likely to erode and will be difficult to retrieve.

DOI: 10.4324/9781003171737-6

The third ingredient concerns trust of a different kind. The Prime Minister will need to put trust in experts, most of whom they will not have met and who will probably have been brought together very quickly to form ad hoc teams. They will provide the expertise on which the national leadership will base their decisions. This is an unusual situation for political leaders who are used to being in control of the agenda, whereas in a crisis, this is seldom the case. Indeed, most of the time, they are just trying to get ahead of the curve. Furthermore, given the typical profile of those who rise to high office, it is also especially difficult for political leaders as their behaviours may change when under pressure. Attributes that serve them well in normal circumstances may appear to be ineffective and dysfunctional. For example, reasoned decision-making may be replaced by narcissism, and mutual trust discarded for passive-aggressive behaviour, leading to a profound loss of leadership effectiveness (Dotlich and Cairo, 2003).

The final point is about logistics. In a national crisis, the key to successful resolution will inevitably involve having enough resources deployed at the right time. This embraces sufficiency, as well as the ability to deploy on a national scale. This is not an easy combination, which once again places political leaders in unfamiliar territory; they can often be impatient for quick results when long-term success is usually based on sound, painstaking logistical planning and delivery. These difficulties can be off-set by proper contingency planning, provided they have been exercised. This occurred during the two episodes of BSE (bovine spongiform encephalopathy, or 'mad cow disease') in the 1980s and 1990s, when the UK government was slow to apply the lessons from the first episode to the second a few years later, despite the disease following a similar pattern.

Having considered these aspects, we will now look at two case studies before assessing how the UK government matched up to the criteria.

The Falklands Crisis – 1982

The Royal Marines officer usually cycled from his flat in London to the Ministry of Defence (MoD), but this time he took a taxi; it was 4.30 in the morning, and this was the beginning of a very different day. As he paid off the taxi, he met a senior officer at the main entrance.

'Morning, Admiral. What's up?'

We're mobilising the whole fleet.'

What, *all* of it?'

'Yes. It's going to be a long day, so I'm off to get some breakfast while I can.'

As one went off for an early breakfast, the other entered the building to join the first meeting by the Naval Staff to plan the re-capture of the Falkland Islands from the Argentinians. It was the morning of 1 April, only hours after the Prime Minister had taken the decision to mobilise, and a day before the Argentinians invaded.

The UK government had been taken completely by surprise when alerted that an Argentinian fleet had set sail for the Falklands, and this caused considerable alarm amongst the Prime Minister's closest colleagues as they discussed options with her the previous evening. Against the strong advice for caution stood a resolute Margaret Thatcher: 'If the islands were invaded, I knew what we must do – we must get them back' (Woodward and Robinson, 1992: xi). But how? The answer came from an unlikely source when the First Sea Lord, Admiral Sir Henry Leach, joined the group: 'I can put a Task Force together . . . it can be ready to leave in forty-eight hours' (Ibid.: xi).

From a standing start, events moved very quickly. On 2 April, Royal Naval ships and the Royal Marines 3 Commando Brigade were mobilised (a sizeable proportion of the brigade were already on Easter leave). On 3 April, there was an emergency Parliamentary sitting (one of the rare occasions that the House of Commons had met to debate on a Saturday since the Second World War) and the *SS Canberra* was requisitioned as a troop ship (she was on her way home from a three-month world cruise).

The following day, the United Nations condemned Argentinian aggression, and on 5 April, the Foreign Secretary, Lord Carrington, resigned because of the failure of the Foreign and Commonwealth Office to anticipate the invasion (this deprived Thatcher of a trusted and experienced minister just when she needed his wise council). The same day, the initial part of the task force sailed including *HMS Hermes, HMS Invincible* and *HMS Fearless* (with the leading elements of the Commando Brigade embarked) – just five days after the PM's order to go to war. On 9 April, the *Canberra* and other ships set sail with the balance of the Commando Brigade reinforced by two Parachute battalions and substantial logistic support which included 4,500 tonnes of war maintenance reserve of ammunition, fuel, stores and spares. During the course of the three-month conflict, the UK deployed 51 warships, 54 ships taken up from trade (STUFT – 15 fitted with helipads), 30,000 tonnes of ammunition and stores and 500,000 tonnes of fuel (all transported by sea) (Oakley, 1989). This was a huge logistical operation which sustained the landing force over 8,000 miles by sea for several weeks.

If the activities over these hectic early days of the crisis were impressive, the same could not be said of the preceding months. It all started to go wrong when the UK government announced in the autumn of 1981 that *HMS Endurance* would be paid off at the end of her current deployment (she was the maritime presence in the Antarctic and the Falklands waters). This indicated to the military junta in Argentina, headed by General Leopoldo Galtieri, that the UK did not have the will to counter an invasion of the Falklands, which had long been claimed by Argentina. Furthermore, the UK had announced at the same time that both *HMS Hermes* and *HMS Illustrious* were to be sold and the two amphibious ships to be scrapped. If the junta had waited a couple of years, the Royal Navy would not have had the ships to retake the islands; however, they had more pressing economic problems at home, so the recovery of 'las Malvinas' provided a popular diversion for their people.

The other problem for the UK was that there were no contingency plans. Although the possibility of invasion was reviewed periodically, it was thought so unlikely that such plans that did exist realised that nothing short of a deployment of the whole fleet would suffice. At least they got that right! The military commanders therefore had to react extremely quickly when ordered to mobilise on 2 April. Their solution was to adapt the plans for deploying the Commando Brigade to Norway (part of the North Atlantic Treaty Organisation [NATO] contingency deployment to the Northern Flank to counter a possible Soviet invasion there). This made sense because it was exercised annually (indeed, part of the Brigade and *Illustrious* were deployed there in the winter of 1981), and there was also a regular 'paper' contingency exercise carried out by MoD.

Another problem for the military concerned the command and control over the task force. There was no proper joint force command across the three services at that at time. Furthermore, in late March, the Chief of the Defence Staff, Admiral Sir Terence Lewin, was in the United States at a NATO planning conference. However, the seizing the initiative by Admiral Leach (the First Sea Lord) when he met the Prime Minister in the House of Commons automatically resulted in a decision that, as this was an amphibious operation, it would be led by the Royal Navy and would feature the Commando Brigade.

All of this indicates how key were the decisions that the leaders took at the beginning of this crisis. It also illustrates the importance of adapting contingency plans to meet the new criteria – and the role that luck played. The Falklands Campaign was a close-run affair, and only the professionalism and rugged determination of the British Forces saw them through just in time. Had the war gone on for another month into a South Atlantic winter, then it is doubtful whether the ships could have sustained their presence at the required level. As it was, the Royal Navy lost six vessels plus the merchant ship *Atlantic Conveyor* and ten others suffered varying degrees of battle damage. This was in addition to the 255 military personnel killed and over 700 wounded. All of which indicates the dire consequences of going to war.

The other aspect that did not go well was the handling of the press and public information. There were no contingency plans for handling the media. As a result, when the task force was put together so quickly, both the military and the media were caught out. Sensing that this was going to be 'the big story' of the moment, the media quickly assembled reporters and TV crews, only to discover that the Royal Navy decided to restrict the number of press to those they could accommodate on board. As a background, before the campaign, the British government had been openly critical of the way that news was being handled in general (House of Commons Report, 1982), and this suspicion was shared by the Navy. This led to angry exchanges between the media and the military before a decision to take just 29 UK media representatives on board (those news agencies not represented agreed to receive 'pooled' reports). No members of the foreign press were included, which left the UK at considerable disadvantage trying to sway world opinion to counter the stream of information constantly available from Argentina. But that was just the start of the problems. The embarked press soon discovered that they were entirely dependent on the Navy for transmission of copy, that reports were censored on site and that no TV pictures could be transmitted. Whilst there were genuine technical reasons for some of the restrictions, this confrontation reflected the tension between the media's desire to publish and the military concern for maintaining the security of a very difficult operation, the outcome of which was by no means certain (Hooper, 1982).

Once embarked, the military and the press gradually developed 'an understanding'. This improved significantly once the landing force disembarked and the press had to share the dangers of combat and the brutal primitive conditions alongside the troops. Even so, the assault by 2 Para on Goose Green early in the war was given away inadvertently by a BBC radio report before the attack which alerted the Argentinians (Thomson, 1985) due to a misunderstanding about the timing of the broadcast. Back in the UK, the MoD at last got itself organised with daily briefings given by the Acting Head of Public Relations, Ian McDonald. He was not a trained public relations officer, and his delivery was staid and slow, which initially attracted criticism and some incredulity. However, as the campaign progressed and the Navy started to take casualties (such as the sinking of the first ship, *HMS Sheffield*) his credibility grew, and so did the reputation of the UK. It became evident that his reporting of the dramatic events in the South Atlantic was accurate and therefore became increasingly trusted – a crucial development in the media battle with Argentina for world opinion.

The handling of public information by the UK was so poor that the House of Commons set up a Defence Committee immediately after the war to investigate what had gone wrong (the war ended on 14 June and the committee's report was published on 8 December). Many lessons were learnt and formed the basis of subsequent ongoing relations between the military and the media.

This was a short conflict with significant casualties and equipment loss for both sides. For Britain, it was considered a great military victory which enhanced her reputation in the world considerably and also enabled Thatcher's Conservative government to achieve popularity at home (prior to the conflict, the government was deeply unpopular after a shaky start to their its administration).

For Argentina, it led to the downfall of the military junta. The British victory was due to highly skilled military professionalism and effective leadership at all levels from general to corporal; from admiral to junior rating. However, it all stemmed from clear decisiveness by the Prime Minister and also by impressive adaptability by both industry and the military at the beginning of the crisis. That said, it was a close-run thing and many lessons were learnt which had impact on future UK policy.

The 2020 Pandemic

By the end of January 2021, the UK had surpassed 100,000 deaths (only the fifth country in the world to do so). In contrast, it had vaccinated nearly nine million of its people – as many as Germany, France, Italy and Spain combined. And yet, a year earlier, no one was really aware that an awful tsunami was about to engulf the world resulting in over 100 million cases recorded worldwide and two million lives lost a year later. How did this all start – and how did the UK respond?

The COVID pandemic emerged in early December 2019 with mysterious and bewildering pneumonia-like symptoms in a small group of Chinese citizens in the largely unknown city of Wuhan. The Chinese state informed the World Health Organisation (WHO) Country Office on 31 December 2019 (WHO website, 2020), initial disease control mechanisms were deployed and diplomatic reporting started to pick up. Yet, despite a global crisis response, unprecedented diversion of national wealth and elevation to the overriding issue for national governments and multinational institutions, the virus has so far proved to be a stubborn and resilient antagonist. It has generated some of the most innovative changes in pharmaceutical, financial and support services, has truncated vaccination approval pathways significantly and brought the UK together around the National Health Service (NHS) more profoundly than could possibly have been imagined. Indeed, the scale of constraint on personal freedoms and the size of the national debt focussed on the crisis was unconscionable.

Pandemics have sat at the top of National Risk Registers for many years (Cabinet Office, 2008). They represent one of the single biggest disruptions to our way of life, and until the biology of a virus is mapped, they have unknowing containment, treatment and recovery mechanisms whereby impacts can only be measured in years. They equate to enormous strategic financial disasters. Their prominence is underwritten by periodic and catastrophic events – the 1919 'Spanish flu' (H1N1) led to 20–40 million deaths worldwide, the 1957 'Asian flu' (H2N2) to 1.1 million deaths, and the 1968 'Hong Kong' flu (H3N2) an estimated one million deaths (Centers for Disease Prevention and Control website, January, 2020). Indeed, over the past 25 years, more than 30 new, or newly recognised, infections have been identified around the world. The pattern of known infections changes constantly as diseases thrive through expansion beyond boundaries – geographic, cultural and biological.

From a UK perspective, plans to protect the country against a pandemic had been top priority and had been well funded since the 9/11 attacks in the United States in 2001. This culminated in Exercise Cygnus in 2016 which predicted that the NHS would collapse in a pandemic and accordingly made a number of recommendations. Unfortunately, these deficiencies were not implemented because the preparations for a no-deal Brexit 'sucked all the blood out of pandemic planning' in the following years (Calvert et al., *Sunday Times*, 2020). This was to be the start of the problems for the UK.

Boris Johnson had won an election in December 2019 with a surprisingly large majority of over 80 due largely to his determination to take the UK out of Europe. It was the end of bitter division within the country which had dominated politics since the 2016 European

Referendum and was not to end until the following year with an 'eleventh hour' deal with the European Union (EU) on Christmas Eve 2020. This left the government with little time or energy to consider other issues, let alone identify the crisis about to hit them. Besides, there were other issues dominating the headlines such as the celebration of 'Brexit' day on 31 January 2020 with a rousing optimistic speech by the Prime Minister. However, the day before the WHO had announced that the coronavirus was a global emergency, and on 6 February, the UK had its second outbreak. The good news was that all the contacts of that case were traced and tested, but this encouraging response led to a false assumption: that the country was facing a *flu* virus and therefore the best option was to let it run its course; there was no need for mass testing. This in turn led to 'drift' throughout most of February, with no attempt to acquire further testing equipment. Furthermore, there had been a failure to replenish gowns and masks, essential for health and care workers, which were then discovered to be out of date.

By 21 February, 76,000 people were infected worldwide and there were 2,300 deaths in China, but Nervtag, a government advisory committee, still decided to keep the threat level in UK at 'moderate.' This all changed five days later when another advisory committee warned the government that the country was facing a catastrophe if it did not take drastic action. Finally, the government realised just how serious this was – and on 28 February, with the virus taking increasing hold in UK, the Prime Minister took to the airwaves to admit that COVID was now the top priority and that he would be chairing the next Cabinet Office Briefing Room (Cobra) meeting on 2 March. The stock markets immediately plunged.

But why was the government so slow on the uptake, especially as other countries around the world had gone into lockdown some three weeks earlier? As already mentioned, wrongly identifying the type of pandemic was one reason, out of date stock was another and there was also differing advice from a variety of experts. However, there was a more fundamental issue: the Prime Minister had been absent. After signing the EU Withdrawal Agreement and reshuffling his cabinet, he spent two weeks over the spring half-term with his pregnant fiancée, Carrie Symonds, relaxing at Chevening. He missed the first Cobra meeting on COVID in late January and did not attend another one until 2 March, missing five crucial weekly meetings. The claim from the Prime Minister's Office was that he was kept informed, but the evidence does not bear this out. Furthermore, what was missing was the large personality of Johnson. This became more evident when he was hospitalised on 5 April with COVID and then placed in intensive care for a week, not returning to work until 27 April. During that period, although the Foreign Secretary stood in for him, it became evident that no contingency had been made for a Deputy Prime Minister with proper accountability. To try to deal with a crisis – let alone one as complicated as this – without a nominated deputy was an extraordinary oversight. This is why the military always have a deputy commander; a lesson learnt from bitter experience in war.

Mr Johnson chaired his first pandemic Cobra meeting on 2 March and the decision-making process started to crank up with the Scientific Advisory Group for Emergencies (SAGE) raising the threat level to 'severe' on 12 March. However, it was not until 23 March that the Prime Minister announced that the country would go into a lockdown. It is appreciated that this was a hugely difficult decision to take. However, this delay cost many lives and also enabled the Cheltenham Festival to go ahead with at least 60,000 people crowded together each afternoon to watch the four-day horse racing event – a magnet for the virus. So, some seven weeks after the first case was identified in the UK, a strategic decision was finally taken, but it was far too late and well behind other countries. This was surprising as the virus had spread to other nations ahead of Britain (Italy being a prime example), and the government had ample warning of the approaching danger.

The announcement of the first lockdown (there were to be another two within a year) is an appropriate place to assess the effectiveness of the leadership and decision-making at the beginning of this crisis. Failure to follow up on contingency plans, 'absent' leadership and an understandable fixation on the complexity of the Brexit negotiations all combined to overwhelm the government with the result that it did not have the spare capacity to deal with a pandemic of this nature. Identification of the size of the problem came far too late, and as a result, there was little proper analysis or strategic direction in the crucial early days. Furthermore, shortages of intensive care ventilators, personal protective equipment (forcing some nurses to wear bin bags) and insufficient supplies of testing equipment all exacerbated the problem (Calvert et al., *Sunday Times*, 2020). Even worse, there were boasts of unsubstantiated 'world class' performances, lack of awareness of what was happening in the rest of the world, failure to listen to experts warning of catastrophe and a tendency to over-promise and under-deliver. It is not clear whether this was due to a misplaced overconfidence, lack of appropriate experience and talent at the top of government, or sheer bad luck of the timing of major events coinciding at the same time. Whichever it was, it resulted in the UK being 'behind the curve' at the beginning of the pandemic and it took a very long time for the government to recover its balance. There were, however, some impressive achievements which may indicate how the country could be better prepared for the next major crisis.

The first was a willingness to engage with the public via regular press briefings at which the government explained what it was trying to achieve. There was an evident transparency, especially by the Prime Minister and the Secretary of Health (often flanked by the Chief Medical Officer and the Chief Scientific Adviser) which was fundamental in getting the public to change their daily habits in order to protect themselves and others from the deadly virus, and crucially, to prevent the NHS from being overwhelmed. Such open communication is essential in a democracy, where it is better to persuade than to dictate, but there are dangers to this approach, as it leaves the government open to challenge (as occurred this time with a vocal minority denying that there was a virus at all) and it requires the spokesperson to adopt the right tone. After a difficult start, including the Prime Minister's occasional eccentric phraseology and exaggerated claims: 'our fantastic testing system' and 'we are very, very, well prepared' (Editorial, *Sunday Times*, 2020), the communication gradually improved and was instrumental in getting the public to agree to the tightest restriction on their personal life since the Second World War some 70 years earlier. That said, the over optimistic promises by the government gradually undermined its credibility.

The second achievement concerns the NHS. Well trained to deal with crises at individual and clinical levels, it was less well prepared for a national organisational crisis of a pandemic. It rose to the challenge magnificently through adaptive, flexible, innovative leadership and performance, despite many hundreds of clinicians, nurses and support staff being infected (50 had died of the virus by mid-April). In spite of their heroic efforts, it soon became apparent that hospitals would become overwhelmed by the number of patients being admitted (by mid-April, over 100,000 people had been infected and 15,000 had died). This problem was solved by the MoD agreeing to help with the building and staffing of the Nightingale Hospitals network across the country, thus providing thousands of extra intensive care beds through the 'COVID Support Force' (MOD website, 2020). This impressive initiative enabled a number of temporary hospitals to be established across the country. The first was built at the ExCel London convention centre on 3 April – constructed in just nine days. It was a good example of the government delegating this task to an organisation well practised in crisis management: the military.

The third achievement was somewhat different and demonstrated proper strategic think-ing. As soon as bio-scientists were aware of the spread of the virus at the beginning of 2020, there was unprecedented activity across the world to develop an effective vaccine. It involved extraordinary cooperation across nations in a race to find a solution. The prospects did not look good (for instance, there is still no vaccine effective against acquired immune deficiency syndrome [AIDS]). In April, the Prime Minister asked Kate Bingham (a venture capitalist and also trained as a biochemist) to head up a British vaccine task force with the simple remit to stop people dying. She immediately selected a small team with the appropriate expertise, and within two weeks, they had identified 23 possible vaccines. This was narrowed down to seven options and the government signed contracts with those selected pharmaceutical companies, paying £900 million up front to fund research – whilst appreciating that most of this money would not be recoverable if a vaccine failed. However, the contracts were care-fully written whereby the UK was guaranteed a specific number of any successful vaccines.

This proved to be a far-sighted approach, as in November (only seven months later), Pfizer-BioNTech announced that their vaccine had passed clinical trials, swiftly follow by Oxford-AstraZeneca, with a combined total of 140 million injections. These two vaccines received approval by the British regulatory authority in December and the first inocula-tion was delivered on 4 January 2021. By the end of that month, three vaccines had been approved, there were four in the pipeline and over nine million people had been vaccinated in UK. The country had 'amassed an order book of 407 million doses, enough for more than six jabs for ever member of the population' (O'Neill and Whipple, *The Times*, 2 February 2021). This was an astonishing achievement.

It had taken a very long time for the UK to recover from its poor response at the beginning of the crisis. However, at last it could properly claim to be the first country in the Western world to commence a mass vaccination programme.

Analysis

So, set against the criteria outlined at the beginning of this chapter, what are the lessons to emerge from these two case studies?

In both examples, the UK government was taken by surprise and missed the cues of the approaching crisis. The difference was that Thatcher took decisive action from the outset and her rapid decision to act enabled the planning process to commence and set in train a series of actions which led to an unlikely military victory three months later. In contrast, Johnson did not properly engage for five weeks, resulting in his government remaining behind the curve for months. There was also a distinct difference in style; Thatcher displayed a calm-ness under pressure (whatever her inner feelings) which affected those around her, whereas Johnson often appeared indecisive and unsure. Neither had the appropriate experience or expertise for their particular crisis; however, it was remarked that Thatcher asked a series of searching questions at her early briefings to enable her to have sufficient knowledge to make the necessary key decisions later on (such as the order to sink the Argentinian cruiser *ARA General Belgrano*).

With regard to credibility, the Johnson government held a series of regular press confer-ences, supported by media interviews by ministers, both to inform the public and also to persuade them of the need to adopt a very restrictive lifestyle. This open persuasive approach worked; however, their credibility was frequently undermined by exaggerated promises. In contrast, the Thatcher government adopted a stilted old-fashioned public relations approach in which the Prime Minister scarcely featured at all. However, the nation, and increasingly the world, grew to trust the official pronouncements which were underpinned by admission of setbacks (such as ship losses). Establishing trust with the public, especially with today's 24/7 media coverage, is essential. In both cases, the government found this difficult, and it is not clear whether a slick media campaign hinders or helps. However, it is interesting that, over time, Johnson gained more credibility via numerous press conferences through more transparency and realistic pronouncements, but it took a year to achieve this.

Both governments learnt to trust their experts. Thatcher empowered the military, and Johnson 'followed the science' – and, on the whole, they both avoided the temptation to interfere too much. This is an unnatural situation for a politician, as it means that they are not in control. However, in both cases, the restraint paid off; Britain won the war in the Falklands and eventually overcame the virus. There were a good examples of politicians and experts working well together in the development and roll-out of the vaccine programme. Johnson identified the right person to address a key problem, Kate Bingham resolved the issue within six months, and the Health Department ensured a good commercial contract.

In both examples, the government faced significant logistical challenges. At the beginning, in spite of no contingency plans, the Thatcher government succeeded by adapting the plans from regular military exercises, whereas the Johnson government failed due to underestimating the size of the problem and also poor administration. In both cases, there was clear evidence of quick adaptability (converting the cruise ship *Canberra* and building the Nightingale hospitals). There was also considerable ingenuity and flexibility shown by the professional experts (the military and the NHS). Over time, the politicians grew to appreciate the complexity of the logistical issues, and then started to issue 'stretch' targets. Some of these were unrealistic, but these political pressures provided a constant sense of urgency. Interestingly, there was a tendency for the public to blame the politicians, rather than the professionals, for any shortfalls.

The Lessons

The main lessons for the beginning of a crisis are the need to identify the key essential issue, take decisive action from the outset, start the planning process and delegate to and trust the professionals. Failure to address these matters means that it will probably take months to recover, if recovery happens at all.

Furthermore, political leaders should expect and be prepared for crises. This involves developmental training. Whenever one surveys the names of those attending senior leadership and management courses in UK, the absence of politicians is both marked and remarked on. Why is it that political parties do not identify their high potential individuals and sponsor them on appropriate courses? Do they think that politicians do not require the same careful development that other organisations do? There are some very good existing short senior programmes which would be most beneficial for individuals who have the potential to become government ministers.

Once an individual has been appointed as a minister, they should be expected to participate in regular exercises based on possible crisis scenarios. After all, this is a normal procedure for the emergency services and the armed forces, and it is strange that political leaders do not see the need to do the same. Contingency plans should be written and exercised regularly with full participation by ministers. Although the precise nature of the crisis may be difficult to identify in advance, regular exercising of contingency plans enables the key players in governmental agencies to identify potential flaws and also build up cohesion and relation-ships which are essential at the beginning of a crisis. Adapting 'a plan' is much easier than starting from cold.

Perhaps the key lesson from the pandemic is that 'the business of government' is far too important to rely on gifted amateurs any longer, especially when the consequences of national failure in a crisis are so dire.

References

Cabinet Office (2008) *National Risk Register*, London: HMSO.

Calvert, J, Arbuthnott, G. and Leake, J. (19 April 2020) When Britain sleep walked into disaster, *Sunday Times*.

Centers for Disease Control and Prevention website (13 January 2021) *Influenza.*

Dotlich, D. and Cairo, C. (2003) *Why CEOs Fail*, San Francisco: Jossey-Bass.

Hooper, A. (1982) *The Military and the Media*, Aldershot: Gower.

House of Commons Report (1982) *The Handling of Press and Public Information during the Falklands Conflict*, London: HMSO.

MOD website (23 March 2020) COVID-19 Support Force: The MODs contribution to the coronavirus response.

Oakley, D. (1989) *The Falklands Military Machine*, Tunbridge Wells: Spellmount.

O'Neill, S. and Whipple, T. (2 February 2021) How Britain placed its bets boldly and reaped rewards, *The Times.*

Spector, B (2019) *Constructing Crisis: Leaders, Crisis, and Claims of Urgency*, Cambridge: Cambridge University Press.

Sunday Times Editorial (24 May 2020) Three weeks of inertia that led to the worst of all worlds, *Sunday Times*.

Thomson, J. (1985) *No Picnic*, London: Leo Cooper.

WHO website (5 January 2020) Pneumonia of unknown causes -China, *Disease Outbreak News.*

Woodward, J. and Robinson, P. (1992) *One Hundred Days*, London: HarperCollins.

6 Spontaneous leadership

Ian MacQueen

***

Whether John Kenneth Galbraith's statement that "all of the great leaders have had one characteristic in common . . . the willingness to confront unequivocally the major anxiety of their people in their time" (Galbraith, 1977, p. 330) is accurate is debatable; however, for anybody in a leadership position, it should be their defining attribute. The current COVID pandemic is unique in my lifetime and many others. It is also unique in the sense that it affects every country in the world at the same time. As a result, we have witnessed an extraordinary collaborative approach across borders to find a vaccine. Less collaborative has been the execution and methodology needed to handle the crisis both in the now, the coming out of the crisis and the world post-crisis.

Vivid acts of compassion at many levels have inspired and ignited leadership in people who would not necessarily have ever thought of themselves as leaders. The analysis of this previously untapped and diverse leadership resource in the current pandemic across so many strata of society should inform the debate on the shape and characteristics of what is required of leadership in the 21st century. Arguably there is a devolvement of leadership to many more levels of society in contrast to some of the more hierarchal "command and control" models of history. This "devolvement" is not a transfer or relinquishment of leadership, but more of a partnership of leaders to address a common or "higher" cause. It is like a community partnership project on a national or even international level. This requires from leaders a quite different perception of their role in society, one that is empathetic to resolving issues not normally considered to be within their professional remit and in ways unfamiliar to traditional definitions of a "leader".

It is important to emphasise that this does not refer to public-private partnerships which have been implemented with varying success in multiple sectors but failed spectacularly during the pandemic, most notably in the test-and-trace system. Rather than rely on local, community-based organisations which have been proven to trace eight times more contacts (BMJ, 2020), the government created a secretive, centralised and inefficient behemoth. By October of 2020, the government system was reaching just 62.6% of contacts, while local authorities were reaching 97%. This is despite the fact that they [had] been denied access to government data, and were given just £300 million, in contrast with the £12 billion for national test and trace' (Monbiot, 2020). This is not the place to discuss governmental cronyism, or the huge profits handed to these well-connected companies, but to draw attention to the outstanding performance of local institutions and their partners which are further discussed later in this chapter.

DOI: 10.4324/9781003171737-7

What is leadership?

Before leadership is discussed, a working definition of the term might be helpful. In essence, it is simple. "Leadership is not about titles. It is not about seniority. It is not about status, and it is not about management. Leadership is about power and the ability to know when and how to use it" (Allen, 2018). Whether in the military, politics, business, a street gang or the schoolyard, "leadership inevitably requires using power to influence the thoughts and actions of other people" (Zaleznik, 2004). One must also make a clear differentiation between management and leadership. Management is concerned with the functional processes of an organisation – keeping to a schedule or plan, staffing, budgeting, performance assessment, etc. Leadership is dependent upon integrity to the cause or objective, then having the communication skills to motivate others to commit to the same objective. The use of clear and concise language is central to leadership. One must ensure that there is no ambivalence or room for interpretation, and that intent is clearly understood by all involved. Unfortunately, during the pandemic, the populace of many countries has felt lost in a fog of confusing and often contradictory instructions. To use an old maxim, "the first casualty of war is truth".

Unequivocal language

The pandemic has also seen leaders in all sectors and of all persuasions engage in the unprecedented misuse of the word unprecedented. There is nothing "unprecedented" about the COVID pandemic. Nor is there anything unprecedented about the discourse and controversy that has come with it. As schoolchildren, most of us were taught that "The Black Death" of the Middle Ages was a case of bubonic plague transferred to humans by rats (not bats). This has since been refuted by modern science, and it is now thought to have been a haemorrhagic fever caused by a virus similar to Ebola. It, too, originated in China and was transferred through the Central Asian steppes, the Middle East and into Europe by the trade route of the day, the Silk Road.

> Immediately on its arrival in 1347 . . . the Great Pestilence . . . was recognised as a directly infectious disease . . . when it had burnt itself out, 40% of the population of Europe had been killed. This outbreak was a pandemic on a scale never before experienced (or since).
>
> (Duncan & Scott, 2005)

I would argue that this is the pandemic that was, and remains, unprecedented. Over decades, the insidious creep of hyperbolic language, along with management buzz words and phrases, have done nothing to improve the standards of political, public or private leadership. Effective leadership does not operate – and never has operated – at such a profound or philosophical level that it requires anyone to learn another language. So, let's leave "pushing the envelope" to the mathematicians and test pilots who understand its meaning, abandon presentation platitudes and lead with clear and concise communication.

The only real way to measure the standard of leadership is by asking: does anyone follow, and do they get results? Winston Churchill is not remembered for his managerial prowess but his inspirational leadership during the UK's "darkest hour". His earnest and solemn honesty to the British people demonstrated his integrity and empathy and was evident from his first speech as Prime Minister to the House of Commons, in May 1940, when he told them clearly that he had "nothing to offer but blood, toil, tears and sweat". He went on:

> We have before us an ordeal of the most grievous kind. We have before us many, many long months of struggle and of suffering. . . . But I take up my task with buoyancy and hope. I feel sure that our cause will not be suffered to fail among men. At this time I feel entitled to claim the aid of all, and I say, "come then, let us go forward together with our united strength".
>
> (Churchill, 1940)

Whether one considers Churchill a good politician or strategist, it cannot be disputed that he was perceived by the British people to be a worthy leader and that they resolutely followed him. He had the "willingness to confront unequivocally the major anxiety" of his time. The current situation cannot be compared to the crisis facing Churchill in 1940, but it has been a major test of political leadership.

Problems for political leaders

There are many suitable frameworks within the military and emergency response sectors for leadership in crises; however, the rapidly changing environment of the pandemic, particularly at the beginning, requires a rapid and adaptive response unfamiliar to political leadership. The resulting success or failure of governmental response can be attributed to the style, decisions, and actions of national leaderships. Perhaps it is unfair to criticise political leaders when those concerned have, largely, a managerial background and no real training or experience in the principles of leadership. They also appear to be conditioned to behave in certain ways by the political systems they inhabit.

Without getting too political, and perhaps simplistically, it appears the countries that have emphasised individuality in their socio-economic policies have not performed as well as those with more "progressive" social agendas. Federal systems have also not responded well, and this might be explained by the deliberate devolution of power in these systems, for example in the United States. My proposition appears to be supported by a recent study published in *The Lancet: Planetary Health* (Gelfand et al., 2021) that explains it much better than I do. Though effective and strong governmental institutions, particularly public health, have been the main instrument for dealing with the pandemic it now appears that on their own they are not sufficient; we also need the assistance of society. The study argues that the key difference in success is whether a country has a "tight" or "loose" culture. Tight cultures like China, Singapore and South Korea tend to be highly respectful of rules and norms. Loose ones like Brazil, Spain, the United States and the UK tend to defy and break them. The difference between these cultures is not an innate difference between East and West, but are a direct result of historic reality. Societies that have faced chronic threats – war, invasion, famine, plagues – tend to develop tight cultures in which following rules becomes a mode of survival. One of the study's authors, Michele Gelfand, said that "whether you are a country, a company or even a family, sometimes you want to be tight, sometimes loose. The key is, do you know how to move from one side of the spectrum to the other?". She points out that New Zealand, generally considered a loose country, tightened up when confronting COVID. Greece, under the leadership of an extremely able Prime Minister, did the same. "The goal should be", she said, "to be ambidextrous – tight or loose, depending on the problem we face" (Gelfand, cited in Zakaria, 2021) In other words, to have "the willingness to confront unequivocally the major anxiety of the time". As she points out, this has been achieved in some countries by "extremely able" leadership.

Empathy and compassion in leadership

Mo Mowlem, when as Northern Ireland Secretary in Tony Blair's government, was largely credited with bringing about the 1998 Good Friday Agreement with the use of skilful and empathetic leadership.

The response to the pandemic by New Zealand Prime Minister Jacinda Arden has again demonstrated what *CEO Magazine* called her "outstanding leadership" (Pigeon, 2020). Two months after becoming the leader of the Labour party in 2017, she became the Prime Minister and one of the world's youngest leaders. In just over three years, she has been globally recognised for her response to her country's first terrorist attack, dealt with a massive and deadly volcanic eruption, responded to the pandemic and won a landslide re-election victory, with support for her party at a 50-year high. A key element of effective leadership is good decision making based on reliable intelligence or data, and Ardern had this at hand. The private sector has access to sources of data just not available to governmental agencies. The New Zealand government was able to access analytics services that "brokers relationships between government and the private sector. The access to insights derived from private-sector data increased the level and quality of information available to support subsequent decision-making" (data.govt.nz, 2021). A similar data exchange partnership happened between a charity and local government in Manchester (see later in this chapter).

Ardern's approach to leadership can be seen in many of her actions. For instance, rather than just regurgitating the political platitude of "we are in it together", she and her ministers took a 20% pay cut at the start of the pandemic in a display of solidarity with the people of New Zealand. She stated that this was "about leadership" and that "if there were ever a time to close the gap between groups of people across New Zealand in different positions, it is now" (Giordano, 2020).

> The arguments for a "female advantage" in leadership generally stem from the belief that women are more likely than men to adopt collaborative and empowering leadership styles, while men are disadvantaged because their leadership styles include more command-and-control behaviours and the assertion of power.
>
> (Paustian-Underdahl et al., 2014, p. 655)

If, regarding leadership, perception is nine-tenths of the law, then clearly, Arden's style works. This is because she has had the "willingness to confront unequivocally the major anxiety" of her time. When asked to summarise what qualities had underpinned her path to the Premiership, she responded:

> Kindness, and not being afraid to be kind, or to focus on, or be really driven by empathy. I think one of the sad things that I've seen in political leadership is – because we've placed over time so much emphasis on notions of assertiveness and strength – that we probably have assumed that it means you can't have those other qualities of kindness and empathy . . . if we focus only on being seen to be the strongest, most powerful person in the room, then I think we lose what we're meant to be here for. So, I'm proudly focused on empathy because you can be both empathetic and strong'.
>
> (Ardern, 2020)

What she critiques here is almost exactly the approach taken by the president of the United States. Writing for the conservative website *The Federalist* in May of 2020, David Marcus insisted that

> an image of Donald Trump wearing a protective face mask while performing his duties, behind the Resolute Desk . . . would be a searing image of weakness. It would signal that the United States is so powerless against this invisible enemy sprung from China that even its president must cower behind a mask.
>
> (Marcus, 2020)

The President disparaged the use of masks and vacillated over the US response to COVID all the way to the November election – when he was voted out of office. He showed distain for science in general and the head of the US Centers for Disease Control and Prevention in particular. He made no attempt to utilise the information and data resources at his immediate disposal, let alone try to negotiate partnerships with the private sector. It could be argued that he did not have the "willingness to confront unequivocally the major anxiety" of his time. However, that depends on whether one considers the pandemic "the major anxiety" – and it would appear that many of his followers did not.

Messianic leadership

Why supporters of the President did not consider the pandemic their "major anxiety" may be a result of his style of leadership, or it may have been his allegiance to – and promotion of – a growing popular cultural-political mindset in the United States that got him elected in the first place. To me, this appears to be a case of what the eminent psychologist Carl Jung referred to when he wrote:

> it is becoming ever more obvious that it is not famine, not earthquakes, not microbes, not cancer but man himself who is man's greatest danger to man, for the simple reason that there is no adequate protection against psychic epidemics, which are infinitely more devastating than the worst of natural catastrophes The supreme danger which threatens individuals, as well as whole nations, is a psychic danger.
>
> (Jung, 2021)

Jung identifies several possible "psychic dangers", but classifies a "mass psychosis" as the most dangerous. This occurs when large sections of society lose touch with reality and unconscious fears become collectivised which in turn, descends into delusion. This societal, delusional, collective unconscious then searches for some type of messiah to "save" it. In turn, the leadership itself falls prey to paranoia and exhorts the populace to join them in an ever-expanding paranoic delusion. History records many episodes of mass psychosis including, at the national level, the rise of totalitarianism in the 20th century, such as the Stalinist Soviet Union and the Cambodian Khmer Rouge. There are more localised events such as the witch hunts and dancing plagues of the 17th century and more extreme episodes like the Jonestown Massacre and the Rwandan genocide. It should at least be considered that the global response to COVID might also be a collectivised delusion. In the early stages of the pandemic, the Director of the Institute for Scientific Freedom in Copenhagen wrote in the *British Medical Journal* that he had "suspected for a long time that we are the victims of mass panic" (Gøtzsche, 2020); time will tell.

For Jung, the largest case of mass psychosis was the one he had witnessed in Nazi Germany. Writing after World War Two, he stated that "the most dangerous things in the world are immense accumulations of human beings who are manipulated by only a few heads" (Jung, 1973). There is no valid or helpful comparison to be made between Hitler and Trump; nor is this a polemic on his presidency. It is, however, a historical warning about menticidal leadership, that pandering to or promoting fear, denying facts and not defending integrity and truth has serious consequences for societies. "In lunatic asylums, it is a well-known fact that patients are far more dangerous when suffering from fear than when moved by rage or hatred" (Jung, 1978) – and it is evident that many political leaders are using fear as the basis for both popularity and policy.

Self-interest and leadership

There are countless examples of when business leadership has also abandoned both personal and professional integrity, embraced venality and criminality and still been successful, but it is usually short term and ultimately self-destructive for both the individuals and the business. For instance, in the 1788 impeachment trial of Warren Hastings, the first Governor-General of Bengal and head of the East India Company (EIC), the prosecutor, MP and political philosopher Edmund Burke stated that he was impeaching Hastings "in the name of human nature itself, which [Hastings] has cruelly outraged, injured and oppressed, in both sexes, in every age, rank, situation and condition of life" (Burke, 1839). He went on to accuse Hastings of:

> impoverishing and depopulating the whole country. . . . With a wanton, and unjust, and pernicious, exercise of his powers . . . in overturning the ancient establishments of the country. . . . With cruelties unheard of and devastations almost without name. . . . Crimes which have their rise in the wicked dispositions of men – in avarice, rapacity, pride, cruelty, malignity, haughtiness, insolence, ferocity, treachery, malignity of temper. . . . We have brought before you the head, the Captain general of Iniquity – one in whom all the frauds, all the peculations, all the violence all the tyranny in India are embodied.
>
> (Burke, cited in Dalrymple, 2019, p. 308)

Though Hastings was eventually acquitted, after a seven-year trial, he was by no means the worst head of the EIC, and the charges brought against him were an accurate depiction of most of its leadership. After the suicide of another former head of the EIC, Robert Clive of India, the playwright and essayist Samuel Johnson wrote that Clive "had acquired his fortune by such crimes that his consciousness of them impelled him to cut his own throat" (Johnson, cited in Nechtman, 2010, p. 299). Corporate criminal leadership has not, unfortunately, been eradicated – though, thankfully, a lot of the bloodshed has. For instance, since the year 2000, Deutsche Bank has been fined $18,286,625,302 (yes, billion) for its global criminal activities including money laundering, violating economic sanctions, accounting and securities fraud, and a multitude of other financial crimes (Violation Tracker, 2020). Paradoxically, it could be said that the leadership of Deutsche Bank did have the "willingness to confront unequivocally the major anxiety of their people in their time", as most of their people were highly anxious to personally enrich themselves and did so ruthlessly – much like the leadership of the EIC – at the expense of the business.

More recently, the Group CEO of Barclays Bank, Jes Staley, was fined £642,430 by the Financial Conduct Authortiy (FCA) for bullying tactics in hounding a Barclays employee for whistleblowing. He was further sanctioned by Barclays, who cut his bonus by £500,000. Incredibly, he remains in post.

Another very recent example of failed leadership is the performance of Paula Vennells, who as CEO of The Post Office, (2012–2019), together with her senior management team and Chairman Tim Parker (who still remains in post), prosecuted hundreds of sub-postmasters for fraud, despite knowing that the financial discrepancies were actually arising from computer errors for which her own company were responsible.

Though greed and arrogance are often the cause of a failure of leadership, by far the most common is fear. This fear of outcome is often present in "great" leaders, but they have the self-confidence to do what they believe is the right thing – regardless of the consequences. When an outcome is not assured, the situation is developing very rapidly or is just something not encountered before the tendency is to play safe and search for affirmation on a course of action before engaging in it. Two pests in effective leadership are hurry and indecision, and they must be controlled or exterminated from the outset.

Over-managed and under-led

This is perfectly demonstrated by the US federal response to Hurricane Katrina in 2005. A congressional investigation into the response by the Federal Emergency Management Agency (FEMA) was, tellingly, titled "A Failure of Initiative", and the first paragraph on Page 1 states that "The Select Committee identified failures at all levels of government that significantly undermined and detracted from the heroic efforts of first responders, private individuals and organizations, faith-based groups, and others" (US Congress, 2006). In the aftermath of the accurately predicted hurricane, FEMA officials were reported to have turned away Walmart trucks carrying water, prevented the US Coast Guard from delivering 1,000 gallons of fuel, turned away 50 private aircraft responding to local hospital requests for evacuation assistance and even cut a local emergency communications line, leading the sheriff to restore it and post armed guards to protect it from FEMA. These actions, and countless others like them, were justified because they had not been authorised. The leadership of FEMA was far too concerned with the correct procedure and how they were going to be perceived and forgot the quality of leadership that Jacinda Arden referred to when she said that "kindness, and not being afraid to be kind or to focus on, or be really driven by empathy" was fundamental to her success as a leader. "We wanted soldiers, helicopters, food and water", said Denise Bottcher, press secretary for Gov. Kathleen Babineaux Blanco of Louisiana. "They wanted to negotiate an organizational chart" (Cited in Shane et al., 2005).

The failure of initiative shown by the leaders of FEMA could have been avoided if they had acted with empathy for the people of New Orleans who were clearly suffering. It was the fear of getting it wrong that lead them to rush around getting in the way of the localised efforts to respond.

The end of Hobbesian leadership?

Compassionate and empathic leadership at the political level may be appropriate to meet societal commitments, but is it good business? Is it even appropriate for a company – that has no social responsibilities, a bottom line and responsibility to stakeholders – to engage in such behaviour? One example that may answer this question is the credit card processing and financial services company Gravity Payments. In 2015, the CEO, Dan Price, heard that "an employee was secretly working a 2nd job at McDonald's". He stated that he felt that he "was an awful CEO who was failing his employees" and said he "gave her a raise to quit that job. No one should have to work two jobs to make ends meet" (Price, 2021). He then took a personal pay cut from $1.1 million a year to $70,000 – which he also made the minimum wage for all employees in the company. Since his decision in 2015, Dan Price has been constantly derided by all and sundry including Fox News, a company whose own CEO was forced to resign for sexually assaulting his employees. In a *New York Times* article, Patrick R. Rogers, an associate professor of strategic management at the School of Business and Economics at North Carolina A&T State University, is quoted as saying,

> the sad thing is that Mr Price probably thinks happy workers are productive workers. However, there's just no evidence that this is true. So, he'll improve happiness, only in the short term, and will not improve productivity. Which doesn't bode well for his long-term viability as a firm.
>
> (Cohen, 2015)

Rush Limbaugh, quoted in the same article, insisted that it was "pure, unadulterated socialism, which has never worked", and that he hoped "this company is a case study in M.B.A. programs on how socialism does not work, because it's going to fail". I am with Price and sincerely hope that it is used as a case study in MBA programs! Six years later, the company reports that:

> our revenue tripled . . . head count grew 70% . . . customer base doubled . . . 70% of employees paid down debt . . . homes bought by employees grew 10× . . . 401(k) contributions grew 155% . . . turnover dropped in half . . . 76% of employees are engaged at work, 2× the national average . . . customer attrition fell to 25% below nat'l average. . . . At the start of the pandemic, we lost 55% of our revenue overnight. Our employees were so invested they volunteered to take temporary pay cuts to prevent any layoffs. We weathered the storm, paid everyone back and are now giving out raises.
>
> (Price, 2021)

This should answer the question regarding compassion and empathy in leadership. It also shows the kind of following a leader with integrity can inspire.

Leadership and partners

There has always been a symbiotic relationship between political and corporate leadership, and there is nothing inherently wrong with that. In times of national crisis, a common cause emerges which encourages both to behave in ways they might not in more "normal" times. A good example of this during the pandemic is Taiwan.

At the earliest stages of the COVID outbreak in January of 2020, the president of Taiwan, Tsai Ing-Wen, established the Central Epidemic Command Centre to coordinate prevention measures. Writing in *Time Magazine*, she said:

> Taiwan is no stranger to hardship, and our resilience stems from our willingness to unite to surmount even the toughest obstacles. This, above all else, is what I hope Taiwan can share with the world: the human capacity to overcome challenges together is limitless.
>
> (Ing-Wen, 2020)

She went on:

> With the cooperation of private machine-tool and medical-supply companies, the Ministry of Economic Affairs coordinated additional production lines for surgical masks, multiplying production capacity. Supported by technology experts, pharmacies, and convenience stores, we devised a system for distributing rationed masks. Here, masks are available and affordable to both hospitals and the general public. The joint efforts of government and private companies – a partnership we have deemed "Team Taiwan" – have also enabled us to donate supplies to seriously affected countries.
>
> (Ibid.)

The process that was quickly implemented in Taiwan may well have been a result of their "tight culture", but it is also their willingness to overcome the challenge together. There are many similar examples in the UK's response to the pandemic, with one notable omission: our central government.

In theory, the (Localism Act, 2011) should have addressed this issue and decentralised power away from Whitehall and back into the hands of local councils, communities and individuals to act on local priorities like a pandemic. It would appear that this has not happened in any meaningful way that could have been co-opted, in the Taiwanese model, to assist in the pandemic response.

Perhaps one place we can credit our government for good leadership and cooperative efforts is in the vaccine response. Regarding a vaccine, the Health Secretary, Matt Hancock, demonstrated foresight from the start and showed that a leader can take their inspiration from any source; in this case the 2011 film *Contagion*. He has said that "in the film, it shows that the moment of highest stress around the vaccination programme is not in fact before it's rolled out . . . it's afterwards, when there is a huge row about the order of priority" (Hancock, cited in Sleigh, 2021) He was advised to order 30 million doses but ordered 100 million instead. In early December 2020, the UK became the first country in the world to approve a COVID vaccine for emergency use. This was mainly due to the Department of Health and Social Care having, reportedly, begun planning a mass vaccination programme before a single case of COVID had been reported. Meanwhile, the Oxford University scientists who would go on to develop a vaccine began meeting to discuss it in January 2020, before the World Health Organisation (WHO) had even come up with the name COVID – again, showing great foresight and decision making. The UK government's vaccines taskforce, set up by chief scientific adviser Patrick Vallance and led by venture capitalist Kate Bingham, was established to help accelerate the acquisition and distribution of vaccine doses. Since May 2020, the task force, consisting of experts in science, technology and logistics, has secured orders from seven different vaccine manufacturers – a total of 400 million doses, or enough to vaccinate the entire UK population three times over (Baraniuk, 2021). This is a response in the "Team Taiwan" model and one that should be applauded. However, in the future, governments could – and should – go further in adopting cooperative partnerships.

Pluralistic leadership

In the executive summary of a recent report by Locality, an organisation set up to support community organisations, says that "at heart, we need a concerted effort to shift public policy: away from an ethos of competition organised around the individual [with] power centralised; towards an ethos of collaboration organised around the community where power is widely dispersed" (Locality, 2020, p. 9). This dispersal of power is the key to the success community organisations have demonstrated in responding to the pandemic; over 95% of respondents to the New Local Government Network Leadership Index said the contribution of community groups to their coronavirus response has been "very significant" or "significant" (New Local, 2020). In the conclusion, the study asserts that "to solve the big social, economic, and environmental challenges we face as a society, government must look to the local, harness the capabilities within our communities, and empower devolved leadership" (Locality, 2020, p. 69). Key to the success of these community groups is their local communication networks, with many of them sharing the same office space in repurposed buildings. One example of this is the Charles Burrel Centre (CBC) in Thetford, Norfolk, located in a previously abandoned secondary school building; councillors and residents campaigned for the building to be repurposed for community use in 2013. The organisation was officially set up as a Community Benefit Society in 2015 and the Centre is now home to 56 organisations. Its tenants range from the local MP to community nurses, a foodbank to local manufacturers. Half the organisations are start-up businesses – a cake maker, a seamstress, a tattoo artist, a hypnotherapist. The CBC chief executive, Danny Whitehouse, has said that "the pandemic has given CBC an opportunity to enhance partnership working. Each part of the system is working in a coordinated to way to build on their specific strengths. This was not due to a decision being taken – it fell into place in an organic way" (Locality, 2020, p. 30). In Levenshulme, Manchester, a community group called Inspire took responsibility for the "intermediary" level of work, slotting in between the street level mutual aid and the formal, city-wide services run by Manchester City Council and the NHS. This has involved three main activities: food delivery for older people, a food bag scheme, and telephone and online support. Over the last five years, Inspire's projects have built up a database of 800 older people locally. They immediately got on the phone to all of them to identify who was isolating and in need of support (Locality, 2020, p. 39). Up and down the country, organisations such as chambers of commerce, Rotary and Lions clubs, and local residents and traders have all got together to support the community with initiatives designed to maintain the necessities of life and ensure that the country is not paralysed in a morass of confusion, fear and indecision. Examples of this are endless and readers of this will no doubt have experienced and maybe even been a beneficiary of one or several of these initiatives. Again, there is no typical leadership involved; a community came together in a time of need, and calmly got on with the job in hand together.

Black flag leadership

As stated at the beginning, leadership is about power and the ability to know when and how to use it, and this dispersal of power has therefore required a dispersal of leadership. This is not an original proposition; it is the essence of political anarchist theory which is not a rejection of authority, law and order or leadership. A basic tenet is that, in the absence of the state, for whatever reason, ordinary people will voluntarily form community associations/federations, provide services to their community (think of Dunkirk) and peacefully administer and regulate themselves. One of the most influential figures in anarchist ideology, Mikhail Bakunin, described in the 1880s the kinds of action highlighted in the Locality study. He said that:

> At the moment of action, in the midst of the struggle, there is a natural division of roles according to the aptitude of each, assessed and judged by the collective whole: some

direct and command, others execute orders. Hierarchical order and promotion do not exist, so the commander of yesterday can become a subordinate tomorrow. No one rises above others, or if he does rise, it is only to fall back a moment later, like the waves of the sea forever returning to the salutary level of equality.

(Bakunin, cited in Western, 2014)

In recent years, we have seen the establishment of many kinds of protest movements and community associations across the globe, with most using social media as their communication networks, and almost none have a typical leadership structure. I refer to the likes of the "Arab Spring", "Black Lives Matter", the "#Me Too Movement" and boycotting groups. The problem that many "protest movements" have faced is their antagonism to authority in general and leadership in particular. A present-day anarchist, Chas Bufe, posits that leadership is inevitable in social groups:

In the 60s and 70s many leftist, anarchist and feminist groups agonised over how to eliminate leadership, equating all leadership with authoritarian leadership. Their fruitless efforts confirm what the more astute anarchists have been saying for over a century – that it's a mistake to think that any kind of group or organization can exist without leadership; the question is, what kind of leadership is it going to be?

(Bufe, cited in Western, 2019, p. 75)

Here is the crux of the matter. What has been conceived as effective leadership practices in the past may not work in the future. With the potential for more global-scale issues like climate change, overpopulation, water shortages, etc., a collectivised and localised leadership approach is essential. There are many claimed authors for the aphorism "those who fail to learn from history are doomed to repeat it", including Edmund Burke, George Santayana and Winston Churchill. Both the historical and contemporary examples of leadership recounted here have been an attempt to show that as far as leadership in a crisis goes, there is not really anything that has not happened before. What matters the most in a crisis is the character of the leader, and character is forged in the furnace of experience. Good judgement comes from experience, and most experience comes from bad judgement. Leadership has to be learnt, tried and tested, again and again.

The novelist John Masters – who led a brigade of the famous, ethnically diverse Chindits behind enemy lines during World War Two – said that a leader must have a quality that is easy to recognise but hard to define "a strength of character, a determination with no obstinacy in it, something that inspires, but does not arouse febrile excitement". They "need wisdom rather than cleverness, thoughtfulness rather than mental dexterity" (Masters, 1961, p. 207). He cautioned his officers against mistaking motion for action and when it came to decision making, like Confucius, Aristotle and Voltaire, he propounded the principle of the Golden Mean – more usually defined as "the best is the enemy of the good". Most things are beyond our control; however, we can always demand from ourselves honesty, integrity, empathy and compassion.

References

Allen, T., 2018. *What Is the Difference Between Management and Leadership?* [Online] Available at: www.forbes.com/sites/terinaallen/2018/10/09/what-is-the-difference-between-management-and-leadership/?sh=5a1b23d374d6 [Accessed 28 March 2021].

Ardern, J., 2020. *Jacinda Ardern: 'Political Leaders Can Be Both Empathetic and Strong.* [Online] Available at: www.theguardian.com/world/2020/may/31/jacinda-ardern-political-leaders-can-be-both-empathetic-and-strong [Accessed 25 March 2021].

Baraniuk, C., 2021. *Covid-19: How the UK Vaccine Rollout Delivered Success, so Far.* [Online] Available at: www.bmj.com/content/372/bmj.n421 [Accessed 21 April 2021].

BMJ, 2020. *Covid-19: Local Health Teams Trace Eight Times More Contacts Than National Service.* [Online] Available at: www.bmj.com/content/369/bmj.m2486 [Accessed 20 May 2021].

Burke, E., 1839. *The Works of Edmund Burke.* Boston: C.C. Little & J. Brown, Vol. 7, p. 267.

Churchill, W., 1940. *Blood, Toil, Tears and Sweat. May 13, 1940. First Speech as Prime Minister to House of Commons.* [Online] Available at: https://winstonchurchill.org/resources/speeches/1940-the-finest-hour/blood-toil-tears-and-sweat-2/ [Accessed 28 March 2021].

Cohen, P., 2015. *Praise and Skepticism as One Executive Sets Minimum Wage to $70,000 a Year.* [Online] Available at: www.nytimes.com/2015/04/20/business/praise-and-skepticism-as-one-executive-sets-minimum-wage-to-70000-a-year.html [Accessed 14 April 2021].

Dalrymple, W., 2019. *The Anarchy: The Relentless Rise of the East India Company.* London: Bloomsbury, p. 308.

data.govt.nz, 2021. *Report: COVID-19 Lessons Learnt.* [Online] Available at: www.data.govt.nz/docs/covid-19-recs-report/ [Accessed 20 May 2021].

Duncan, C., & Scott, S., 2005. What Caused the Black Death? *Post Graduate Medical Journal*, Vol. 81, pp. 315–320.

Galbraith, J. K., 1977. *The Age of Uncertanty.* Boston: Houghton Mifflin.

Gelfand, M. J. et al., 2021. *The Relationship between Cultural Tightness – Looseness and COVID-19 Cases and Deaths: A Global Analysis.* [Online] Available at: www.thelancet.com/journals/lanplh/article/PIIS2542-5196(20)30301-6/fulltext [Accessed 14 April 2021].

Giordano, C., 2020. *Coronavirus: New Zealand PM Jacinda Ardern to Take 20% Pay Cut as Show of Solidarity During Covid-19 Pandemic.* [Online] Available at: www.independent.co.uk/news/world/australasia/coronavirus-new-zealand-jacinda-ardern-prime-minister-pay-cut-a9465756.html [Accessed 25 March 2021].

Gøtzsche, P. C., 2020. *Rapid Response: Covid-19: Are We the Victims of Mass Panic?* [Online] Available at: www.bmj.com/content/368/bmj.m800/rr-1 [Accessed 31 March 2021].

Ing-Wen, T., 2020. *President of Taiwan: How My Country Prevented a Major Outbreak of COVID-19.* [Online] Available at: https://time.com/collection/finding-hope-coronavirus-pandemic/5820596/taiwan-coronavirus-lessons/ [Accessed 29 March 2021].

Jung, C. G., 1973. *Collected Works of C.G. Jung: The First Complete English Edition of the Works of C.G. Jung.* [Online] Available at: www.google.co.uk/books/edition/Collected_Works_of_C_G_Jung/9eY4CQAAQBAJ?hl=en&gbpv=0 [Accessed 30 March 2021].

Jung, C. G., 1978. The Individual and the Community. In: J. Jacobi & R. Hull, eds. *C.G. Jung, Psychological Reflections: A New Anthology of His Writings 1905–1961.* Princeton, NJ: Princeton University Press, p. 163.

Jung, C. G., 2021. *The Spirit in Man, Art, & Literature (Collected Works of Jung Vol. 15).* [Online] Available at: https://carljungdepthpsychologysite.blog/2020/02/06/carl-jung-the-psyche-is-the-science-of-the-future/ [Accessed 27 March 2021].

Localism Act, 2011. *Legislation.gov.uk.* [Online] Available at: www.legislation.gov.uk/ukpga/2011/20/contents/enacted [Accessed 18 April 2021].

Locality, 2020. *We Were Built for This: How Community Organisations Helped us through the Coronavirus Crisis – and How We Can Build a Better Future.* [Online] Available at: https://locality.org.uk/wp-content/uploads/2020/06/We-were-built-for-this-Locality-2020.06.13.pdf [Accessed 18 April 2021].

Marcus, D., 2020. *The President of the United States Should Not Wear a Mask.* [Online] Available at: https://thefederalist.com/2020/05/11/the-president-of-the-united-states-should-not-wear-a-mask/ [Accessed 29 March 2021].

Masters, J., 1961. *The Road Past Mandalay.* London: Michael Joseph.

Monbiot, G., 2020. *The Government's Secretive Covid Contracts Are Heaping Misery on Britain.* [Online] Available at: www.theguardian.com/commentisfree/2020/oct/21/government-covid-contracts-britain-nhs-corporate-executives-test-and-trace [Accessed 20 May 2021].

Nechtman, T. W., 2010. *Nabobs: Empire and Identity in Eighteenth-Century Britain.* New York: Cambridge University Press.

New Local, 2020. *Edition 9: Councils' Response to COVID-19.* [Online] Available at: www.newlocal.org.uk/publications/leadership-index-publications/edition-9special-topic-covid-19/ [Accessed 18 April 2021].

Paustian-Underdahl, S. C., Walker, L. S. & Woehr, D. J., 2014. *Gender and Perceptions of Leadership Effectiveness: A Meta-Analysis of Contextual Moderators.* [Online] Available at: www.researchgate.net/publication/261952862_Gender_and_Perceptions_of_Leadership_Effectiveness_A_Meta-Analysis_of_Contextual_Moderators [Accessed 24 March 2021].

Pigeon, E., 2020. *Five Reasons Why Jacinda Is What the World Needs Now.* [Online] Available at: www.theceomagazine.com/business/politics/jacinda-ardern-leadership/ [Accessed 24 March 2021].

Price, D., 2021. *Twiter.* [Online] Available at: https://twitter.com/DanPriceSeattle/status/1382018355985588228?ref_src=twsrc%5Etfw%7Ctwcamp%5Etweetembed%7Ctwterm%5E1382018355985588228%7Ctwgr%5E%7Ctwcon%5Es1_&ref_url=https%3A%2F%2Fwww.huffpost.com%2Fentry%2Fdan-price-gravity-payments-cut-salary_n_60760c [Accessed 14 April 2021].

Shane, S., Lipton, E. & Drew, C., 2005. *Storm and Crisis: The Fallout.* [Online] Available at: www.nytimes.com/2005/09/05/us/nationalspecial/after-failures-government-officials-play-blame-game.html [Accessed 6 April 2021].

Sleigh, S., 2021. *Matt Hancock Reveals Matt Damon Film Contagion Inspired UK Vaccine Strategy.* [Online] Available at: www.standard.co.uk/news/politics/matt-hancock-matt-damon-film-contagion-covid-vaccine-strategy-b918422.html [Accessed 21 April 2021].

US Congress, 2006. *A Failure of Initiative: Final Report of the Select Bipartisan Committee to Investigate the Preparation for and Response to Hurricane Katrina.* [Online] Available at: www.govinfo.gov/content/pkg/CRPT-109hrpt377/pdf/CRPT-109hrpt377.pdf [Accessed 06 April 2021].

Violation Tracker, 2020. *Good Jobs First.* [Online] Available at: https://violationtracker.goodjobsfirst.org/parent/deutsche-bank [Accessed 31 March 2021].

Western, S., 2014. *Ephemera: Theory & Politics in Organization.* [Online] Available at: www.ephemerajournal.org/contribution/autonomist-leadership-leaderless-movements-anarchists-leading-way [Accessed 19 March 2021].

Western, S., 2019. *Leadership: A Critical Test.* 3rd ed. London: Sage.

Zakaria, F., 2021. *Opinion: A New Key to Covid Success: Not States but Societies.* [Online] Available at: www.washingtonpost.com/opinions/global-opinions/a-new-key-to-covid-success-not-states-but-societies/2021/04/08/31142d74-98a7-11eb-a6d0-13d207aadb78_story.html [Accessed 14 April 2021].

Zaleznik, A., 2004. *Managers and Leaders: Are They Different?* [Online] Available at: https://hbr.org/2004/01/managers-and-leaders-are-they-different [Accessed 28 March 2021].

7 Calling time on leadership myths

Stefan Stern

***

It is understandable if, after many months of disruption and confusion, people are yearning for certainty and a return to a more familiar world. A running joke on social media during the roll-out of COVID vaccines has been the hopeful observation that "nature is healing." Another sign that the status quo ante was trying to make a comeback came in an email (which this author received) with the subject line: "Five simple steps to future-proof your business." It might not be fair to identify the firm that was pushing its services in this way – it was a marketing company – but the significant point is this: even after the shock of the pandemic, some still want to believe that something called "future proofing" might be possible, or is even a sensible goal to aim for.

In fact, radical uncertainty seems to characterise our times and likely future, and this is the context in which leadership will be tested. Nothing is proof against an essentially unknowable future. If leadership has been in crisis in the past 18 months or so, this is partly because the quest for easy certainty has been a foolish one.

Not everything is completely unpredictable, however. In their recent book *Radical Uncertainty: Decision-Making for an Unknowable Future*, published in 2020 but written before anyone had heard of COVID, John Kay and Sir Mervyn King wrote this:

> The impact of a pandemic is determined as much or more by the state of medical knowledge as by the pathogens of disease . . . we must expect to be hit by an epidemic of an infectious disease resulting from a virus which does not yet exist. [1]

Announcing yet another lockdown at the end of October 2020, the British prime minister, Boris Johnson, said: "We've got to be humble in the face of nature." [2]

Alas, as we shall see, humility has not necessarily been the virtue one would most likely associate with Mr Johnson's behaviour as a leader in recent times. And he has not been alone in this regard. Around the world, a rather different sort of leadership – clinging on to popular if misguided notions of what leadership is – has been visible during the pandemic. In this chapter, I shall consider a few of those leadership myths and describe how they have been tested and found wanting.

Myth 1: The people want a heroic figure out front

When the going gets tough, the tough put on colourful sportswear and jump on a jet-ski. That, at least, seemed to be the attitude of Jair Bolsonaro, president of Brazil, as he headed

DOI: 10.4324/9781003171737-8

to Brasilia's Paranoá Lake in May 2020 for some high-profile leisure activity. [3] He was captured on video dismissing fears over COVID as a "neurosis." This was his consistent view through the first half of 2020. The world's (over-)reaction to the disease was "madness," he said. He would not wear one of those silly, emasculating face-masks. He would shake hands with everybody and lead from the front. Besides, his manly history "as an athlete" would keep him safe from the virus. It was just "a little flu," he argued – a diagnosis which did not turn out to be accurate. In July 2020, President Bolsonaro tested positive for COVID.

Narcissistic leaders feel validated by their position of prominence in business or society. Success teaches them that whatever it is that got them to the top – their skill, courage, superior gifts (and never, of course, luck) – will see them safely through, no matter what crisis emerges to confront them. Theirs is a rather slim playbook, containing only a limited repertoire of moves. But they will stick to them come what may, because . . . well, how else could they have got so far already?

Former US President Donald Trump clearly took a similar view of his role in the fight against COVID in 2020. He appeared to believe, in public at least, that he could simply reassert control over the virus by force of his personality. Henry Mintzberg, professor of management studies at McGill University, Montreal, has criticised what he has called "management by deeming" – "I deem that this will happen," and so on. [4]

Trump was a deemer par excellence. He claimed over and again that the virus would simply "go away." [5] But by October 2020, he, too, would be infected with COVID. Noisy heroic poses and assertion was no match for the microscopic virus.

Another, less heroic and grandiose approach to leadership in this time of crisis had been possible all along, and it was possibly displayed most impressively by the prime minister of New Zealand, Jacinda Ardern. Having become prime minister in 2017 at the age of 37, she had already led her country through the trauma of the Christchurch mosque shootings in 2019. When COVID hit in early 2020, her firmness and calm under pressure were striking.

This leadership style was a deliberate choice. As she had told the *New York Times* in 2018:

> One of the criticisms I've faced over the years is that I'm not aggressive enough or assertive enough, or maybe somehow, because I'm empathetic, it means I'm weak. I totally rebel against that. I refuse to believe that you cannot be both compassionate and strong. [6]

It was not necessary to strike a macho pose to grapple with the challenge of dealing with COVID. In fact, lucid thought and analysis was to prove a more important weapon in trying control the spread of infections. Those countries whose leaders displayed genuine humility in the face of nature seem to have fared better than others, where leadership was performative, brash and ineffectual.

If life has carried on surprisingly well in some parts of the world, it has been because of unflashy professionalism and the dedication of people who probably do not see themselves as leaders at all. In the UK, there have been public displays of appreciation for the health care workers who have been under so much unrelenting pressure, and have continued to work at no small risk to their own health. Other workers – delivery drivers, transport workers, supermarket staff, care workers – have shown themselves to be truly essential, even if this fact is not obviously represented in their levels of pay.

Perhaps there may be times for leaders to strut and attempt to present a heroic attitude. But the last year and a half has not been one of those times. The leadership we needed was less showy and less grand than that.

Myth 2: The big picture matters most of all

Monday the 3rd of February 2020 was an apparently triumphant moment for the British prime minister, Boris Johnson. On the previous Friday, 31st January, the UK had formally ceased to be a member of the European Union. Brexit – in a legal sense, at any rate – had been achieved. Now the PM stood in the grand setting of Sir Christopher Wren's Royal Naval College in Greenwich, London, where he had summoned diplomats, business leaders and the media, to witness his latest oration.

"It is great to welcome everyone here to Greenwich and I invite you first to raise your eyes to the heavens," he began. "The Vatican has Michelangelo," he went on, "Greenwich has [Sir James] Thornhill," who had painted the impressive ceiling which loomed over the audience's heads. "This painting above you was started in 1707, the very year when the union with Scotland was agreed – and does it not speak of supreme national self-confidence?" he asked, rhetorically. "This is the settlement of a long and divisive political question about who gets to sit on the throne of England" [7] After his decisive election victory the previous December, Johnson, too, must have felt that England (if not the Celtic nations) belonged to him.

This was a swaggering and hubristic speech. Only one distant development threatened to spoil the celebratory party: news that a respiratory disease, caused by a new virus, was taking hold in parts of China and seemed likely to spread further.

But Johnson was not dismayed. He was ready to see off any danger and make sure that business could continue as usual:

> When there is a risk that new diseases such as coronavirus will trigger a panic and a desire for market segregation that go beyond what is medically rational to the point of doing real and unnecessary economic damage, then at that moment humanity needs some government somewhere that is willing at least to make the case powerfully for freedom of exchange, some country ready to take off its Clark Kent spectacles and leap into the phone booth and emerge with its cloak flowing as the supercharged champion, of the right of the populations of the earth to buy and sell freely among each other. And here in Greenwich in the first week of February 2020, I can tell you in all humility that the UK is ready for that role." [7]

This was the biggest of big picture speeches. But it was a false picture that was being offered to the foreign dignitaries gathered in Greenwich, as well as to the home audience. It was inaccurate and complacent, built on shaky foundations.

This was actually a moment that called for sober attention to minute detail. Prior to this speech, Johnson had already missed two emergency Cabinet Office Briefing Room (Cobra) meetings called to discuss the coronavirus. In the course of February 2020, three more Cobra meetings were held, but the prime minister was regrettably absent for all of them.

At the beginning of March 2020, Johnson was still boasting of shaking hands with coronavirus victims. And on March 22nd, the day before a severe lockdown was finally and belatedly announced, a journalist from the *Daily Mail* asked when it might be necessary to bring in the police to enforce restraint. "Bring in the police?" Johnson replied, with astonishment in his voice. [8]

Johnson had been good at the big picture and bad at the crucial detail. By late March, he was in isolation, infected with COVID. And in early April, he spent a few days in intensive care, requiring oxygen to keep his lungs working.

The day after Johnson's speech in Greenwich, Trump had delivered the State of the Union address in the US Congress, which if anything surpassed Johnson's effort in its grandiloquence and hyperbole. He, too, kept to the big picture – in his case, a grand, glowing big picture which bore little relation to reality. (At the end of the speech, House Speaker Nancy Pelosi tore up her copy of the text before the loyal applause had died down. [9])

Trump did mention coronavirus once, however. "My administration will take all necessary steps to safeguard our citizens from this threat," he said.

But that, of course, is not how things turned out.

Myth 3: boosterism and assertion will keep the show on the road

The calamitous scenes which developed in India this year were not supposed to happen. In early March, the government, led by prime minister Narendra Modi, declared that the country was in the COVID "endgame." India had become the "pharmacy of the world," a key manufacturer of vaccines at its Serum Institute and other sites. [10]

In January 2021, Modi had tweeted: "It would make every Indian proud that the two vaccines that have been given emergency use approval are made in India! This shows the eagerness of our scientific community to fulfil the dream of an Aatmanirbhar Bharat ["self-reliant India"], at the root of which is care and compassion." [11]

After imposing a severe lockdown in 2020, the Indian government seems to have relaxed its controls too soon. "It was policymakers and elected leaders who tacitly encouraged crowding in festivals (Holi at end March 2021), election rallies in five states (March-April 2021) and religious congregation (Kumbh Mela in Haridwar, March-April 2021)," wrote Dr Chandrakant Lahariya in an opinion piece for *India Today*. [12]

Modi has been an uncompromising populist, an "India first" nationalist to match Donald Trump's "America first" template. Grandiose claims and a lack of humility are characteristics common to both these men. But the ingenuity and virulence of COVID has made fools out of those who would proclaim victory too soon, or seek to boost morale with empty declarations of success.

The mistake made by leaders such as these was to "believe your own bullshit." Of course, if you are intolerant of criticism and prefer to be surrounded only by those who agree with you, there is less chance of realising in time that you are heading down the wrong path.

In the UK, Boris Johnson has been the booster-in-chief. On the 19th March 2020, he tried to sound an optimistic note about the prospects for dealing with COVID. "I think, looking at it all, that we can turn the tide within the next 12 weeks and I'm absolutely confident that we can send coronavirus packing in this country," he said at a press conference. [13]

In July of 2020, a little over his earlier 12 week deadline, Johnson again declared that the end would soon be in sight. "It is my strong and sincere hope that we will be able to review the outstanding restrictions and allow a more significant return to normality from November at the earliest – possibly in time for Christmas," he said. [14]

And when a much-delayed second lockdown was finally announced for the start of November 2020 – delayed in part because the prime minister was reluctant to concede that his earlier boosterism had been misplaced – Johnson said:

> If we follow this package of measures in the way that we can and we have done before, I have no doubt people will be able to have as normal a Christmas as possible and that we will be able to get things open before Christmas as well. [15]

That normal Christmas was, of course, to be cancelled on the 19th December when Johnson had another late rethink about his initial plans, which had been to allow households to mix. "Yes, Christmas this year will be different, very different," he said at a rapidly arranged press briefing. "We're sacrificing the chance to see loved ones so we have a better chance of protecting their lives, so we can see them at future Christmases." [16]

This is the drearily predictable cycle of statements and corrections that the overly assertive, boosterist leader is condemned to follow. After the bold over-claiming will come the downbeat and at times even shamefaced admission of failure.

After almost declaring victory over COVID in March 2021, prime minister Modi was forced to adopt a different tone only a month later. "The country is today fighting a very big battle against COVID," he said. He continued:

> The situation had improved for a while, but the second COVID wave has come like a storm. I express my condolences to all those who have lost their loved ones due to COVID. Just like a member of your family, I am with you in this hour of sadness. The battle is long and difficult, but we have to overcome it together with our dedication and courage. [17]

These last words were perhaps intended to offer a boost to morale, but by this stage it was too little, too late. The death toll was spiralling upwards and out of control, even as the supplies of oxygen were running out.

Sometimes the boosterism just has to stop.

Myth 4: this is a man's world

So far in this chapter we have looked at the track records of a few prominent leaders: Jair Bolsanaro of Brazil, Boris Johnson of the UK, Donald Trump of the United States and Narendra Modi of India.

But now it is time to mention a few other names: Angela Merkel of Germany, Erna Solberg of Norway, Sanna Marin of Finland, Katrín Jakobsdóttir of Iceland, Mette Frederiksen of Denmark and Tsai Ing-wen of Taiwan, as well as the afore-mentioned Jacinda Ardern of New Zealand. All of these people have provided largely effective leadership in the time of the pandemic.

The alert reader may have noticed that these two lists divide along gender lines. It would be too simplistic to suggest that only women leaders have shown themselves capable of knowing how to operate during the past year of crisis. Many countries have had their ups and downs, and moments of relative success followed by further problems. Countries with male leaders – such as South Korea, Singapore, Israel and Japan – have fared comparatively well. [18]

But it is clear that a certain sort of male leader, such as the less-than-fabulous four mentioned above, has been especially ill-suited to being in charge at a time like this. Boasting and bravado have not been needed. Competence has been.

Angela Merkel, chancellor of Germany for 16 years, has personified sober competence better than any other leader. In mid-March 2020, while others were still struggling to grasp the seriousness of the situation, Merkel said on German television: "This is serious. You should take it seriously, too. Since German unification – no, since World War II – there has been no challenge like this one, where our common solidarity matters so much." [19]

Germany, like other European countries, has struggled to distribute vaccines efficiently, and Merkel's party, the CDU, is a much less appealing prospect without "Mutti" ("mummy") at the helm (she is finally stepping down in 2021). Yet no-one has embodied calm and mature leadership as convincingly as Merkel over the past decade and a half. She is the ultimate proof that this need not be a man's world.

Another man who for a time was held up as an example of effective leadership during the crisis was Andrew Cuomo, the former governor of the US state of New York. His confident, plain-speaking press conferences were seen as an exemplary way to communicate with a worried public. By the summer of 2020, plans were afoot for Cuomo to write a book about his leadership, *American Crisis: Leadership Lessons from the COVID Pandemic*, which eventually was bought by Crown Publishing for around $4 million, according to the *New York Times*. [20]

Unfortunately, it subsequently became clear that the governor's track record was not quite as outstanding as all that, and that in particular nursing home deaths in New York state had been higher than originally thought. It was alleged by the *New York Times* that the governor's team made efforts to camouflage or massage the figures down while the book deal was being negotiated.

Early and subsequently edited out passages from the book do not read so well in the light of later revelations. "I have experience and a skill set that qualifies me as a good governor," Cuomo wrote in the early draft. "I have accomplished by any objective standard more than any governor in modern history. But I am not a superhero."

He also wrote in that earlier version: "People are smart, and after a while if they can watch you long enough, they can figure out who you are." (Cuomo was subsequently accused of multiple counts of sexual harassment and forced to resign.)

Fortunately, at least one male leader has come to prominence in recent times to give encouragement to men everywhere that they are not a hopeless cause when it comes to leadership: the 46th president of the United States, Joe Biden. Supposedly "Sleepy Joe" has impressed critics with his firmness and decisiveness. The contrast with his vainglorious predecessor has been helpful, of course. But those who under-estimated Biden have been forced to reconsider their views.

In the *Financial Times*, the seasoned Washington observer Ed Luce offered this insight into Biden's unexpected success. "By past standards Biden's ego is modest. At 78 it's hard to claim you personify the future." And Luce added: "The best politics is to govern rather than fret about your brand. This sets him apart from both Obama and Trump. Not everything needs to be about him." [21]

The writer Arwa Mahdawi observed in *The Guardian* recently that there could be benefits in some leaders experiencing so-called "imposter syndrome," as this might guard against over-confidence. [22] Too often, she added, it is women who experience this imposter syndrome. And this does not seem quite right, or justified. She wrote: "Wouldn't it be more helpful, however, if we encouraged mediocre men to aspire to the competence of a middle-aged woman who is overqualified and underpaid?"

In support of this point of view, Mahdawi cited an interview with Jacinda Ardern, who had also discussed this question of over- or under-confidence. [23] "Some of the people I admire the most have that self-consciousness and that slight gnawing lack of confidence," Ardern had said. And what does she ask herself if she too is lacking a bit of confidence? It is this: "Does it mean I need to do a bit more prep, do I need to think more about my decision making?"

Amen to that.

Conclusion

Can we hope that some of the myths of leadership will be challenged and even shattered by the events of the last 18 months? That might be expecting too much. It may take a while before a final reckoning can be made, by which time memories will have faded. And a new swaggering over-confident leader will step forward, promising once again to solve all our problems.

Already we can see that some things have absolutely not changed – excessive pay at the top, for example. According to the *Wall Street Journal*, median pay for 322 executives was $13.7 million (£9.9 million) in 2020 – a rise of $1.1 million on the year before. [24]

But there are perhaps tentative signs that a bit more serious thinking is going on about what leadership after the pandemic should look like. In a discussion between Rory Stewart, a former Conservative politician, and the BBC's Evan Davis, there was a good attempt to identify where leadership has been going wrong and what an improved version of it might entail. [25]

Stewart described one his biggest concerns. "Three[-]word slogans, very simple messages have become mainstream," he said. "We have created a politics which is about permanent campaigning. A lot of our leadership problems are about people who are focused more on how to get elected than they are on how you govern well."

And he added: "These politicians are not incentivised to focus on crises, they're not likely to put in the time to get to know the experts – they are professionals in charming and winning over voters, they are not professionals at crisis management."

Evan Davis responded: "Good leaders would know what their instincts are and say to themselves: 'I'm always a bit of an optimist, I ought to lean against the wind of my own instincts to make sure that my bias is not affecting my judgment'."

On March 9th 2021, the UK's chief medical officer, Prof Chris Whitty, gave his candid assessment of the past year to a parliamentary science committee. The world, he said, is "full of leaders who wish they'd acted quicker and then been more careful as they take things off. . . . That's the history of this everywhere in the world . . ." [26]

We can at least hope our leaders will acknowledge that and learn from it.

References

1. Kay, J. and King, M. (2020) *Radical uncertainty – decision-making for an unknowable future*. London, UK: Bridge Street Press.
2. "Prime Minister's statement on coronavirus (COVID-19)", 31 October 2020. www.gov.uk/government/speeches/prime-ministers-statement-on-coronavirus-covid-19-31-october-2020
3. "Bolsonaro attends floating barbecue as Brazil's Covid-19 toll tops 10,000", *The Guardian*, 10 May 2020. www.theguardian.com/world/2020/may/10/bolsonaro-attends-floating-barbeque-as-brazils-covid-19-toll-tops-10000
4. "The scary world of Mr Mintzberg", *The Observer*, 26 January 2003. www.theguardian.com/business/2003/jan/26/theobserver.observerbusiness11
5. "Six months of Trump's Covid denials – 'It'll go away . . . It's fading'", *The Guardian*, 29 July 2020. www.theguardian.com/world/2020/jul/29/trump-coronavirus-science-denial-timeline-what-has-he-said
6. "Lady of the rings: Jacinda rules", *The New York Times*, 8 September 2018. www.nytimes.com/2018/09/08/opinion/sunday/jacinda-ardern-new-zealand-prime-minister.html
7. "PM speech in Greenwich", 3 February 2020. www.gov.uk/government/speeches/pm-speech-in-greenwich-3-february-2020
8. "Boris Johnson UK coronavirus briefing transcript March 22: Warns Italy-style lockdown is possible". www.rev.com/blog/transcripts/boris-johnson-uk-coronavirus-briefing-transcript-march-22-warns-italy-style-lockdown-is-possible

9. "State of the Union: Pelosi rips up copy of Trump's speech", *BBC website*, 5 February 2020. www.bbc.co.uk/news/av/world-us-canada-51381948

10. "Modi's govt mistakes are to blame for latest Covid crisis", *The Print*, 13 April 2021. https://theprint.in/opinion/modi-govts-mistakes-are-to-blame-for-indias-latest-covid-crisis/638943/

11. "Every Indian proud that vaccines given approval made in India: PM Modi after DCGI nod", *The Indian Express*, 3 January 2021. https://indianexpress.com/article/india/narendra-modi-coronavirus-vaccine-dcgi-covishield-covaxin-serum-bharat-biotech-oxford-7130827/

12. "Covid 2.0: Pandemic lessons India should have taken from second influenza wave of 1918", *India Today*, 15 April 2021. www.indiatoday.in/news-analysis/story/covid-2-pandemic-lessons-india-should-have-taken-from-second-influenza-wave-of-1918-1791386-2021-04-15

13. "UK can turn the tide against virus in the next 12 weeks: PM Johnson', *Reuters*, 19 March 2020. www.reuters.com/article/us-health-coronavirus-britain-johnson/uk-can-turn-the-tide-against-virus-in-next-12-weeks-pm-johnson-idUSKBN2163A4

14. "Coronovirus: Johnson sets out plan for 'considerable normality' by Christmas", *BBC website*, 17 July 2020. www.bbc.co.uk/news/uk-53441912

15. "Covid: Boris Johnson 'confident' UK will have 'as normal a Christmas as possible'", *ITV website*, 5 November 2020. www.itv.com/news/2020-11-05/covid-boris-johnson-confident-uk-will-have-as-normal-a-christmas-as-possible

16. "Johnson U turn leaves nation's plans for Christmas in tatters", *The Guardian*, 19 December 2020. www.theguardian.com/world/2020/dec/19/johnson-u-turn-leaves-nations-plans-for-christmas-in-tatters

17. "Narendra Modi: Covid resurgence in India like being 'hit by a storm'", *The Guardian*, 20 April 2021. www.theguardian.com/world/2021/apr/20/narendra-modi-covid-resurgence-in-india-like-being-hit-by-a-storm

18. https://theconversation.com/are-women-leaders-really-doing-better-on-coronavirus-the-data-backs-it-up-144809

19. "The singular chancellor – the Merkel model and its limits", *Foreign Affairs*, May/June 2021. www.foreignaffairs.com/articles/europe/2021-04-20/angela-merkel-singular-chancellor?utm_source=newsletter&utm_medium=email&utm_campaign=21%2F04%2F2021&cmid=b7c80f8e-4a52-4f35-a6e6-0f216c7a45d4

20. "As Cuomo sought $4 Million book deal, aides hid damaging death toll", *The New York Times*, 31 March 2021. www.nytimes.com/2021/03/31/nyregion/cuomo-book-nursing-homes.html?campaign_id=2&emc=edit_th_20210401&instance_id=28707&nl=todaysheadlines&regi_id=23234248&segment_id=54652&user_id=5c26e8843be709c8df116e0b95ca2d99

21. "Joe Biden's quietly revolutionary first 100 days", *Financial Times*, 18 March 2021. www.ft.com/content/22b39e9b-9b21-4d82-ba5b-8cc427c13cd8

22. "What do Boris Johnson and other Tory leaders really need? Far less self-confidence", *The Guardian*, 23 March 2021. www.theguardian.com/commentisfree/2021/mar/23/what-do-boris-johnson-and-other-tory-leaders-really-need-far-less-self-confidence

23. "Open Minded", *Ep 5 Rt Hon Jacinda Ardern*, 20 December 2020. www.youtube.com/watch?v=MGKwczxm0pQ

24. "CEOs at top 300 companies earned more during the pandemic", *The Independent*, 11 April 2021. www.independent.co.uk/news/world/americas/covid-ceos-pay-income-increase-b1829863.html

25. "Lessons on a crisis", *BBC Radio*, 4, 23 March 2021. www.bbc.co.uk/programmes/m000td0h

26. "Science and technology committee oral evidence: UK Science, research and technology capability and influence in global disease outbreaks, HC 136", 9 March 2021. https://committees.parliament.uk/oralevidence/1845/html/

8 By Force or Fire

African Leadership Must Change or Leave

Tawanda Mhindurwa

***

Africa is burning and there are little fires everywhere. If you look onto the front lawn, that's the high unemployment figures; if you see the burning garage, it's the dreams of the freedom fighters. In the driveway, the children's toys are melting; that's the brain drain leaving the continent and going abroad. The foundation has cracked into a spherical shape, and those are its leaders refusing to give up power when the time is up. The World Bank Group tells us:

> Africa, home to more than *1 billion people, half of whom will be under 25 years old by 2050*, is a diverse continent offering human and natural resources that have the potential to yield inclusive growth and wipe out poverty in the region, enabling Africans across the continent to live healthier and more prosperous lives. With the world's largest free trade area and a 1.2 billion-person market, the continent is creating an entirely new development path, harnessing the potential of its resources and people.
>
> (The World Bank Group, 2020, emphasis in original)

Governments aren't even achieving current goals, so how can they even plan forward?

By 2030 it is predicted that Africa will have the youngest working population in the world. Africa's population currently is very young, with 60% of the continent under the age of 25. What is the continent doing to ensure that they are creating enough employment to build strong sustainable economies of these numbers? Are we creating a culture that allows transformational leadership?

Africa is suffering, and it's because the continent is not being led or governed in a dignified and empathetic manner. We are seeing a growing concern and distrust of leadership from citizens. We have cities like Harare in Zimbabwe and Johannesburg in South Africa where citizens have taken it upon themselves to create their own livelihoods separate from the state, be it sources of electricity and water to schooling and banking. We are a people burnt from experience and afraid because we can still feel the heat.

So between femicide, a brain drain, high unemployment, corruption, lack of accountability and poor health systems, what needs to fall first? Where do we start? How do we begin creating the continent that will not leave anyone behind, and serve its peoples' aspirations before selfish needs? Do we have to restructure our governments? What is standing in the way of Africa being great?

We are not fighting a physical war anymore, but we are now fighting the war on ideas and information. Independent Africa is only 60 years old, and like any regular 60 year old, there are ideas that they still might be grappling to understand or contextualise and it's up to the

DOI: 10.4324/9781003171737-9

younger people or those that know better to engage them in order to get the wisdom of the ages whilst envisioning a future that fits into the global village. When you see the violence against women, the lack of accountability when it comes to public funds, the terror that is unleashed on anyone who dares to speak up or push back, you realise that it's the hegemonic structure that needs to change. The ideological state apparatuses are not working for the people anymore.

The COVID Pandemic

There has never in history been a bigger or globally felt reckoning of leadership in the world than now. The COVID pandemic has forced us to not only sit at home and keep safe, but it seems this time spent at home has allowed us to think deeply and interrogate the ways we are being governed. I think leadership has had such a big spotlight on it because we have finally experienced how much power our leadership has and the ways in which the abuse of that power can affect our lives. COVID has put state capacity under a microscope accelerated by digitalisation.

For the first time in a while, at least globally, we had to listen to and watch our government leaders tell us what to do every single day, in developed worlds where things run smoothly and "politics" is something you *can ignore* if you're in a certain demographic and class (white and/or middle class). It gave them a shock to see that their lauded governments were able to mistreat and disregard them, too, whether due to lack of COVID preparedness or just ineptitude. The disregard that some Western governments were showing at a time when the citizens of their countries needed them the most was appalling, to say the least. The difference – pandemic aside – between which countries lost hundreds of thousands and those that didn't solely lay in the ways the government ran and presided over the situation.

In the Western world, it was the first time that the populace saw or were able to see in real time the government at work without any interruptions from tabloids and from campaigners and other everyday diversions. There was no opposition to cast blame upon, and there were no immigrants to blame, either, although the hate crimes against the Asian communities went up by almost 300% due to perceptions that the pandemic was "born" in China. All eyes and responsibility were on the governments of the day. People of the Western world for the first time quietened down and were able to fully realise, reflect on and analyse the awful or great ways in which their countries were being run. Every single day, people watched television to find out the different ways in which funds were being misappropriated; they watched numbers go up, and they saw their loved ones die because of poor governance. Many were pleasantly surprised to see that the people they had voted in were doing an amazing job, whilst many were horrified day after day.

The pandemic exacerbated and highlighted the poor leadership around the world – and for the first time, the privileged folk among us started witnessing and recognising what minority groups have been saying for years about poor governance, unequal distribution of state resources, underdevelopment and poor resourcing in underprivileged communities. We are finally recognising the importance of good leadership. The COVID era has finally exposed and demonstrated the life-and-death consequences of leadership.

In Africa, we are facing a melee of problems across the continent, from decaying healthcare systems, lack of education, infrastructural problems and empowerment of women. Those of us living in Africa have witnessed this and have been at the receiving end of it all, but we know that good meaningful change will only arrive if our leaders choose the same thing.

What is good leadership? How do we quantify it? Can it be quantified? What are the outputs of good leadership? Can we recognise good leadership even though we've never experienced it? Can we train or retrain leaders or does the fact that one is a leader mean they must constantly be amenable to change? Is the theory and work on leadership exhaustive enough? Have we figured out how to successfully lead without a hitch? Do we need an overhaul of leadership continent wide? Or does it take one or a few "good" leaders to shape a country and probably serve as role models for the rest of the continent?

Globalisation has opened the world and our access to it. I think it would be unfair to say that only Africans suffer from a leadership deficit demonstrated through a lack of accountability, According to the UK government's gov.uk (Government, 2021), the role of the government is to decide how the country is run and for managing things, day to day. They set taxes, choose what to spend public money on and decide how best to deliver public services.

The government is responsible for the quality of life that its citizens will have. With that in mind, we can deduce that leadership in Africa is quantified by the quality of life being lived by its citizens. The quality of an average African life is directly proportional to how good or bad the leadership is in one's country.

Africa's Young Population Presents Opportunities and Challenges

Africa has a leadership crisis, and we are currently the fastest growing youth population in the world (UN deputy chief, 2021). With this information comes two problems: we do not have the means to look after and nurture said population, and our leaders are either not interested or are failing to create a future for this population and its aspirations. We also do not have any young people leading in Africa or in top government, so even if the government wanted to find a ways to create new economies or systems, there is no one in leadership to give meaningful insights into the needs of the younger generation. The average age of an African president is 62 years old, and yet the average age of an African is 19; these figures are worrying because we are the youngest continent and yet our leaders do not represent or reflect that. Our continents' leaders are not representing its people, and the inability to do that means leaders are very out of touch and will – like most of their peers – mis-prioritise resources, funds and policy. Marian Wright Edelman, American children's rights activist and founder of the Children's Defense Fund, famously said that "you can't be what you can't see" (HATCH, 2021). How are African leaders inspiring the youth to lead?

Sixty per cent of Africa is younger than the age of 25. This is not necessarily a negative; this growth has been attributed to declining child mortality, better health care and no interruption from colonisers who aimed to sterilise indigenous Africans (Noko, 2020). However, it then becomes a challenge because we currently do not have the means to empower and nurture our continent's youth (Foundation, 2019). A younger population is great for a burgeoning/working economy; however, an Africa that does not empower its youth will only continue to benefit the Western world which will always open doors for their skills. The continued growth of the African population is both an opportunity and a challenge for the continent. Africa's future success depends on it. On the positive side, the population provides an opportunity for the continent to address Africa's sustainable development challenges.

Whilst the continent's natural resources are vital, the creativity and innovation of its youthful population can play a key role in the continent's economic transformation (Kariba, 2020). Africa is growing younger and younger – and yet, one look at our leadership and the policies that they dole out demonstrates a different story.

Educate a Woman and You Educate a Village

How many of our African leaders know these facts – or care to know them? If they do know, what are they doing to ensure that the country that they lead can leverage on this important aspect? What are the consequences of not creating a sustainable environment for youth? The outcomes are disastrous. The World Bank estimates that 40% of people who join rebel movements are motivated by a lack of economic opportunity (Kariba, 2020). Mozambique is a case in point. Additionally, the plight of women will continue; women already face challenges with a lack of access to reproductive health services and education. This will only become worse if Africa's leadership doesn't put measures into place looking after the continent's women, who besides having a lot of intellectual talent, find themselves bearing the brunt of poor leadership.

Furthermore, by not looking after the continent's women, we are doing ourselves a massive disservice, because women when educated are more likely to look after family; educating women is educating a village (Suen, 2013). The World Bank Group also tells us that investing in the education of the girl child has massive benefits which include breaking cycles of poverty and aiding economic growth; the data show that educating girls saves lives and builds stronger families, communities and economies (Kattan, 2020). The United Nations tells us that African economies lose a billion USD in revenue by not investing in the girl child. Women account for more than 50% of Africa's combined population, but in 2018 generated only 33% of the continent's collective GDP. This reinforces and fuels inequality and compromises Africa's long-term economic health (Moodley et al. 2019.). To our definition of good leadership, we can add another quantifier: the ability and safety of the girl child to live a safe life and have access to education and resources is a requirement in determining good leadership.

Accelerating progress in gender parity is great for women; however, it is not enough to want to include women just because they can *help* the economy. African leaders have an obligation of duty and care to ensure that African women begin to feel safe in the communities that they build and look after, and that they are able to partake, contribute and lead in a meaningful way towards their own development and the countries that they live in.

Greed and Clout Will Finish My People

There's a Shona proverb which says "ushe madzoro", which means that with every new leader, there must be change and that change must be good; it also speaks to working with people for the greater good. When you look at a country like Zimbabwe which had one leader for 40 years and juxtapose it next to a country like South Africa which has had four very *different* leaders with four very different agendas and leadership styles, it is easy to trace as a nation *what* and *who worked*, and *what* and *who did not*.

Forty years is far too long to be the consistent leader of a country; so much happened and changed.

In 40 years, we went from the inventions of PCs and the Walkman to iPads and iPods. We even went through several musical revolutions from The Police and ABBA to Michael Jackson to Beyoncé and Britney Spears to "Gangnam Style", "Crazy Frog", "Despacito" and Kendrick Lamar. Civil society globally had a huge shift as one would expect: 9/11 and the war on Iraq, Saddam Hussein's capture and death, the death of Osama bin Laden, the Arab Spring, Black Lives Matter and the rise of online activism. I could go on and on. The point is that the global world changed – and Zimbabwe did not. Zimbabwe had a leader and a system that refused to relinquish power, and leaders who couldn't read emails on their phones because the font was too small didn't know how to send an email. How does a country like Zimbabwe even begin to reconcile economic growth, people and culture when the country had a false start from the beginning?

What really is the difference between countries like Zimbabwe and South Africa? Both countries were colonised and fought for their freedom. Both countries had free and fair elections that culminated in the majority ruling, but *what* did they do differently after independence that changed the trajectories of both countries? The answers: transition and authoritarian rule.

In the book *The Five Minds of a Manager* by Gosling and Mintzberg (2003), reflection is defined as "the space suspended between explanation and experience". There were four years between Nelson Mandela being released from a South African prison and Mandela being elected as the president of South Africa. Mandela and his team did not waste a moment of this. They used this time to think, reflect and decide the way they wanted to run their country; they spoke to fringe groups and even started lobbying members of the public to contribute to the new incoming Constitution. This period of transition was also a learning and a stabilising curve for the economy, which did not drop or destabilise; the incoming team saw the importance of listening and in that period deciding the kind of leaders people wanted and deserved after years of racial abuse, war and segregation.

"Successful visions are not immaculately conceived, they are painted stroke by stroke" (Gosling & Mintzberg, 2003, p. 1). You have to have a healthy respect for history in order to come to terms with the past and map a future. Zimbabwe gained independence and has continued to exact the trauma and abuse of its colonisers on its own people; this I believe is in part due to the failure of the Robert Mugabe government to take time to transition and acclimatise, whilst providing space for the chimurenga fighters and the country as whole to reflect on hundreds of years of trauma and atrocities, and allow for the nation to share aspirations as they heal.

We have to understand that Zimbabweans had not started fighting in 1965 when the Rhodesian government declared independence from the British, but from at least 1870 when the scramble for Africa begun. We gloss over the actual effects and damage of colonialism like it was a walk in the park, but colonialism is and was the highest form of genocide and systemic erasure and dehumanisation. There are parts of countries, monuments and people that don't exist anymore because of colonialism. There are cultures and systems that have been forgotten and destroyed because of colonialism. There are hundreds of years of distress to unpack and appease. Being independent doesn't absolve that. Mugabe inherited one of the most structurally sound and diversified economies not only in sub-Saharan Africa, but also among emerging global markets. It was very promising, and yet by the time he was ousted, Zimbabwe's economy resembled the Weimar Republic economy that was crippled by hyperinflationary policymaking. Mugabe at the time cannot be held fully responsible for the lack of time during the transition. This was also the then-Rhodesian government's responsibility, as it was trying to end this era as quickly as possible due to the shame and embarrassment felt after losing a war to people it believed were incapable and incompetent. Mugabe was not the only one who suffered the effects of the lack of a transitional period: so did the comrades, colleagues and citizens.

I would like to imagine that his colleagues look back in dismay that it only took seven years for him to start creating a one-party system, or maybe he did not want a period of transition because he knew people would see through him and how power hungry he was. Former Zimbabwe African National Union–Patriotic Front secretary-general Edgar Tekere disagreed with Mugabe when Mugabe started voicing his belief in a one-party state, and was consequently fired from the party for his divergent views. In this instance, Tekere showed courage. Imagine if Tekere had not been the only one in that room who stood up to Mugabe at the time. Imagine if the rest of the party had disagreed with and forced him to change his opinions and the course of governance for Zimbabwe? Imagine if all it took to change the course of modern Zimbabwean history was to be courageous and stand for common good in that moment? Another determinant for a good African leader is to be courageous in the face of adversity. The continent needs more people in positions of power who will stand strong in their convictions and speak for those with no voice or influence. I believe that many bad decisions that are made in African governments would never come to the light of day if the people at the top did not choose to stand up to their colleagues for the common good.

History and psychology has shown us time and time again that you need time to heal, and not taking this time can have severe negative impacts. Zimbabwe did not even change its *own* Constitution until 2013! For 33 years, after a bruising liberation struggle, Zimbabwe was still using the colonisers' Constitution. The greed for power and political clout kept them captive. I am incredulous that no one thought or brought up the fact that the country had not created its own Constitution for so long. And strangely enough, Mugabe's popularity never even dipped after that; did no one know better? Because what happens when you lead with an iron fist is that you create a nation that is mentally paralysed by fear. It is no secret that thousands of political activists and opposition members have disappeared and never returned (Mwananyanda, 2020; Silika, 2020).

To further prove my point, Mugabe never wrote a book or an article; people with less colourful lives have written more. This is speculative, but I think my point remains that most people who write reflect, and healthy reflection is important as a leader. Good leaders need to have the ability to stop, think, step back and thoughtfully interrogate their experiences and use these to inform their future decisions. Zambia's first president, Kenneth Kaunda, famously wrote that "The inability of those in power to still the voices of their own consciences is the great force leading to change".

Liberation Leaders Should Not Lead Countries

Africa is home to many of the world's longest serving heads of state. Since 1960, ten heads of states in Africa have held office for more than 30 years. The council on foreign relations tells us that "Military coups have become less common, but incumbents have increasingly used so-called constitutional coups to secure longer terms" (Felter, 2020). Liberation is defined by struggle. This is not to say that as a foundational basis and inspiration for the beginning of a nations start is a bad thing; it is a great place to start afresh and the values of those who have fought and died for their country must be remembered and emulated. The problem comes when those struggle ideals, attitudes, behaviours and leadership qualities persist within the *rebuilding* of the state. Clapham (2012) speaks of the fact that participating in the struggle is such a life defining moment and those who participated in the liberation don't acknowledge how much of an effect and toll it can have on the mind. He goes on to say:

> even long after the struggle has ended, and its former participants have achieved leading positions in government, it remains extraordinarily vivid in the minds of former fighters with it a deep sense of conviction in the rightness of the cause, and the entitlement and responsibility of the survivors to continue to exercise the power, and pursue the objectives, for which they fought. In the case of bitter and protracted wars of liberation, these

survivors carry with them abiding memories of the comrades who perished along the way, and a sense of obligation not to betray those who sacrificed their lives for the cause.

(pp. 5–7)

Liberation leaders not only suffer from undiagnosed post-traumatic stress disorder (PTSD) that they never get help for, but they ultimately feel entitled to power because they were on the front lines. This might be a an unpopular opinion, but every Black person who was alive during colonial rule suffered, fought and assisted in their personal capacity at some level of the struggle. Liberation leaders demand a permanent claim to the state – are those who did not participate in the same way expected to sit and accept their claim to power *forever*? What also ends up happening when liberation leaders and their parties rule for longer than two terms is that they begin to believe or propagate lies and propaganda that any opposition party formed is fighting against the "liberation" of its people. Because what characterised liberation movements was thus the stress on unity and the rejection of partisan divisions as destructive of the new nation and the illusion that an entire country could have a single purpose and accept a single representative to speak as the mouthpiece of an oppressed nation. They are never open to dialogue, because in their liberation mindset anyone who is not for them and anyone who disagrees is a dissident or treasonous, but that mindset doesn't lead to successful outputs in governance. Aaron Eckhart's character Harvey Dent in the film *The Dark Knight* says: "You either die a hero, or live long enough to see yourself become the villain"; this is an African leaders proverb.

Conclusion: Waiting for God . . . Or?

Leaders around the world and throughout history have long used religion as a tool to subjugate and extract wealth from the citizens of their states and other nations. However, as the world has moved towards more liberalism (if by name only in many cases) and sustainability under the banner of environmental, social and governance (ESG) considerations and a less theocratic system, we still have African leaders who use biblical rhetoric, form and words to impart fear and ultimately violate their people. The history speaks for itself: violence on the continent has long-been meted out in the name of Christianity, from the slave trade to colonisation to the forced sterilisation of women and the structural violence of widespread poverty in a continent with resource abundance. Therefore, for African leaders to use rhetoric such as the "the will of God is the will of people" when they are actively involved in oppressing their citizens' lives is particularly disturbing and violent – and is, in effect, gaslighting.

> Religion holds power. It was through the cross and the bullet that the continent was dissected by European powers. It was through the pages of the Bible that apartheid was theologically justified, and it was through the Dutch Reformed Church of white Afrikaners that "the races" were declared separate as mandated by God.
>
> (O'Connor, 2018)

The 2001 South African Census found that 57% of Zimbabweans in South Africa were male and 43% female. In 2005, SAMP found a very similar ratio still pertaining (56% and 44%, respectively). Many more migrants were married than unmarried (58% versus 31%) with another 10% widowed, separated or divorced. Around a third of migrants were sons and daughters in the household, 28% were heads of households and another 13% were spouses or partners of household heads. All of this suggests a broadening and deepening of participation in migration from Zimbabwe.

The majority of migrants were relatively young (72% are younger than the age of 40) and well educated. Less than 1% had no schooling, and over 50% had a post-secondary diploma, undergraduate degree or post-graduate degree. Migrants were employed in a wide variety of skilled, semi-skilled and unskilled jobs outside Zimbabwe. In other words, this is a generalised out-movement of people, not confined to one or two professions or sectors. Twenty percent of migrants were in the informal sector as traders, vendors, hawkers or producers. Also significant were skilled professionals (15%), health workers (12%), services (9%), teachers (7%), manual workers (6%) and office workers (5%).

According to the World Bank in 2020, remittances into Zimbabwe stood at around 2 billion USD whilst they also accounted for 10% of the country's GDP. The gross irony is that Zimbabweans outside the country face taxes and high charges on remittances, despite their significant contribution to looking after their families in Zimbabwe. Whilst state taxes are high, on remittances and workers in Zimbabwe, service delivery leaves a lot to be desired.

African citizens deserve better, and until our leaders lead with empathy and wisdom, little will change. They say God only helps those who want to help themselves, but what about those who literally cannot help themselves – those so disenfranchised, tortured and broken that the thought of speaking up leaves them frozen, the thought of whose lives getting worse or being made worse makes them rather spend another hour selling tomatoes or attempting to steal from their fellow citizen? What about those who will never see or experience the good that their country can give, and what about those who have been rejected by their own countries because our leaders and churches would rather lead with terror than do some reading and research and realise that being gay or trans is not "un-African", but has been a part of the African way of life for centuries? Those whose sisters, brothers, husbands, wives and colleagues have been killed or have disappeared without a trace or word or answer – who is looking after those families? Is God coming to save them? Can they help themselves? Are they waiting for a sign, for hope, a God, a call to action? Who is thinking of the Africans getting fucked from each side? What does an African renaissance mean for those nations that rely on its current parlous state of subjugation? You try to escape from politics and find respite in God, but God has taxes too. You are paying and you pay until you have nothing left to give; your body is on the line every day, and so are your menial wages. The country of your birth and heritage takes and takes away from you, and at no point does anyone try to give you a break. No one *can* give you a break. You try to find respite in civil society, and even they can only do so much. We speak of how rigid European countries are when giving us access, but do we speak enough on the reasons why we're fleeing? In the words of Zimbabwean lawyer and writer Petina Gappah, "For as long as politicians see the poor in purely transactional terms, as just there to provide votes and a backdrop to speeches[,] this (cruelty) will not change".

To conclude my fighting words: being an African leader is not an easy feat, but they know that. African countries fought for years to be free of colonial powers in *their own* countries and homes. Anyone who knows anything of war and specifically *colonial* strife knows that enemies do not rest where profit and power is at play. They will try to "fix" your economies; they will destabilise your industries; they may even try to spark conflict – but those who *know* this, those who have *decided* that they want to lead should *know* this, right? They should *know* that they have to be extra careful; know that the line between good and bad *for them* is so *thin*; know that despite everything you try and do for your country you may be the painted as the villain forever; know that being pro-Black and fighting for the indigenisation of your countries industries will not get you invited to world stages, but will at least keep your people fed, most times. We do not have a seat at the table.

The final determinant is *knowing better and doing better*. A good African leader knows better; knows what they're getting into; knows how to fight international battles; knows what is on the line for the citizens of the country that they lead and not just their reputation. They must be willing and able to be knowledgeable, which also means they must be willing to admit when they are wrong and know to change course when new information is presented; knowledge is a two-way street. Economic prosperity for the citizens needs to be their main priority. What is political freedom without economic freedom?

The extractive systems upon which the world runs and is set in are deeply problematic. African countries are running the race 15 seconds after the starting gun has been fired. We definitely need to investigate how bad leadership is further entrenched in the way we are doing capitalism globally. African countries are falling because of poor leadership *and* a system that is set up for mineral-rich African countries to fail, which in turn reinforces bad leadership that tends to have freer rein to go authoritarian – which quashes any hope of viable opposition, and the system perpetuates and worsens. Meanwhile, the siphoning continues – and this explains why commodities and exchange markets are in London (they have no gold resources or cocoa) and why Switzerland is the world's largest exporter of gold.

Leaders are made and not born. The will of God is not the will of the people; the will of the people is the will of the people.

References

Clapham, C., 2012. From Liberation Movement to Government. *The Journal of Modern African Studies*, 12(3), pp. 1–14.

Cotterill, J., 2020. *Workers abroad offer lifeline for Zimbabwe's economy.* [online] Ft.com. Available at: <https://www.ft.com/content/6303aede-b2c3-11e9-bec9-fdcab53d6959> [Accessed 22 January 2021].

Felter, C., 2020. *Africas Leaders for Life.* [Online] Available at: www.cfr.org/backgrounder/africas-leaders-life [Accessed 12 April 2021].

Foundation, M. I., 2019. *Africas First Challenge: The Youth Bulge Stuck in Waithood.* [Online] Available at: https://mo.ibrahim.foundation/news/2019/africas-first-challenge-youth-bulge-stuck-wait hood [Accessed 15 April 2021].

Gosling, J. and Mintzberg, H., 2003. The Five Minds of a Manager. *Harvard Business Review*, November.

Kariba, F., 2020. *The Burgeoning Africa Youth Population: Potential or Challenge?* [Online] Available at: citiesalliance.org [Accessed 15 April 2021].

Kattan, R. B., 2020. *Girls Education.* Washington, DC: The World Bank.

Moodley, Lohini et al. (2019) 'The power of parity: advancing women's rights in Africa, McKinsey Global Institute report, 24 November, https://www.mckinsey.com/featured-insights/gender-equality/the-power-of-parity-advancing-womens-equality-in-africa.

Mwananyanda, M., 2020. *Zimbabwe: Five Years on Whereabouts of Journalist and Pro-Democracy Activist Still a Mystery.* [Online] Available at: www.amnesty.org/en/latest/news/2020/03/zimbabwe-five-years-on-whereabouts-of-journalist-and-pro-democracy-activist-still-a-mystery/ [Accessed 17 April 2021].

Noko, K., 2020. *aljazeera.com.* [Online] Available at: www.aljazeera.com/opinions/2020/4/8/medical-colonialism-in-africa-is-not-new [Accessed 15 April 2021].

O'Connor, T., 2018. *Religion in South Africa: The Power to Destroy and Heal a Nation.* [Online] Available at: https://berkleycenter.georgetown.edu/posts/religion-in-south-africa-the-power-to-destroy-and-heal-a-nation [Accessed 24 June 2021].

Silika, K., 2020. *Thousands of Unidentified Zimbabweans Lie in Secret Mass Graves – and I Want to Find Them.* [Online] Available at: https://theconversation.com/thousands-of-unidentified-zimbabweans-lie-in-secret-mass-graves-and-i-want-to-find-them-122586 [Accessed 20 April 2021].

Suen, S., 2013. *The Education of Women as a Tool in Development: Challenging the African Maxim.* Scotland: Open Journal Systems.

The World Bank Group, 2020. *The World Bank in Africa.* [Online] Available at: www.worldbank.org/en/region/afr/overview [Accessed 22 April 2021].

Crush, J. and Williams, V., 2005. *UNITED NATIONS EXPERT GROUP MEETING ON INTERNA-TIONAL MIGRATION AND DEVELOPMENT.* [online] Un.org. Available at: <https://www.un.org/en/development/desa/population/events/pdf/expert/8/P05_Crush&Williams.pdf> [Accessed 22 April 2021].

HATCH, T., 2021. *Representation Matters: Madam Vice President. [online] Childrens Defense Fund.* Available at: <https://www.childrensdefense.org/blog/madam-vice-president-representation-matters/> [Accessed 13 March 2021].

United Nations Sustainable Development. 2021. *With fast-growing youth population, Africa boasts enormous market potential – UN deputy chief.* [online] Available at: <https://www.un.org/sustainabledevelopment/blog/2017/10/with-fast-growing-youth-population-africa-boasts-enormous-market-potential-un-deputy-chief/> [Accessed 22 March 2021].

Parliament.uk. 2021. *Government.* [online] Available at: <https://www.parliament.uk/site-information/glossary/government/> [Accessed 22 March 2021].

Part II

Future Directions

9 Seeds Beneath the Snow

Insights on Leadership from Anarchism

Alison Hogan

***

The scale of the impact of the COVID pandemic, locally and globally, has shown that the world is neither stable nor predictable. It has heightened awareness of the seriousness of other existential threats from future pandemics to climate change to cyber-induced chaos. In the face of such an uncertain future, many believe that to survive and thrive requires a re-boot and re-imagining of how we get things done – and that many established organisational structures and processes are no longer fit for purpose.

Anarchism offers a perhaps surprising but insightful lens through which to explore this future of radical uncertainty, particularly the dynamics and distribution of power and the implications for leading and leadership. As Parker et al. (2020, p. 80) propose:

> The beginning of creativity, of an innovative response to a situation, must involve a challenge to common sense, to what everyone else seems to think. That is what we think that anarchists encourage, a call to be radical and brave in our questioning of the world. Because if we don't do that, we might not have a world left that is worth saving.

They suggest that "it is inherent in the experimental nature of anarchy that there will be tension and often fierce debate about what it is or what it is not". This is because " 'anarchism is not one thing, not a single set of beliefs, which is agreed upon' but perhaps [is] better defined as 'a network or web of ideas'" (Parker et al. 2020, p. 5).

Acknowledging the caveat about what exactly it is or is not, anarchism poses a fundamental challenge to mainstream organisational theory in its rejection of hierarchical and authoritarian structures within which management and leaders hold "power over" others, whereby power is a form of control. Anarchism seeks alternative organisational structures committed to "power-with" or "power among" people, whereby groups and organisations are based on principles of self-management, equality, mutual support and co-operation.

Many organisations, though they may not be described as anarchist, have adopted such principles, including Buurtzorg, a neighbourhood health care organisation founded in the Netherlands which is based on a "leaderless", nurse-led model, committed to patient self-management and empowerment and adopting a whole care-process of assessment, intervention and outcomes. Growing from one to 850 teams in ten years in the Netherlands, it has collaborated with care organisations in 24 other countries (Buurtzorg n.d.).

Social movements that have roots in anarchism include the Occupy Wall Street Movement, a response to the global financial crisis which by November 2011 was estimated to have spread to some 82 countries (*The Guardian* 2011), and Extinction Rebellion, an

DOI: 10.4324/9781003171737-11

international movement that uses non-violent civil disobedience in an attempt to halt mass extinction and minimise the risk of social collapse (Extinction Rebellion n.d.).

In contrast, hierarchical organisations hold a fundamental assumption that, to succeed, management must retain some level of control, "power over" employees – for the good of the employees and the good of the organisation. They will grant some levels of autonomy for the motivation of employees, but the assumption is that employees need and want to be led, that they lack the will or agency to self-manage and that without some level of control and structured leadership, disorder will result.

Fear of disorder is often used as justification for authority, control and the need for "power over". At times of widespread disruption, protesters will often be described as "anarchists", as being synonymous with chaos and unlawfulness. It is a sobriquet used from both ends of the political spectrum. Thus, in the United States when, in May 2020, there were protests in the streets over the death of George Floyd and the White House was locked down, President Trump retweeted a video saying "Anarchists we see you". The implication was that the man in the video was paying protesters to incite violence when it was explained later that he was helping other protesters buy medical supplies (*The Washington Post* 2020).

Some months later, in January 2021, when pro-Trump supporters stormed the US Capitol building, generating global media coverage, "Anarchy in the USA" was the headline in the British "i" newspaper, as well as the *Daily Express*.

Contemporary anarchism, whilst supporting direct action when necessary, rejects the characterisation of anarchy as chaos and disorder. In the place of control and hierarchy, it is committed to embracing both individual autonomy and collective responsibility. This requires order, the evolving of principles and practices to underpin an effective self-managing, self-regulating organisation.

The symbol of anarchy, the letter A for anarchy surrounded by O for order, captures the indivisible link between the two. As Pierre-Joseph Proudhon wrote in *What is Property*, published in 1840, "[a]s man seeks justice in equality, so society seeks order in anarchy". For Proudhon, anarchy "is not the daughter but the mother of order" (Proudhon 1831).

The paradox for hierarchical organisations is to achieve an optimum balance between individual autonomy and control. For anarchic organisations, it is the balance between individual autonomy and collective responsibility. However, as we will explore in this chapter, the ultimate paradox for any organisation is the recognition that human nature is both naturally selfish and naturally co-operative. The task is to acknowledge and seek ways to harness these contradictory forces for the common good and well-being of human beings at every level of our society and, ultimately, for the survival of our planet.

Seed beneath the snow

Far from being an unrealisable utopia, an anarchist society, based on everyday collaboration and mutual support, is described by Colin Ward (2018, p. 14) as "like a seed beneath the snow", always in existence but "buried beneath the weight of the state and its bureaucracy, capitalism and its waste, privileges and its injustices". Ward suggests that:

> given a common need, a collection of people will, by trial and error, by improvisation and experiment evolve order out of the situation – this order being more durable and more closely related to their needs than any kind of externally imposed authority could provide.

(Ward 2018, p. 30)

During the extended period of the global pandemic, people were driven to experiment and improvise in the way they worked and in how they lived their lives. Like seeds beneath the snow, communities came together to support each other. At work, employees discovered a new level of agency, tapping into sources of initiative and creativity, often to survive. Volunteers supported those in self-isolation; local councils provided accommodation for the homeless; restaurants and pubs, no longer able to open their premises, found innovative ways to provide products and services, using the internet and home deliveries.

Some companies completely re-purposed production lines to produce different products such as PPE (personal protective equipment), tackling issues including re-design, sourcing of materials, re-skilling and remote working.

Such a communal response to an urgent need and a shared purpose is not new. What is different about the pandemic is the scale and reach of the impact and the length of time that it has endured – long enough for the old order to be questioned, new ways of working and collaborating to become established and well-being given a higher priority. This has been reinforced by a wider recognition of the urgency of addressing the impact of climate change as more countries and communities experience disruptive weather patterns. When faced with the harsh reality of some of these existential threats, the paradox that human nature is both naturally selfish and naturally co-operative becomes starkly prescient.

In the past, a criticism of anarchism was that the focus on bottom-up, grassroots initiatives would always have limited impact. Attempts to scale up would inevitably be thwarted by coercive powers and control. Horizontal networking and federal structures would often atrophy. However, these limitations are gradually being reduced through the harnessing of digitalisation, the World Wide Web and social media. The potential is increasing for networks to connect, for practices and experience to be reinforced, and for levels of support and collaboration to grow.

The growth of place-based initiatives and leadership is one example. In the city of Bristol, local civic leaders have used the place-based model to develop a One City Approach, with leaders, acting as one, coming from five different realms of political, public managerial/professional, community, business and trade union backgrounds. The plan is to co-create a fair, healthy and sustainable city, with all its actions mapped against the 17 UN Sustainable Development Goals (Hambleton 2021; Bristol One City 2021).

In Wales, the Well-Being of Future Generations (Wales) Act 2015 was passed with the aim of making sustainability its central organising principle, encouraging people to work together to improve the environment, economy, society and its culture. It has appointed a Future Generations Commissioner whose duty, in particular, is to act as a guardian of the ability of future generations to meet their needs and to encourage public bodies to take greater account of the long-term impact of the things that they do. Though the Commissioner can only advise, the position is supported by the Auditor General to help ensure that public bodies are held to account for their performance in relation to the act's requirements.

Contemporary anarchism does not seek to overthrow formal structures of power, including the state, as history has proven that far from withering away, new structures – equally or more repressive – will emerge. Instead, it takes a prefigurative approach to change and seeks to "form the structure of the new society within the shell of the old" through a developmental, evolving process of experiment and practice from within and connecting with others, horizontally, like a rhizome root which sends out shoots in different directions.

Whilst not anarchist, initiatives like place-based leadership are seeking to take a prefigurative approach and build the new in the shell of the old and share the commitment to address the paradox of balancing individual autonomy and collective responsibility.

Contemporary anarchism seeks to evolve structures that are non-hierarchical and non-authoritarian, based on co-operation rather than competition. The process of decision-making, based on dialogue and consensus, is fundamental to this. Consensus does not mean that everyone agrees or thinks the same about something. Indeed, disagreement is a natural and necessary way to enable people to voice contrary views. However, the process needs to be built on a foundation of trust, openness, active participation, dialogue and listening, and be clear enough and provide sufficient time for everyone to feel safe and confident to express their views.

Where there is a unity of purpose or shared goal, the objective is "to find solutions to problems in which expressed interests of different groups of people are in balance with each other" (Laihonen in Parker et al. 2020, p. 92).

The attention that the anarchist theory of organisation gives to process, as an ever-evolving, developmental practice, is known as constitutionalising. For a state, a constitution is a set of principles, which may be written or unwritten, that set out the distribution of power within a political system. It includes relationships between political institutions, the limits of government jurisdiction, the rights of citizens and the method of amending the constitution itself (McNaughton 2006, pp. 131–136). In anarchism, constitutionalising is defined as "a continual process of defining and redefining the identity of an ethos of a community and developing and changing the rules that govern the behaviour of the community and its members". It is a process of continuous learning and development, of an acceptance that rules and processes based on past events cannot regulate current and future actions (Laihonen, p. 92).

Thus, a study of minutes of meetings of the General Assemblies of three Occupy Wall Street camps shows how the movement constitutionalised over a period of time. This included developing key documents outlining its principles, its institutions, and formal and informal rules. It also evolved the adoption of decision-making procedures to enable and empower participants, preferring consensus and supermajorities to lobbying and voting by simple majority. In their research, R. Kinna et al. argue that:

> the anarchist constitutional politics of Occupy was designed primarily to challenge and constrain different forms of global and local power, whilst providing a template for anarchistic constitutional forms that can be mimicked and linked up, as opposed to scaled up.
>
> (Kinna et al. 2019, p. 358)

Constitutionalising, including developing decision-making procedures, can be a frustrating and time-consuming process, but one that is likely to result in greater traction and success than a decision-making process in a hierarchical organisation whereby, when consultation ends, ultimately, control and decisions lie with management, and rules and regulations become fixed rather than continually evolving.

Leading in leaderless movements

In anarchist thought, leadership has been inextricably linked with power and control, if not domination and coercion. Because of this, there has been an emphasis on forms of organisation characterised as leaderless, where all are equal. However, as Jo Freeman demonstrated in her research into the women's liberation movement, the adherence to a structure without leaders simply masked power. When the structure of a group is informal, the rules of how decisions are made are known only to a few; awareness of power is limited to those who know the rules. She suggests that when the existence of leadership is denied, stealth leadership occurs and elite in-groups or powerful individuals will take leadership without it being named, and without consent (Freeman 1972–73).

The way to counter stealth leadership is to ensure that the rules of decision-making are open, formalised and made available to everyone. This includes acknowledging the possibility that leadership will emerge in some form; for example, when the knowledge, skills or expertise of particular individuals may offer some benefit to the wider collective or organisation. In such circumstances, their contribution will be explicitly named and the parameters agreed, that the leadership will be temporary and without a formal position of power or authority over others.

Occupy Wall Street described the role of leading as follows:

> Occupy Wall Street is structured on anarchist organising principles. This means that there are no formal leaders and no formal hierarchy. Rather, the movement is full of people who lead by example. We are leader-full, and this makes us strong.
> (cited by Kinna et al. 2019, p. 366)

Simon Western has addressed this paradox of leading in a leaderless movement by proposing a particular type of leadership which he describes as autonomist leadership, a "non-hierarchical, informal and distributed form of leadership". It is not connected with elitism, authoritarianism and coercion, but mobilises a collective leadership agency (Western 2014, p. 673). He suggests that, rather than rejecting leadership in social movements, anarchists and other radicals ought to recognise that leadership is not synonymous with hierarchical structures and fixed leaders. Western draws on Lacanian psychoanalysis to describe the potential of leadership as an emergent process that occurs in social movements.

> When autonomist leadership is transparently acknowledged, tensions and conflicts do not disappear, but become developmental rather than regressive. This means working through difficult challenges such as addressing power dynamics and struggling for meaning and ideas.
> (Western 2014, p. 676)

Western suggests that mutualism offers a balance to excessive individualism.

> The principles of mutualism are central to the anarchists' approach to leadership, whereby leaders do not hold power over others and any formalisation of a leadership position is temporary, open to recall and dissolvable at any time. . . . A leader can be a follower and vice versa at any appropriate moment.
> (p. 678)

This is expressed by Bakunin as follows:

> At the moment of action, in the midst of the struggle, there is a natural division of roles. . . . Hierarchical order and promotion do not exist, so the commander of yesterday can become a subordinate tomorrow. No one rises above others, or if he does rise, it is only to fall back a moment later, like the waves of the sea forever returning to the salutary level of equality.
> (Bakunin, cited in Joll 1979, p. 92)

For Western, autonomist leadership is committed to no ranking or hierarchy and has a heightened awareness and commitment to the autonomy of all, guarding against coercion and the manipulation of power. It always works between the two tensions and forces of mutualism and collaboration, on the one hand, and competing individual and group interests on the other hand.

Within the Zapatista movement in Mexico, political decisions are deliberated and decided in community assemblies, and military and organisational matters are decided by the Zapatista area elders. Their aspiration is to do politics in a new, participatory way, from the "bottom up" instead of "top down". They have a process of communication called *preguntado caminamos*, walking we ask questions. The Zapatistas consider the contemporary political system of Mexico inherently flawed due to what they consider its purely representative nature and its disconnection from the people and their needs (Henck 2007).

Extinction Rebellion (abbreviated as XR) is experimenting with models of self-organising systems, based on a set of nested interlocking circles. Chris Taylor, a member of XR, explains that there are circles that look at how the movement develops, at the culture, values, non-violence; others look at training, how to run meetings, plan actions and set overall strategy. "This structure of circles managing the organism as a whole, supported by local autonomous groups then creates a system that releases energy and potential into the movement" (Taylor 2019, p. 62).

Western (2014) suggests that digital platforms have enabled the mobilisation of autonomous leadership in ways which were inconceivable before.

"Autonomous leadership is embedded within networks as an active leadership dynamic that is fluid, changing and dispersed throughout the network. . . . it pops up, disappears, reappears, is beyond any single individual or elite group and is potentially within all individuals" (p. 681).

As such, it is a type of leadership that particularly "thrives in the digital and physical networks of contemporary social movements, utilising mobile communications and digital platforms such as Twitter and Facebook" (p. 673).

How organisations are moving into the space – but not giving up control

Looking more closely at some of the theories and models that have been proposed for organisations to reinvent themselves, to be re-imagined and "future-ready" for a post–COVID world, many ideas are closely aligned with core anarchist principles.

In seeking agility in an uncertain and volatile environment, organisations are encouraging more consultative, supportive leadership rather than authoritative leadership, favouring networks of teams and encouraging more dialogue and empowerment. They have had to take more seriously issues of mental health and the psychological safety of their people. At a wider systemic level, a primary focus on shareholder value and bottom-line profits has had to be tempered with a very real engagement in wider societal, environmental and governance issues.

However, although companies have undergone "near-constant transformation through downsizing, delayering, culture change and the introduction of self-managed teams, . . . managerial control persists and in many ways is tighter than ever" through controls including key performance indicators, big data, management by objectives, rankings and measurements of progress (Wierman et al., in Parker et al. 2020, p. 62).

According to Blair Taylor, contemporary activist movements may have changed
tions – but not the world – and

> often unwittingly act as social entrepreneurs that offer not only ethical legitimation,
> the very engine of a new spirit of capitalism, where social problems are dealt with
> enlightened consumption, and soul-deadening work is transformed into "meaningful",
> flexible/part time and self-directed labor.
>
> (Taylor 2013)

One framework gaining credence explores the shifting of power in the world between
old power and new power with their contrasting values. For example, old power values of
managerialism, institutionalism and representative government compare with new power
values of informal, opt-in decision-making, self-organisation and networked governance
(Heimans & Timms 2014).

Old power is closed, inaccessible, and leader-driven. New power is open, participatory
and peer-driven. Heimans and Timms suggest that organisations that share the new power
model and values "celebrate the power of the crowd". Such organisations include companies
like Google, whose parent company is Alphabet, one of the world's top five technology companies by revenue – which, along with Microsoft, Amazon, Apple and Facebook, together
constitute a huge concentration of power and influence globally.

However, they also include a distributed activist groups like Occupy and the free content
on-line encyclopaedia, Wikipedia, whose models are closer to the principles of anarchism
in their distribution of power. According to Heimans and Timms, what is distinctive about
organisations like Wikipedia and also Linux, the open source software operating system, is
that "they effectively 'upload' power from a source that is diffuse but enormous – the pas-
sions and energies of the many. Technology underpins these models, but what drives them is
a heightened sense of human agency" (Heimans & Timms 2014).

Re-asserting our agency

The lens of anarchy throws some light on the paradox of control and autonomy and of individual freedom and collective responsibility, particularly relevant in this disruptive world
of radical uncertainty and ambiguity. Yet, as the research of Parker et al. and Western demonstrates, anarchism as a theory of organisation – with its challenge to some fundamental
assumptions and practices of hierarchical organisations and leadership – is largely absent
from both management and critical studies.

At a time when we need to re-imagine the future of organisations, an appreciation of
anarchist practices could help organisations and business educators, to understand better the
distinction between hierarchical and authoritarian structures and horizontalism and mutuality; and how to "encourage us to recognise our own agency and think creatively about power
and how we use it" (Parker et al. 2020, p. 234).

According to Margaret Heffernan, we stand at a crossroads, and the price of seeking certainty is high. It means "surrendering to a limited experience of life, designed by individuals and corporations who do not know us, whose interests are not ours. In this condition,
convenience is passivity and choice obedience". The question she poses is whether, "in our
hunger to know the future, is the alleviation of doubt and uncertainty sufficient reward for the
loss of agency, of autonomy?" (Heffernan 2020, p. 102).

For Western,

> the radical emancipatory task is to live openly with the knowledge that authoritarianism and other misuses of power are potentially within us all, a social symptom in all social relations. The challenge is to contain the excess and to work toward the desired emancipatory society, whilst acknowledging that it is never to be found in its purest form.
>
> (Western 2014, p. 694)

Do we strive to root out all forms of coercion, or is it sufficient to work towards the dissolution of power? John Holloway, in his book *Change the World without Taking Power*, suggests:

> If revolution through the winning of state power has proved to be an illusion, this does not mean that we should abandon the question of revolution. But we must think of it in other terms: not as the taking of power, but as the dissolution of power.
>
> (Holloway 2002, cited by Taylor 2013, p. 734)

A former chairman of a FTSE 100 company observed:

> If you look at failures and problems and you were to correlate those with the degree of ego, arrogance and hubris, you would find a fantastic match. The one ingredient on which all the others depend is objectivity, and it is the objectivity which power corrupts – slowly, imperceptibly, remorselessly, possibly fatally.
>
> (Hogan 2013)

If human nature is both naturally selfish and naturally co-operative, each of us has a choice in our lives how we manage that paradox and whether we strive to lead wisely within the communities and systems of which we are a part.

References

Bakunin cited by S Western from Joll, 1979:92, p. 677

Bristol One City, *About the One City Plan*, 2021. www.bristolonecity.com/about-the-one-city-plan/

Buurtzorg, n.d. www.buurtzorg.com/about-us/

Extinction, Rebellion, n.d. https://extinctionrebellion.uk/the-truth/about-us/

Freeman, Jo, *The Tyranny of Structurelessness*. https://www.jofreeman.com/joreen/tyranny.htm

The Guardian 2011. https://www.theguardian.com/news/datablog/2011/oct/17/occupy-protests-world-list-map

Hambleton, Robin, *Place, Power and Post Covid-19 recovery*, RSA, March 2021. www.thersa.org/comment/2021/03/place-power-post-covid-19-recovery

Heffernan, Margaret, *Unchartered*, London: Simon & Schuster, 2020, p. 102

Heimans, J. and H Timms, Understanding "New Power". *Harvard Business Review*, December 2014

Henck, Nick, *Subcommandante Marcos: The Man and the Mask*, Durham: Duke University Press, 2007

Hogan, A, *The Development and Practice of Excellence in Board Leadership*, Unpublished, 2013

Jo Freeman aka Joreen, *The Tyranny of Structurelessness*, 1972, www.jofreeman.com/joreen/tyranny.htm

John Holloway, 2002, cited by B Taylor

Kinna, R., A. Prichard and T. Swann, *Occupy and the Constitution of Anarchy, Seeds for Change & the Anarchy Rules Project, Anarchic Agreements*, Loughborough: Global Constitutionalism, 2019, 8:2, p. 358

Laihonen, M., from Parker et al., p. 92

McNaughton, Neil, *Success in AS Politics*, London: Hodder Education, 2006, pp. 131–136

Occupy protests around the world: Full list visualised. https;//www.theguardian.com/news/datablot/2011/oct/17/occupy-protests-world-list-map

Parker, Martin, Konstantin Stoborod and Thomas Swann, *Anarchism, Organisation and Management*, New York: Routledge, 2020, p. 8

Proudhon, Pierre-Joseph, *What is Property*, 1831, https://theanarchistlibrary.org/library/pierre-joseph-proudhon-what-is-property-an-inquiry-into-the-principle-of-right-and-of-governmen

Taylor, Blair, *From Alterglobalization to Occupy Wall Street, City*, Routledge, 2013, www.tandfonline.com/doi/abs/10.1080/13604813.2013.849127

Taylor, Chris, *Circles or Power: Extinction Rebellion's Approach to Organising, the Brewery*, London: Ltd Forward Institute, 2019

Ward, Colin, *Anarchy in Action*, Oakland: PM Press, 2018, p. 14

The Washington Post, Stop blaming everything bad on anarchists, 4 June 2020

Welsh Government, *Well-being of Future Generations (Wales) Act 2015: The Essentials*. https://gov.wales/well-being-future-generations-act-essentials-html#section-60684

Western, Simon, Autonomist Leadership in Leaderless Movements: Anarchists Leading the Way, *Ephemera*, 2014, p. 673

Wierman, B., E. Granter and L. McCann in Parker et al. p. 32

10 Leadersmithing, Mistakes and Remorse

Eve Poole and Anthony Bash

***

Introduction

Living with COVID has forced a particular focus on how to offer strong leadership in the face of acute and unprecedented global uncertainty. Specifically, it has drawn attention to the extreme risk that attends decision-making when so much is unknown or changing by the hour. Models of leadership and scholarship about leadership are usually developed retrospectively, predicated on learning lessons from successful leaders. In the COVID crisis, we will not know for some time who the successful leaders have been, but we really need the models and the scholarship now. In the meantime, given the continuing uncertainty, how do we best identify, develop and consolidate leadership skills for unknown situations, and as well as hone excellence in decision-making amidst ambiguity? Further, what might leaders do to develop resilience in an environment where some of their decisions may, with the benefit of hindsight, turn out to have been wrong?

This chapter will look at how the leadersmithing approach (Poole, 2017) can yield promising resources, and how the templating approach it advocates can help to develop the character necessary for navigating the unknown. It will also offer new resources about what to do when your decisions don't prosper, and about ways to move on from setbacks and failure (Bash, 2020).

Leadersmithing

Way back in 2003 at Ashridge Business School, we decided to solve the problem of what to teach leaders by travelling into the future. We had a notion that 20/20 hindsight might be reversed into 20/20 foresight, so that leaders could become job-ready before the fact. So we set about asking all the senior leaders we could get our hands on what they knew then about themselves as leaders that they wished they'd known ten years earlier. We used this data to distil a list of critical incidents that, in all the years since we've tested them, still seem to constitute the perennial list of challenges all leaders face. We also developed the idea of amygdala templates, those hard-wired ways of responding well both in the present and the future to typical leadership situations that might safely be deployed under pressure. This approach, dubbed 'leadersmithing,' is one which takes seriously the nature of leadership as a life-long craft discipline and not just a profession. It is an approach that attends to the development of core practices and apprentice-pieces. The overall aim of

DOI: 10.4324/9781003171737-12

leadersmithing is to build up a portfolio of templates that tend towards leadership mastery. The result is that leaders can develop skills and attributes that are more useful than the kind of things they can usually pick up from a book. Such skills and attributes also mean that leaders are better prepared for the unknown and the unknowable, and less likely to dread being mugged by fate.

The Key Critical Incidents

In our research into what constituted those crucible leadership moments (Poole, 2017), there were five such moments which have a direct resonance with leading in a COVID–style crisis. These were: stepping up, taking key leadership decisions, managing ambiguity, taking a risk, and accepting when you get it wrong.

Stepping Up

Many of the leaders we interviewed had not realised that they could do the job – or could not – until they got it. They talked about that awful feeling when you realise, finally, that the buck stops with you. There is no-one else. You have to make the decision, or take responsibility, even if the situation is not of your making. There is nothing that can really prepare you for how it will actually feel when you are finally responsible, and COVID has forced all leaders into the limelight, requiring raw leadership at its clearest and most public. Seasoned leaders may have found it easier, and were those who had been able to prepare by finding ways to flex their leadership muscles to build the core strength for stepping up when the day comes. Others were thrust into positions of leadership with little or no experience, and have had to learn painfully on the job, the hard way. But all are now learning very quickly whether they can hack it or not.

Taking Key Leadership Decisions

Along with this existential feeling of final responsibility, leaders told us that decision-making feels different at the top. Organisations are typically pyramid-shaped and have a management logic. This means that the enterprise can only proceed if decisions are taken. Slow decision-making acts as a brake, freezing the organisation until a decision allows it to move on. So leaders find themselves taking decisions not necessarily at a time of their own choosing, but at a time dictated by the needs of the organisation and its operating environment.

We know from psychological profiling that preferences about decision-making vary. Some people love making decisions, and may make them too early or too hastily, because they are in a hurry to move on. Some want the best possible data before they are willing to make a call, so feel bounced and vulnerable when the organisation harries them about making a decision now. In either case, bending to the needs of the organisation can feel uncomfortable. But if leaders are nothing else, they are decision-making machines – that is their function in the organisational model.

Leading in a COVID environment has been particularly hard, because at the beginning, a lot of decisions had to be made quickly, and with imperfect information. Then as each new policy change was announced, fresh decisions were needed, either to confirm or to change previous ones, with many leaders feeling both exhausted and bewildered by the relentless and unrecognisable terrain.

Managing Ambiguity

Ashridge's Phil Hodgson used to talk about the 'ambiguity pump' in organisations (Ward and Kirkbride, 2001, p. 289). Someone junior does not know what to do, so they escalate it to their boss. Their boss escalates it to their boss, who escalates it to their boss, and so on. As the top leader, by the time you get to hear about it, a veritable tsunami of uncertainty is breaking on your desk. And you are expected to say something impressive, wise and final about the matter. COVID has been a masterclass in discerning when to wait for clarity to emerge, and when to forge on in spite of the mist, because a decision is now required. Choosing when to act is the stuff of wisdom. The Greeks had a word for it: *kairos*. Unlike their other word for time, *chronos* (chronological time), *kairos* is about tim*ing*. It means the right or opportune time, the 'supreme moment' when the leader has perfect timing.

Surfing the wave of panic that uncertainty can represent is quite a skill, but it does get easier with practice. Over the years, this need to nurse uncertainty has rejoiced under many different names. In vogue at present is the term 'negative capability,' described by the poet John Keats (1958) in an 1817 letter to his brothers: 'that is when man is capable of being in uncertainties, mysteries, doubts, without any irritable reaching after fact & reason.' Lewis Carroll (1975) puts something similar into the mouth of the Red Queen, when she meets Alice through the looking glass: 'Alice laughed. "There's no use trying," she said. "One can't believe impossible things." "I daresay you haven't had much practice," said the Queen. "When I was your age, I always did it for half-an-hour a day. Why, sometimes I've believed as many as six impossible things before breakfast."'

In the context of COVID, sometimes leaders have just had to accept that there are no 'right' decisions, as whatever they do will have a negative impact to some extent. At best, the decisions they take will amount to no more than the least worst option. This is what is sometimes called 'the dilemma of dirty hands,' when you know that whatever you do will have negative consequences for some (Walzer, 1973, p. 160). It takes courage and maturity to live with this, and even more courage to live with the knowledge of hindsight that one might have chosen a less impactful least worst option.

Taking a Risk

If the reality of decision-making in the midst of ambiguity, in an environment of change, means that it was always likely you would be called upon to take decisions without the right data, then leading an organisation during a global pandemic has certainly brought that reality home. Every decision in this fast-moving environment has been a risk. But even in this context, risk is relative and subjective, and even the most prosaic decision can be deemed to have been risky in retrospect if it does not work out. What might feel to you like a big risk might not seem so to others; and something you regard as not risky at all, given what you know, might feel to the uninitiated as a big leap of faith. So this critical incident is partly about 'feel the fear and do it anyway,' and partly about mopping up afterwards. You would be suspicious if you met children without scabs on their knees. These are their badges of honour for taking risks and learning from them; COVID will now have given you your own battle scars.

Accepting When You Get It Wrong

Statistically speaking, then, you will make some mistakes. Even with the best intentions and the best data, facts change and unforeseen consequences arise – and hindsight can be a harsh judge. It is 'your fault,' yet it is not. This is where the pain of leadership is felt most keenly. Lockdown hits, staff are let go and lives collapse. Then the furlough scheme is announced, and they need not have lost their jobs after all, but it is too late to repair the damage done. How do you bear guilt for your part in misery, even if it was never part of your plan to cause it?

There were already, globally, a host of ex-leaders expiating the sins of office through charity work, and COVID will no doubt add to their number. Some leaders deal with the guilt by internalising their pain, and tend to suffer acute stress and heart disease as a result – heartbroken, indeed. Others deal with it through partition, by divorcing themselves from their role. This tends to show up in an increasingly robotic boss who seems to have hollow eyes and no soul. By far the hardest path is to sit with the pain and try to forgive yourself for it, as a way of addressing the guilt and remorse you feel.

Not coping with getting it wrong otherwise results in exponentially worsening leadership, because each time a decision doesn't play out, the leader will be further paralysed by guilt and, Pavlov-style, become even more risk averse in decision-making to avoid these feelings in the future. And all leaders need to be able to sleep at night, because if they cannot, their ability to make better decisions next time will be eroded. This is because we need sleep to bank the day's data in the memory. If this filing doesn't happen, the database will become increasingly dated and empty, and a leader's ability to make good decisions will reduce – as will their health, without the opportunity for night-time repair that is afforded by deep sleep. Insomnia is bad enough without it being exacerbated by guilt.

What It Feels Like

If, then, these are the particular critical incidents all leaders are facing during COVID, what might be done to make the burden easier to bear? The first step is always to acknowledge how it feels, in order to diagnose potential solutions.

Leaders who have made mistakes talk about experiencing a range of different emotions, depending on how at fault they feel, and how responsible. Leaders often have to take responsibility for the actions of their predecessors, and feeling bad about those feels different from feeling bad about having actually made a mistake on your own watch. It feels different again if you know yourself to have been at fault, or if it's just that circumstances changed. So how might you diagnose your predicament in order to best address it? While all words depend on their use in a particular culture and context, the words in Table 10.1 are commonly used to describe the spectrum of the way we feel about mistakes.

As you can see, remorse is the one that is most freighted with conscience because moral agency is specifically involved, whereas chagrin is more about ego than guilt. All of them have varying mixtures and degrees of guilt and shame about them, of acknowledging personal responsibility and accountability, and of contributing to how people move on in

Table 10.1 Responses to Mistakes

Regret	Feeling sorry about something you did or did not do, whether or not it was your fault
Ruefulness	Feeling that you could have done something different
Remorse	Feeling culpable for having done something morally wrong
Chagrin	Feeling annoyed at having been made to look foolish

a psychologically healthy way after failing in some way. They also reflect the fact that leaders who have made mistakes have to deal not only with how they feel about their mistakes, but also with how they manage their own feelings about others' reactions to their mistakes.

Responding to Mistakes

So how should you respond when a mistake is made? The free school meals controversy is a good contrary example. On 13 January 2021, the UK Health Secretary, Matt Hancock, was interviewed by Piers Morgan and Susanna Reid in a breakfast TV programme called Good Morning Britain. Hancock had voted against the provision of free school meals for children during the COVID lockdown of 2020. As a result of the intervention of a footballer, Marcus Rashford, and strong public support for Rashford's initiative, the government changed its policy and decided to provide free school meals for eligible children. When Hancock said that he was 'glad' that free school meals were now being provided, Piers Morgan asked him whether he 'regretted' originally voting against free school meals. Despite being asked several times, Hancock repeatedly refused to respond with 'yes' or 'no' and kept saying that he was 'glad the situation has been resolved.' Leaders need to develop the practice of candour when they make mistakes. It is the grace of humility in action. This is necessary for the wellbeing of leaders, and necessary for those who are the subjects of the mistakes. If Matt Hancock had said, 'Yes, I do regret my mistake. I have learned from it, and will not make the same mistake again,' the incident would most likely have been at most a footnote in his political biography. Instead, he became for a time the subject of public ridicule and criticism. Candour, then, is the best response.

The Practice of Candour

Owning Up

Of course it is unwise to run away from acknowledging mistakes and accepting personal responsibility. As Liam Donaldson (2018) said, after retiring as Chief Medical Officer, 'To err is human; to attempt to cover it up is unforgivable.' Owning up to mistakes may involve a significant measure of pain, guilt and shame. It may also involve a sense of failure. But if you cover up your mistakes, there is always a risk you will be found out anyway, and you cannot learn from your experience of making a mistake – or come to terms with it – unless you first acknowledge it clearly as a fact: 'I made a mistake. I am responsible.' Owning up means making a clear, unambiguous, unconditional statement of responsibility for the mistake and its consequences. This is owning our mistakes, as well as owning up to them. Such candour will have the incidental effect of offering to all people in our organisations an example that they can follow when they make mistakes. It models the fact that mistakes are a typical part of life, made by even the most senior and experienced of leaders.

Being Straightforward

There is a difference between owning and owning up to a mistake, on the one hand, and clearly and unambiguously identifying the substance of the mistake and why it did not work, on the other hand. The latter is the only way to learn what went wrong and what could have been done differently, and it will offer others the chance to learn from our mistakes, too. Role-modelling straightforwardness in this way contributes to the learning of others, as well as to your own personal and professional development. Usually, it proves that it's possible to make a mistake and to survive. Of course, people often share responsibility for mistakes, as mistakes can be collective as well as individual. In this context, there has rightly been a fashion to avoid 'the blame game' when its outcome is intended to be vindictive or to scapegoat. But avoiding root cause analysis just prevents learning. Investigating what went wrong, and being straightforward both about the process and how the outcomes of the investigation will be dealt with, build a culture of trust and are vital for identifying both what went wrong and lessons for the future. As Liam Donaldson (2018) rightly added in the previously quoted sentence, 'To fail to learn is inexcusable.'

Learning From Mistakes

It was Winston Churchill who said, 'Success is never final; failure is never fatal; what counts is the courage to go on.' While we are only ever as good as our last success, failure is as much part of life as success, and we need to learn from them both. Leaders need to find the courage to go on, and to learn to live with the consequences of failure. In 2016, after Andy Murray (*The Times*, July 11, 2016, p. 66) had won the men's singles title at Wimbledon for the second time, he said 'Failing's OK, providing that you've given your best and put everything into it. Don't be afraid of failing. I have learned from all my losses.' It takes enormous courage to analyse, learn from, and accept one's mistakes, and to see where things went wrong, what could and should have been done differently, and what could be done in the future to avoid the same mistakes. It takes even more courage to be appropriately open about the lessons learned. And sometimes the learning we have to do is to come to terms with the fact that we did what we could with what we had: there was no way we could have done better, and the negative outcome was inevitable. There is no point in blaming yourself for what could not have been different, even though one can still empathise with those hurt or damaged as a result.

Making Amends

But when you can, you must put things right. The word 'repentance' is useful here: it refers not only to a straightforward acknowledgement of having done wrong, but also to restitution, reparation, and repair. Of course, sometimes things cannot be put right, but making amends when possible demonstrates integrity. Owning up and accepting responsibility shows that you really mean it. And if that is not possible, a straightforward expression of contrition for mistakes can go a long way towards healing the emotional scars of those who have been affected by them.

The Fruits of Candour

One of the results of the practice of candour is that it shapes and changes those who have been candid. Truth-telling delivers us from feeling as though we have to live a lie, or expending valuable leadership energy policing others' perceptions of us. It also shapes our personality, and is likely to help us to become better listeners and learners: more understanding, and more forgiving in spirit. Candour models a way of being for others to practise and learn from, thereby shaping institutional and corporate culture, and the way we ourselves would like to be treated when we make mistakes becomes the way we treat others. Candour is, as we said, the grace of humility in action, changing us and changing those around us.

Another result of the practice of candour is that we learn to live with the flaws in ourselves and others, and we learn to roll with the punches. As is ably being demonstrated by the COVID pandemic, events, crises and unexpected disasters can always disrupt the best-laid plans. The legacy of leaders will ultimately be judged by how well they responded to unexpected challenges. A CV with no obstacles overcome shows precious little opportunity for real leadership, and one of the tests of that legacy is how candid a leader was about both their successes and their mistakes.

Mistakes and Remorse

The practice of candour deals with the public effects of mistakes, but what of those situations resulting in feelings of remorse? Leaders carrying the burden of mistakes can experience the gut-wrenching agony of guilt and shame. In empathising with those adversely affected by the consequences of mistakes, leaders may also carry their pain, too. We have learned enough from 150 years of psychology to know that buried and supressed emotions do not disappear in the long term. Those who shrug their shoulders and walk away after they have made serious mistakes, denying to themselves the inner horror of the consequences of what they have done, and who bury in the dark places of their minds the guilt and shame they face, are likely in the longer term to face both physical and psychological damage. Such emotions can lead to decreased functioning of the immune system, making leaders more vulnerable to illness and slower to recover from it. They can also lead to poor mental health, through stress, anxiety and depression. In the long term, we do not escape the guilt of remorse and regret.

Words like 'remorse' and 'penitence' developed in a religious context and refer to deep shame or guilt for moral wrongdoing (Bash, 2020). But given that decisions going wrong are just occupational hazards of senior leadership, there may well be many decisions we make that turn out to be bad which were not in fact the result of moral wrongdoing, but more to do with extreme bad luck. They are the very opposite of serendipity, the equally accidental synchronicity with a beneficial outcome. And while we are used to the graceful acceptance of good luck, we seem to feel that bad luck is somehow our fault.

So although remorse has tended to mean the deep regret or guilt experienced by someone with a very troubled conscience, in our experience of talking to leaders, it seems that it is also present when a decision, made in all integrity, has in hindsight been wrong and caused pain, suffering and loss to others. The lash of one's conscience can be much the same from mistakes with unintended, adverse consequences, whether from a moral or non-moral viewpoint. Additionally, whether one has been morally at fault or not, one may feel emotions similar to the sense of loss one may have after a bereavement.

Hannah Arendt (Arendt, 1958, p. 237) writes of 'the predicament of irreversibility,' the fact that once something has been done, it can never be undone, even though in some circumstances its consequences may be reversed. So how to live with yourself afterwards? Even though there is no escaping the predicament of irreversibility, we would argue that you can learn to live with the predicament wisely, and in ways that prepare you for future failures and setbacks. There are virtues to practise – apart from the virtue of candour – when one is bleeding in conscience from failure. These virtues are not rocket science, but they are easy to forget when one feels overwhelmed by failure (see following sidebar).

Living With Remorse

1 Keep going with the rhythm of daily life – set your alarm, and make time for friends and hobbies.
2 Eat regularly and wisely, neither self-medicating with food nor starving yourself in penance.
3 Take regular exercise – it releases endorphins and will help restore your wellbeing.
4 Beware of using alcohol or drugs as a crutch – they make poor masters.
5 Talk to your friends and family. They may not always be able to help, but they can support you in your loneliness.
6 Find peers who understand. Draw on their experience, and use their understanding to help you heal.
7 Acknowledge your feelings as a type of bereavement, for they are about a death of hope and aspiration about an aspect of the future – and grief takes time to heal.
8 Find someone to talk to confidentially. It is not a moral weakness or failure of character to talk through feelings, and it may help you 'do your grief work' – and do it well.

Building Resilience

Given that leadersmithing is all about developing templates to build resilience before the fact, are there any pre-emptive things a leader might do to build up competence in this area, before they are called on to deliver in earnest?

First, character matters and leaders can develop that long before they achieve seniority. As Michelle Obama (Elizabeth Garrett Anderson School visit) said to the children of the Elizabeth Garrett Anderson School in April 2009, 'Whether you come from a council estate or a country estate, your success will be determined by your own confidence and fortitude. It won't be easy, that's for sure, but you have everything you need.' In leadership, who we are matters as much as what we do. As we know from the Emotional Intelligence literature, self-awareness and being perceived as self-aware are both crucial for developing into a leader with the right sort of character to bear the responsibilities of leadership. Small steps can be used to display this, and to start creating the templates necessary to make remorse easier to bear. For example, can you name and apologise for the next small mistake that you make in a meeting, perhaps over a fact or someone's name? Can you seek out someone you know you have wronged and apologise privately to them? Can you undertake to apologise on behalf of your team or organisation for something minor that has gone wrong? Developing muscle memory for taking responsibility in this way removes an important psychological barrier, which makes the bigger stuff that may come later much easier to confront. Behaving in this way also creates a culture that is curious about learning from mishaps – one in which it becomes safe to take risks.

Second, values matter. Where do your values come from, and do you know what they are? Some people like rules ('do as you would be done by'), and others like to optimise outcomes ('the greatest good for the greatest number'). A more durable approach is simply to live consistently in a way that you think a virtuous person would. The idea of living virtuously as the basis of moral behaviour has its roots in the thinking of Aristotle, who emphasised that a virtuous person is someone who develops and practises virtue: 'we become just by doing just acts, temperate by doing temperate acts, brave by doing brave acts' (Thomson, 1965, p. 56). These traits may be inborn or learned, but if nurtured become a way of life. As we now know from neuroscience, brain plasticity (Doidge, 2007) means we eventually become what we do. Could you take a virtue for a walk today? Could you practise kindness or generosity or humility, just to limber up your virtuosity a bit? Behaviours of probity, integrity and empathy generate inner qualities that radiate out in leadership roles, but of course are attributes that every person can develop as a parent, machinist, plumber, teacher or CEO. This more consistent approach to morality makes a leader more predictable, which signals reliability and builds trust. On the other hand, some people seem to have Jekyll and Hyde characters, and seem to change with the weather. You may know people like this, and their unpredictability probably make you feel very uncomfortable. Few would choose to follow them, and few will be at their best in their company. But a reliably virtuous leader will have an integrated personality and character because they will have synthesised the disparate elements of their personality, identity, and experience. This equips them with the capacity not only to adapt and adjust to changes in circumstance, but to do so in a way that maintains coherence and consistency in a virtuous way.

Finally, a practical suggestion about improving your mastery in ambiguity. The best framing of ambiguity is drawn from the work of Ralph Stacey (2002). Famous for pioneering the field of complexity, he is fond of contrasting two axes: agreement and certainty. Where things are close to both agreement and certainty, there is little ambiguity, like what day of the week it is. But as things move away from either certainty or agreement, the more ambiguous they become: when will this crisis end? A leader's job is to nail down certainties and achieve agreement about them, so that they can be delegated, and leadership attention re-directed to where it can add most value. So next time you face a challenge, ask just these two questions: what is certain, and what is agreed? If you keep working these two angles, you will tease out the known from the unknown, and can save your energy for the things that really matter: the search for new certainties, and your diplomacy for new agreements. A useful by-product of this approach is that you will also generate a paper trail to explain your decisions, should they be questioned in the future.

Conclusion

There is a big difference between being a Teflon® leader, to whom nothing sticks, and a leader who can hold the impact of others' negative views about them with healthy self-esteem and still carry on. This is why developing robust and balanced self-esteem really matters, because it helps leaders to live humbly, knowing that others may hold a diminished view about them because of their mistakes. It is very unlikely that any good leader will have managed to please everyone, but we are more than our successes and we are more than our mistakes. Good leaders learn to discriminate between justified criticism and unwarranted shaming, and they accept the inevitability of mistake-making because it comes with the territory. As for all people, leaders who make mistakes are still worthwhile, lovable and valuable; leaders should expect this courtesy, and be sure to be seen to be extending it to others.

Leadersmithing is a process of character formation involving the deliberate development of templates for the future. Lessons well learned from the modest tasks of yesterday become the foundation of the successful negotiation of the tougher tasks of today. In a COVID world, for which no-one was prepared, we may through no fault of our own make many mistakes.

But adopting a leadersmithing approach means we can learn fast, early and often, in order to make our future leadership of others both more robust and more resilient.

References

Arendt, Hannah (1958) *The Human Condition*, Chicago, IL: Chicago University Press.

Bash, Anthony (2020) *Remorse*, Eugene, OR: Cascade.

Carroll Lewis (1975) *Alice's Adventures in Wonderland and Through the Looking Glass*, London: Penguin, p. 257f.

Doidge, Norman (2007) *The Brain that Changes Itself*, London: Penguin.

Donaldson, L (2018) *The Lancet Editorial*, 391(10135), 2079. https://doi.org/10.1016/S0140-6736(18)31119-X

Poole, Eve (2017) *Leadersmithing*, London: Bloomsbury.

Rollins, HE (1958) *The Letters of John Keats*, 2 vols, Cambridge: Cambridge University Press, i, pp. 193–194.

Stacey, RD (2002) *Strategic Management and Organisational Dynamics*, Harlow: Prentice Hall.

The Herald, 3 April 2009, https://www.heraldscotland.com/default_content/12753141.emotional-first-lady-tells-schoolgirls-counting/

Thomson, JAK (1965) *The Ethics of Aristotle*, London: Penguin.

Walzer, M (1973) Political Action: The Problem of Dirty Hands. *Philosophy & Public Affairs*, 2(2), 160–180.

Ward, K & Kirkbride, P (eds) (2001) *Globalization*, Chichester: Wiley.

11 Addicted to Leadership

From Crisis to Recovery

Lucie Hartley and Richard Bolden

Introduction

Following the events of 2020 (notably Black Lives Matter and COVID), and with the world hurtling towards a climate catastrophe, a rising groundswell of opinion suggests that leadership is changing and indeed must change (Tourish, 2020). Many now advocate moving away from a 'heroic' leadership model toward a more collaborative, inclusive, responsible and compassionate approach, where the *leadership process* is widely distributed and outcomes are more widely owned. Whilst such shifts are to be encouraged, these are not new ideas and this is not the first time writers have urged us to reconsider leadership. Indeed, as far back as the 6th century BC, the philosopher Lao Tzu suggested:

> But of a good leader, who talks little, when his work is done, his task completed, they will say: 'We did it ourselves'.
>
> (Lao Tzu, cited in Manz and Sims, 1991, p. 35)

Despite the pressing need for more collaborative and inclusive leadership, evidence suggests that in both politics and organisations, people are still drawn towards narratives of charismatic, narcissistic and populist leaders (Foroughi et al., 2019). Why is this and how might we break, what appears to be our 'addiction' to many unhealthy and destructive forms of leadership? In this chapter, we suggest that, as leaders, followers and citizens, we have a tendency to default to compulsive, habit-forming, learned patterns of behaviour and thinking regarding the ways in which we view and practice leadership. In exploring the parallels between these and drug and alcohol 'addiction'[1] (including the drivers of addiction and interventions used to support recovery), we attempt to distil key principles, which could support radical change in leadership theory and practice. We use the notion of addiction in both a *metaphorical* sense – by conceptualising the ways in which followers, leaders and wider society may be addicted to forms of leadership – and a *literal* sense – by drawing on real life examples from addiction services and leaders working within them.

We begin by considering the nature of addiction and the kinds of longing and desires that might lead us to become addicted both to forms of leadership and to substances. We then shift our focus to the wider systemic and contextual factors that underlie leadership toxicity and the potential for leaders and followers to be drawn into destructive patterns of thought and behaviour. This is then illustrated through specific examples from drug and alcohol services, which illustrate the potential for senior leaders to mirror similar patterns of thought and behaviour to that of their clients. We conclude by drawing insights from work with people who are dependent on drugs and alcohol to consider the processes through which

DOI: 10.4324/9781003171737-13

we might endeavour to overcome our individual and collective addictions to leadership and begin to navigate the long and challenging road from crisis to recovery.

Addiction and Longing

The process through which people become dependent on drugs, alcohol or anything else occurs over a period of time. Like the ubiquitous frog in a pan of boiling water, the situation deteriorates at a rate that may not be noticed until it's too late. The first step on the road to recovery, therefore, is to acknowledge the nature of the problem and to seek help.

Drug and alcohol addiction is described as a chronically relapsing condition. Whilst a genuine desire and intention to change is an important first step for people who are dependent, it is only the start of what is often a long journey towards recovery, frequently interspersed with lapses and relapses. Classic interventions aim to develop a more conscious awareness of thought processes and behaviours, find ways to sustain a continued level of vigilance around patterned responses and ensure meaningful activity and ongoing support. Recovery is seldom a one-off event and is frequently described as a daily practice, requiring courage, strength and support to sustain, often over many years.

Addressing leadership addictions similarly requires awareness, vigilance, an exploration of new activities and ongoing support to achieve and sustain change. Collaboration, courage, flexibility and a willingness to consciously engage with complexity and uncertainty feature prominently along this road.

Leadership and Longing

Traditional fairy tales have much to teach us about longing. Their beginnings often introduce us to deep desires, and their telling and endings find ways to resolve and contain them. Bettleheim (1976) suggests that the house in the story of Hansel and Gretel, for example, symbolises a fantasy of infantile bliss:

> The house at which Hansel and Gretel are eating away blissfully and without a care stands for the good mother, who offers her body as a source of nourishment. It is the original all-giving mother, whom every child hopes to find again later somewhere out in the world, when his own mother begins to make demands and to impose restrictions.
>
> (p. 161)

The lead author's experience of working with people who are dependent on drugs and alcohol suggests that substances can also symbolise this fantasy. She once asked a client how he would describe a bottle of wine if it were a person. He said it was 'an uncomplaining friend, who met my needs in every way'. He said it 'cocooned' him and let him 'live in a fantasy'. Clients who used heroin also talked about being 'wrapped in cotton wool' and the 'euphoria' of their first heroin 'high'. One woman, in writing about heroin addiction, spoke of her longing for the 'irrevocable glories of the first time' (Marlowe, 1999, p. 1).

Whether we love or hate our leaders, there is a strong draw toward them, and even when they fail us, we continue to make them objects of our attention, vilifying them or hoping that they will come good. Despite a well-earned reputation for flagrant disregard of the truth, a catastrophic start to management of the COVID outbreak and many people saying they didn't trust him, millions of people across the UK tuned into Prime Minister Boris Johnson's addresses to the nation during the pandemic. A similar pattern of events unfolded on the other side of the Atlantic as US President Donald Trump mused on various (frequently unscientific and often dangerous) ways of stopping the virus and Brazil President Jair Bolsonaro described COVID as 'a measly cold'. In repeatedly watching these televised addresses, what is it we were longing for? Were we just looking for information from our nation heads – or were we longing for something more, which was offered by the promise, confidence and charisma of these leaders?

Several academics have written about the 'leadership mystique' (Gabriel, 1997; Kets de Vries, 2001) and the 'romance of leadership' (Meindl et al., 1985). Gabriel (2005), following a 'leaderless' teaching experiment with MBA students, concludes that the 'symbolic space' of leadership insists on being filled and that the importance we accord it seems to represent early parental figures. Grint (2009) references Erich Fromm's (1941) *Fear of Freedom*, when he argues that the decline in communal relationships over time has led to people feeling unbearably lonely and increasingly responsible, the fear of which drives us to seek refuge in leaders. Grint (2009) further suggests we look to leaders to protect us from existential angst:

> It is into this permanently unstable world that leaders, especially charismatics, step, offering certainty, identity, and absolution from guilt and anxiety to replace – and displace – the moral quagmire and purposeless existence that existentialism reveals.
>
> (p. 100)

It could be argued that the compulsive draw toward our leaders is like an addiction, and that this inhibits followers from taking responsibility. Is this dependency, however, a wholly bad thing? Leaders, after all, provide a container for our aspirations, act as permission givers and represent important issues. Greta Thunberg, for example, could be seen as the physical embodiment of the climate change movement, offering the hope and vision her followers long for. Not all addictions are viewed as harmful. Many people, for example, are dependent to tea and coffee, and there are other common addictions in our modern world which many would regard as innocuous (e.g. addictions to exercise or shopping). Some addictions, however, are seen as being particularly toxic and we would suggest that the magnetic pull of a 'toxic' leader can be harmful, especially in crisis situations.

Toxic Leadership

The concept of 'toxic' leaders and leadership (Lipman-Blumen, 2005; Whicker, 1996) suggests that the very traits and tendencies that enable people to rise to senior positions within organisations (such as high levels of self-confidence, drive, competitiveness, etc.) may also be associated with psychological disorders (narcissism, psychopathy, etc.) that may come to have a dysfunctional effect within organisations and wider society. Maak et al. (2021) compared the handling of the COVID crisis by Trump and Bolsonaro to Germany's Angela Merkel and New Zealand's Jacinta Ardern, arguing that narcissism and ideological rigidity are key 'fault lines' in leadership. They point to the way in which Merkel and Ardern cultivated positive relationships with stakeholders, took heed of the evidence base and sent messages of unity and collaboration. By contrast, Trump and Bolsonaro failed to do this, looking only to evidence which propped up their own view of the world and dividing – rather than uniting – diverse stakeholders. Like many writers, Maak et al. (2021) call for more compassionate and responsible leaders.

Understanding Context

Whilst we wholeheartedly endorse the need for responsible and compassionate leadership, we believe that too great a focus on the characteristics and behaviours of individual leaders – the 'villains', 'heroes' and 'heroines' of our fairy tales – fails to recognise the wider context within which they operate, and which got them to where they are in the first place (see Ladkin, 2020 for an insightful example). After all, villains are often the product of toxic experiences and further supported by toxic environments. Heroes and heroines need healthy people, systems and contexts to help them reach the Holy Grail. So, whilst the world cries out for more compassionate and responsible leaders, it is vital that we create the environments which can sustain and support this style of leadership.

There is a parallel here with the way in which people often view addictions; regarding affected individuals through a negative moral lens, as the 'sinners' entirely responsible for their predicament. The reality is that many people who become dependent on drugs and alcohol have been heavily affected by harsh upbringings/environments, including poverty, sexual/physical abuse, parental absence, parental substance abuse and parental mental ill health and/or domestic violence. Evidence suggests that up to two-thirds of drug users have a history of adverse childhood experiences (Tilson, 2018), and there is a strong correlation between substance misuse and other complex needs, such as mental health, criminal behaviour, and homelessness. Studies have found that these adverse experiences can be exacerbated by the 'system', which aims to help, but can be daunting to navigate, with the constant demand to re-tell traumatic events, exacerbating symptoms of post-traumatic stress disorder (PTSD) and potentially re-traumatising individuals. In response, services are increasingly focusing on trauma-informed and system-based approaches, where the focus of responsibility for change is seen as not only residing with the individual, but also with the way in which services can collaborate, reconfigure the system and take a more trauma-informed approach to people's care (Fenney, 2019).

Toxic Triangles

The term 'toxic trio' has been used to describe the issues of domestic abuse, mental ill health and substance misuse, which have been identified as common features of families where harm to children and adults has occurred. In leadership literature, Padilla et al. (2007) refer to the 'toxic triangle', adding the issue of context to argue that, whilst destructive leaders and susceptible followers may be present in many situations, it is only where they are combined within a conducive environment that damaging leadership occurs.

In the wake of the COVID crisis, many leaders in the National Health Service (NHS) emerged emotionally exhausted and bereft, struggling to survive in an environment which is under-funded, target-driven and places huge expectations on individuals. Paradoxically, whilst they operate in an organisation where the founding principles are about responsibility and compassion, they themselves are vulnerable to the toxic impact of witnessing trauma, with staff working in intensive care units during the COVID pandemic showing a 40% likelihood of developing PTSD – twice that of military veterans recently engaged in combat (Greenberg et al., 2021). In such cases, it may be unreasonable to expect them to open their hearts any further to show compassionate leadership, a point noted by Maak and colleagues (2021):

> It cannot be overstated, how demanding it is for a leader to make space for human moments, and to be present for and attentive to those who suffer in a situation in which pressure on the leader is relentless.
>
> (p. 74)

The potential for leadership roles to be toxic or harmful in and of themselves has been high-lighted by Frost and Robinson (1999), who used the notion of the 'toxic handler' to describe the way in which leaders and managers are expected to deal with and absorb distress, anxiety and conflict on a daily basis. Frost (2003) drew an analogy between exposure to these 'toxic emotions' and the exposure of a factory worker to dangerous or carcinogenic chemicals – something which he personally experienced in his own work as a manager and which may well have contributed to his early death from cancer.

Gallos (2008) cites research by cognitive scientists which demonstrates that some people are more attuned to being empathic than others. She suggests that caring leaders are likely to fall into this category and considers factors that enable these leaders, who she refers to as 'toxin magnets', to stay healthy. A report published by the Kings Fund (West et al., 2017) argues that compassionate leadership is critical to creating a culture of innovation and improvement in the NHS to meet the needs of a changing population. They argue, however, that it is unrealistic to expect individual leaders to demonstrate compassion unless a culture of compassionate leadership is embedded throughout the organisation.

Addictive Behaviour in Leaders

In 2013, the authors presented a paper at the International Studying Leadership Conference which explored patterns of addictive behaviour in leadership practice in drug and alcohol charities. At the time, the lead author was chief executive of a drug and alcohol charity. Building on Padilla et al.'s (2007) notion of the 'toxic triangle' and in light of her own experience, she was interested to look at how the potentially toxic nature of leadership roles, and the expectations and aspirations of followers, may draw leaders into dysfunctional and addictive ways of feeling, thinking and behaving that are harmful to themselves, their organisations and others. She conducted a first-person action research case study and semi-structured interviews with three senior-level managers in UK-based addiction charities. The action research was conducted over a period of four months, during which time she experimented with mind-fulness and reflective practice. She consciously reflected on her own leadership and manage-ment practice throughout this period by keeping a regular journal.

Several issues emerged within the case study and interviews that suggest similarities between the experiences of senior managers in drug and alcohol charities and the clients their organisations support. Research participants described feelings and behaviours such as a sense of deprivation and crisis, the feeling of work being 'critical', and the experience of being 'absorbed' to the exclusion of all else. A further parallel which emerged in the case study was that between the leaders' self-destructive working behaviour (e.g. working late, not stopping when tired) and the self-destructive behaviour of addicts. It was noted in the case study that being 'busy' could be experienced as a 'numbing out' or could lead to 'feeling more' due to the stimulation – both feelings that dependent drug and alcohol users will say they use substances to experience. It was further noted that being 'busy' could affect engagement with others and lead to feelings of chaos and disorganisation, again having parallels with the behaviours and feelings of addicts. A further parallel noted in the case study was 'habitual behaviour and associations', such as eating chocolate when working late. It was observed that relentless activity was often followed by a 'crash' – feeling low and empty – and this was likened to the 'crash' and 'come down' of people who use stimulant drugs.

In each of the interviews and in the case study, there was a common theme of the difficulty in managing and maintaining work-life boundaries. These were most frequently expressed in terms of time management, identities and the expectations of others. The theme of boundaries is particularly significant in considering the behaviour of people addicted to substances. People using illegal drugs, for example, break legal boundaries and those injecting drugs break the boundaries of their own skin. In the case study a recurrent sense of 'not enough time' was noted, which may be linked with an underlying sense of deprivation/crisis.

All the research participants talked of the practices they used to manage their stress levels, including acupuncture, yoga, reflection and meditation. Each talked of the need to have someone to talk things through with. Within the case study, the author experimented with mindfulness meditation and keeping a personal reflective journal. She noticed a change in her approach to reflection, from simply thinking about what had happened and how she thought/felt about this to asking herself why she was seeing/feeling things in particular ways. This was facilitated by some informal coaching sessions where the coach modelled this approach with her own reflections. The regular journal writing created a further vehicle for increased reflection during this period.

Although balancing competing identities remained a challenge, reflection helped identify and explore how different roles were constructed and positioned vis-à-vis one another and, over time, it became possible to navigate between them more successfully. Both reflection and mindfulness were found to help in stepping back from personal preoccupations and focusing on the needs of others. When engaged in practising mindfulness, the author found herself better able to avoid more habitual and unhealthy working patterns, to notice things which benefited from her attention and to tolerate the 'not knowing' that often accompanies senior roles (what the poet John Keats termed 'negative capability').[2]

The study suggested that a disciplined approach to reflection and mindfulness can be helpful in managing toxic influences and relating to them differently. The literature review and research further pointed to the importance of self-awareness, so that leaders can be more conscious of and less driven by unconscious thinking and behaviour patterns. Reflection was seen as an important tool in developing self-awareness and managing internal and external expectations and stereotypes. It was also seen as helpful to engaging with and understanding other people better.

The practice of action research was considered as a reflexive practice in itself. This was beneficial in enabling the researcher to critically explore her reflections in an iterative manner. Similarly, with mindfulness, action research enabled her to look at the ways in which mindfulness affected experience of her role, which encouraged her to access this practice more, see the challenges of engaging with it and try different ways of incorporating it into her various identities.

Overall, this study suggests that the demands of senior management roles in drug and alcohol charities (and most likely elsewhere, too) place pressures on their incumbents that may lead to dysfunctional and damaging patterns of affect, thought and behaviour. Mindfulness and reflection are proposed as potential antidotes that enable greater awareness of self and others and the capacity to break out of the 'toxic triangle'. Further exploration of whether these tendencies are more peculiar to this sector (i.e. do leaders mirror the difficulties their clients experience or are people with addictive tendencies attracted to this type of work?) would be useful.

Addiction and Sensemaking

Grint (2008) looks at leaders' addictions to making sense of the world through a particular lens so that they can respond in a way which they find easier or more rewarding. Grint looks at how different levels of certainty call for different responses from leaders. He illustrates this in Figure 11.1, using Rittell and Webber's (1973) classification of different types of problems.

Grint (2010) points out that more complex, 'wicked' problems don't lend themselves to simple solutions, as they usually cross cultural and institutional boundaries. Grint suggests that the lack of obvious solution requires the leader to engage with a broad range of stakeholders and take a more collaborative approach, which many leaders find difficult to do:

> But because we are prisoners of our own cultural preferences we become addicted to them and have great difficulty stepping outside our world to see something differently.

(p. 9)

Although Grint sees what he calls a 'leadership' approach as being the most appropriate response to wicked problems, he points out the privileged position of decision-makers, making them the ones who define the problem. Grint argues that leaders are often addicted to management and command, and therefore tend to define problems as being more urgent or straightforward than they are.

Overly simplistic or blatantly false definitions of problems and solutions also result from a further pernicious addiction prevalent in the modern world: our addiction to social media. Vosoughi and Roy (2018) found that fake news spreads six times faster than genuine news and the recent documentary on Netflix *The Social Dilemma* highlights alarming concerns regarding the impact of fake news and the manipulation of data on democratic processes.

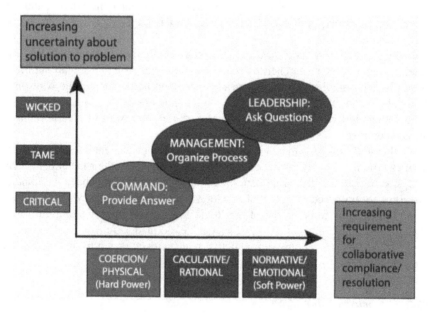

Figure 11.1 Typology of Problems, Power and Authority

Source: Grint, (2008, p. 11)

Maak et al. (2021) suggest it is incumbent upon responsible leaders to challenge erroneous information:

> Responsible leadership that aims to champion evidence-based decision making also needs to actively challenge misinformation and science denialism. Judged by Brandolini's bullshit asymmetry principle that 'the amount of energy necessary to refute bullshit is an order of magnitude bigger than to produce it' (Williamson, 2006), this is a formidable task.
>
> (p. 15)

The impact of cultural context on how we define problems – and indeed, solutions – has parallels in the world of drug and alcohol addictions. In the UK, alcohol and tobacco are legal drugs, regulated by the government, which benefits from taxes levied on the alcohol and tobacco industries. Most people would see heroin as a far more problematic drug, yet alcohol and tobacco cause more deaths by far and detoxing from alcohol carries an inherent risk of fatality, which is not the case with heroin. The way in which drugs are viewed varies across cultural contexts and time. Alcohol, for example, was prohibited in the United States between 1920 and 1933, and of course remains prohibited within much of the Muslim world. By contrast, heroin was legal and widely prescribed for common ailments in the UK in the 1930s.

Giving Up Addictions

There are many forces which cause a gravitational pull towards heroic leaders, the allure of toxic leaders, toxic systems and practices, and distorted lenses through which we view the problems and solutions of leadership. If leadership really is to change, what is it that we have to give up, and how can we maintain recovery from our many addictions?

Relinquishing Pleasures

The transtheoretical model of change[3] suggests that people considering altering their behaviour go through different stages in the process of change. One of these stages is called the 'contemplation stage', during which people are ambivalent about whether they want to make a change or not.

An exercise called 'decisional balance' is a relapse prevention intervention[4] commonly used at this stage with people addicted to drugs or alcohol. It prompts users to weigh up the advantages and disadvantages of continuing to use and examine the short-term and long-term consequences. This enables addicts to acknowledge the pleasures and benefits of their substance use, whilst facing the reality of the consequences.

People in leadership positions are no different, and there are many pleasures to be had from occupying these roles (Gosling, 2019). Some of these may be harmless, but some are unhelpful and may even be toxic. As with addicts, leaders should examine their motivations, ambivalence and the impact the pleasures they enjoy have on others, their organisations and the wider environment within which they operate. DiAngelo (2018), for example, suggests that white leaders must acknowledge their 'white privilege' and face up to their 'white fragility' in order to engage in meaningful conversations and contribute positively to addressing racial inequality.

Disillusion

Using drugs or alcohol can be an attempt to control and regulate the difficult internal or external environments which users experience. This illusion of control comes at a high price, often spiralling individuals into deeper misery and cumulative difficulties. The numbing effects of use to manage physical and psychological pain and the longing for a state of bliss lead people to go from one drink and one fix to the next. In the process of giving up, addicts have to learn to stop, to be with the resulting empty space, to sit with deeply painful feelings, and tackle what are often complex and difficult situations.

The fantasy that leaders (or one model of leadership) can resolve and control the complex issues we face is also an illusion. Followers, seeking refuge from existential angst, can cling to the comfort of the illusion, whilst leaders, supported by the insidious power of social media, can perpetuate it. The process of disillusionment requires a willingness to tolerate uncertainty and complexity.

Heffernan (2020) argues that Silicon Valley has perpetuated a myth that with enough data, we can gain control over the future. However, she points out that certainty doesn't exist and the future can't be predicted. In April 2021, three eminent climate scientists wrote an article which challenged an over-reliance on the notion of 'technological salvation', claiming that computer modelling using anticipated technological solutions to removing greenhouse gases from the air, balanced against forecast carbon emissions, has been overly simplistic and led to erroneous judgements and overly simplistic thinking with regards to when 'net zero' can be achieved:

> Such models represent society as a web of idealised, emotionless buyers and sellers and thus ignore complex social and political realities, or even the impacts of climate change itself.
>
> (Dyke et al., 2021)

Negative Capability – Being and Being Without

A powerful antidote to the illusion of control and the inherently future state of longing is a call to engage with present reality and the uncomfortable feelings which can accompany its intrinsic uncertainty.

Cultivating a quality of 'being' in order to adopt a different kind of attentiveness to the present, using mindfulness and reflexive practices, was explored in the author's research mentioned previously. Von Bülow and Simpson (2020) discuss this in relation to the demand that busy leaders need to be 'more caring', which they say can feel like 'another thing to do' in their demanding jobs. They suggest, instead, that leaders need to foster a quality of being and they point to the concept of 'negative capability' (mentioned earlier) as an alternative way to understand the concept of care. They suggest that negative capability has two aspects: first, the ability to give focused attention to those things which require our attention without the distraction of unhelpful thoughts, feelings and actions; and second, the ability to be with uncertainty in a way which enables an openness to what is true.

> Negative capability, as a radical acceptance of *being* and *being without*, thus creates the conditions for giving a heightened quality of attention in all of its multi-dimensional complexity.
>
> (p. 3)

An openness to the uncertainty and complexity of the world we inhabit would also support leaders and researchers to accept that there are likely no neat and simple solutions to many of the challenges the world faces. Whilst we long for resolutions and fairy tale endings, both the addict's road to recovery and the solutions for leadership are unlikely to be predictable, linear or straightforward. In his analysis of leaders' addiction to defining problems as 'tame' or 'critical' to rationalise the use of simple solutions, Grint (2010, p. 8) suggests we need 'clumsy solutions' to more complex, 'wicked' problems.

Avoiding Cross Addictions

The tendency to give up one dependency and replace it with another is known as 'cross addiction' (e.g. when an addict stops using heroin but starts drinking heavily), which fails to deal with the problems underlying addictions.

In relation to leadership, Grint (2010) points to the danger of replacing the romance of 'heroic leadership' models with an equally dangerous romance of 'distributed leadership' and collaborative working models, which in practice have their own challenges. He contests that groups of people with different philosophical outlooks tend to be addicted to different models of leadership. He suggests that what is needed is an openness to different types of leadership at different times, with followers taking more responsibility and both leaders and followers being prepared to give up their 'addictions':

> We need to be managers, leaders and commanders at different times . . . the addiction to command is not restricted to power-hungry commanders but also involves anxiety-prone and responsibility-avoiding followers . . . getting off the addiction will require the equivalent of 'cold turkey' – the unpleasant period of 'drying out' so that the addiction is gradually halted.
>
> (pp. 310–311)

The Paradox of 'Unleadership'

Jarvis et al. (2020) write about the limitations of both heroic and distributed leadership during the COVID crisis. They point to the many unsung heroes and heroines who shopped, prepared meals for and stood on the doorsteps of neighbours, and who found ways to source and make PPE (personal protective equipment) when the government was failing to provide this. Paradoxically, it seems that when it appeared that the leaders had no solutions, alternative ways forward emerged. Jarvis and colleagues call this 'unleadership', because people acting in these ways don't define themselves *in relation to* leaders or leadership (i.e. they are not focused on opposing or having power over others), but act collaboratively, co-creating an emerging reality. These people, they argue, challenge our obsession with powerful (and power-hungry) leaders, and highlight the importance of *paying* rather than *seeking* attention to make a difference in the world. They also refer to 'the illusion of control' (discussed previously):

> In the UK, COVID has exposed the limitations of strong leaders who cling determinedly to the illusion of control . . . underestimating both their citizens' willingness to limit their individual freedom for the common good, and their creativity and resourcefulness in working around the barriers created by centralised control.
>
> (p. 133)

Services working with addicts and other health and social care services have similarly moved away from models which promote practitioners and clinicians as the only experts, holding a monopoly over the expertise and knowledge required to 'treat patients'. There is an increasing emphasis on 'strength-based' approaches, focusing on the 'recovery capital' (social, physical, human and cultural resources and strengths) of people using services, working *with* rather than *for* people, and on the importance of mutual aid and the co-creation of services.

Checks and Balances

To maintain changes, addicts are encouraged to anticipate situations which may lead to lapse or relapse and to put in place checks and balances. They may, for example, draw up an emergency plan for what they will do in a high-risk situation, and they may complete a 'relapse prevention plan', looking at different strategies, including meaningful activities and forms of support. Social networks are an extremely important feature in recovery, and for many addicts, regular involvement with a mutual aid group (e.g. Alcoholics or Narcotics Anonymous) is an absolute lifeline.

Checks and controls can be put in place to minimise the potential negative impact of narcissism in some leaders. Maccoby (2000) proposes several solutions, including: finding a trusted sidekick who can challenge the leader's assumptions and encourage them to consider alternatives; indoctrinating the organisation to internalise the vision and values of the leader; and getting into psychoanalysis, because through self-awareness and reflection narcissistic leaders will be better placed to exploit the positive aspects of their personality and minimise the negative impacts. Dotlich and Cairo (2003) argue that effective executives regularly commit ten 'unnatural acts' that help mitigate against derailment, including surrounding themselves with people who create some discomfort, connecting instead of creating, trusting first and asking questions later, giving up some control, and coaching and teaching rather than inspiring and leading.

Waking Up

The thinking and behaviours which underlie addictive habits are often unconscious. Relapse prevention and other cognitive behavioural interventions support addicts to become more conscious of, be vigilant about and take responsibility for those things which trigger them, putting them at risk of lapse and relapse. A commonly used relapse prevention technique, based on the principles of mindfulness meditation, is called 'urge surfing'. This technique is used to help an addict deal with urges or cravings by sitting with the feeling and exploring the somatic reality of the sensation, as opposed to reacting to the habitual response of their mind.

Leaders, too, can be supported to become more conscious of patterned responses through reflexive and other types of awareness-raising practices (e.g. mindfulness). Self-assessment instruments, such as the Hogan Developmental Survey, can be helpful in identifying and monitoring behavioural tendencies that may lead to executive derailment and putting in place strategies for mitigating the potential causes and consequences; 360-degree appraisal and executive coaching and mentoring are likewise valuable in raising awareness and creating spaces for leaders to talk through, reflect upon and respond to insights with regard to their leadership practice.

The responsibility for vigilance around toxic influences and indicators of leadership toxicity and addiction, however, should not be left to 'leaders' alone, but also actively promoted and facilitated at organisational and societal levels. In an environment now commonly characterised as VUCA (volatile, uncertain, ambiguous and complex), it is interesting to note that the Zulu word 'vuka' means 'to wake up'. This could enable all of us to be aware of our responsibilities to play an active part in the governance and leadership of the organisations and communities to which we belong. As Grint says:

> Leadership, then, is not just a theoretical arena but one with critical implications for us all and the limits of leadership – what leaders can do and what followers should allow them to do – are foundational aspects of this arena. Leadership, in effect, is too important to be left to leaders.
>
> (Grint, 2005, p. 4)

Conclusion

It would be rather neat to end this chapter with a 'happily ever after' solution to where leadership needs to go, a formulaic recipe for success of the kind which makes bestsellers. This would, however, ignore the wake-up call COVID gave us, the call to grapple with much bigger and substantial issues that our world faces (e.g. climate change, social inequality, polarisation and isolation, and the increasing misery caused by a plethora of addictions). These 'wicked problems' will likely only respond to 'clumsy solutions'. We do, however, suggest that there is merit in drawing together parallels between key principles and approaches in understanding addiction and an emerging discourse regarding the ways in which we need to fundamentally change our narrative about leadership.

There is an important role for drugs in our society. Diamorphine (pure heroin), for example, provides a kinder ending to people who suffer pain in their final days. Equally, there is a role for leaders and for different types of leadership to respond to different types of problems. As people, and as leaders and followers, we need to recognise, however, when our leadership addictions become harmful.

Just as Hansel and Gretel needed to relinquish the fantasy of the 'all-giving' mother, we need to be willing to relinquish the fantasy that drugs and leaders will quell and distract us from our longings and discomfort. This requires a maturation and letting go of the illusion of control by addicts, followers and leaders. We don't suggest that there can never be any straightforward solutions or plans made for the future. Indeed, we uphold that longer-term visions and aspirations are vital to effective leadership. However, strategies of leaders and their organisations need to acknowledge, tolerate and make space for an increasing level of uncertainty, twists and turns, and emergent solutions along the road. Nurturing a quality of attention (e.g. through reflection and mindfulness meditation) supports leaders and followers to do this and to pay attention to the right things. As Jarvis et al. (2020) argue, this paradoxically opens the space in which solutions (familiar and unfamiliar), compassion and responsibility can emerge.

A high level of consciousness regarding situations, tendencies, behaviours and habituated ways of defining and responding to problems that are associated with substance use and leadership toxicity would benefit leaders, addicts and organisations. Leaders should examine their motivations and be prepared to give things up, including privileges, which cause harm to themselves and others. Whilst there are times when the expertise of the clinician or leader is needed, leaders and practitioners (health and social care) need to be prepared to give up on the seduction of being the expert and recognise the part their clients, employees or citizens will play along the road to recovery or in the resolution of 'wicked problems'.

Putting in place checks and balances which root out toxic influences and developing leaders' self-awareness will support this. Addicts need to re-evaluate their social networks, choose their friends wisely and find people who will support them and refuse to collude with their addiction. Similarly, we need to critically appraise and choose our leaders wisely, ensuring they are surrounded by the right people, who will support and challenge them to act wisely.

Tendencies towards addictive behaviour must also be seen within the context of the system, and the forces supporting toxic systems (notably the media) must be held to account. Our leadership systems tend towards an individualistic orientation, emphasising progression, promotion and reward. If we are to nurture compassion and responsibility in leaders, we should ensure that compassion and responsibility are at the heart of the system within which leaders operate, and develop ways to identify and address systems where this is not the case. As some academics would attest (Jarvis et al., 2020), a focus on outcomes – as opposed to the performance of the individual leader – creates the conditions for 'unleadership' to emerge, whereby people get things done because they see that things need doing, as so many people did during the COVID crisis. This is not just about leaders or followers, but about what can happen in the co-created space between them both. Similarly, allowing space within the system for users of drug and alcohol services to co-create services, as experts in their own recovery journeys, can have remarkable outcomes.

Responsible leadership requires a deep sense of self and community – valuing diversity, ethics, the individual and the collective. It is something that involves all of us, leaders and followers, binding us in a moral relationship that can be quickly undermined through neglect, indifference and the sleepy dreaminess of the candy cottage. In much the same way that supporting the recovery of people who are unfortunate enough to fall into addiction is both an individual and a societal responsibility, so, too, is the need to wake up to and call out the harmful aspects of toxic leadership and our collective leadership addictions. Only then can we escape our dependency on villains and travel the long, uncertain and winding road from crisis to recovery.

Notes

1 The term 'addiction' has been used to align with what other writers have written regarding addictions in leadership. It should be noted that this is a contested term, which has its roots in a disease and more individualistic model of addiction. Furthermore, the term 'addict' is often associated with moral overtones, which can 'demonise' individuals. The authors take a more collective perspective (viewing 'addiction' as the outcome of societal and cultural influences, and hence a collective – as well as individual – responsibility). They would usually talk about *people* who are dependent on drugs or alcohol.
2 'The Romantic poet John Keats (1795–1821) coined the phrase "negative capability" in a letter written to his brothers George and Thomas on the 21 December 1817'.
3 This is one of the stages in the Transtheoretical Model of Change described by Prochaska and DiClemente (1983).
4 Relapse prevention is based on a cognitive-behavioural model of the relapse process developed by Marlatt and his colleagues (Marlatt and Gordon, 1985; Parks et al., 2001).

References

Bettleheim, B. (1976) *The Uses of Enchantment: The Meaning and Importance of Fairy Tales*. London: Thames and Hudson.

DiAngelo, R. (2018) *White Fragility: Why It's So Hard for White People to Talk About Racism*. Boston: Beacon Press.

Dotlich, D. and Cairo, P. (2003) *Why CEOs Fail*. San Francisco, CA: Jossey Bass.

Dyke, J., Watson, R. and Knorr, W. (2021) Climate scientists: Concept of net zero is a dangerous trap. *The Conversation*, April 22.

Fenney, D. (2019) Tackling poor health outcomes: The role of trauma-informed care. *Kings Fund blog*, 14 November. www.kingsfund.org.uk/blog/2019/11/trauma-informed-care, accessed 13/05/2021.

Foroughi, H., Gabriel, Y. and Fotaki, M. (2019) Leadership in a post-truth era: A new narrative disorder? *Leadership*, 15(2), 135–151.

Fromm, E. (1941) *The Fear of Freedom*. London: Routledge.

Frost, P. (2003) *Toxic Emotions at Work: How Compassionate Managers Handle Pain and Conflict*. Boston, MA: Harvard Business School Press.

Frost, P. and Robinson, S. (1999) The toxic handler: Organizational hero – and casualty. *Harvard Business Review*, July–August, pp. 96–106.

Gabriel, Y. (1997) Meeting god: When organizational members come face to face with the supreme leader. *Human Relations*, 50(4): 315–342.

Gabriel, Y. (2005) MBA and the education of leaders: The new playing fields of Eton? *Leadership*, 1(2): 147–163.

Gallos, J. (2008) Leading from the toxic trenches: The winding road to healthier organizations and to healthy everyday leaders. *Journal of Management Inquiry*, 17: 354–367.

Gosling, J. (2019) Take your lead: The pleasures of power in universities and beyond. *Journal of Management & Organization*, 25(3): 1–7.

Greenberg, N., Weston, D., Hall, C., Caulfield, T., Williamson, V. and Fong, K. (2021) Mental health of staff working in intensive care during Covid-19. *Occupational Medicine*, 71(2): 62–67.

Grint, K. (2005) *Leadership: Limits and Possibilities*. Basingstoke: Palgrave Macmillan.

Grint, K. (2008) Wicked problems and clumsy solutions. *Clinical Leader*, 1(2): 54–68.

Grint, K. (2009) The sacred in leadership: Separation, sacrifice and silence. *Organization Studies*, 31(1): 89–107.

Grint, K. (2010) The cuckoo clock syndrome: Addicted to command, allergic to leadership. *European Management Journal*, 28: 306–313.

Heffernan, M. (2020) *Unchartered: How to Navigate the Future*. London: Simon & Schuster.

Jarvis, C., Gaggiotti, H. and Kars-Unluoglu, S. (2020) Unleadership. In M. Parker (Ed.), *Life after COVID-19: The Other Side of Crisis*. Bristol: Bristol University Press.

Kets de Vries, M. F. R. (2001) *The Leadership Mystique: An Owner's Manual*. London: Pearson Education.

Ladkin, D. (2020) What Donald Trump's response to COVID-19 teaches us: It's time for our romance with leaders to end. *Leadership*, 16(3): 273–278.

Lipman-Blumen, J. (2005) *The Allure of Toxic Leaders*. New York: Oxford University Press Inc.

Maak, T., Pless, N. M. and Wohlgezogen, F. (2021) The fault lines of leadership: Lessons from the global Covid-19 crisis. *Journal of Change Management*, 21(1): 66–86.

Maccoby, M. (2000) Narcissistic leaders: The incredible pros, the inevitable cons. *Harvard Business Review*, 78(1): 69–77.

Manz, C. C. and Sims, H. P. (1991) Superleadership: Beyond the myth of heroic leadership. *Organizational Dynamics* (Spring): 18–35.

Marlatt, G. A. and Gordon, J. R. (1985) *EDS. Relapse Prevention: Maintenance Strategies in the Treatment of Addictive Behaviors*. New York: Guilford Press.

Marlowe, A. (1999) H is for heroin. *The Observer Review*, September 5.

Meindl, J. R., Ehrlich, S. B. and Dukerich, J. M. (1985) The romance of leadership. *Administrative Science Quarterly*, 30(1): 78–108.

Padilla, A., Hogan, R. and Kaiser, R. (2007) The toxic triangle: Destructive leaders, susceptible followers, and conducive environments. *The Leadership Quarterly*, 18: 176–194.

Parks, G. A., Anderson, B. K. and Marlatt, G. A. (2001) Relapse prevention therapy. In N. Heather, T. J. Peters, and T. Stockwell (Eds.), *International Handbook of Alcohol Dependence and Problems* (pp. 575–592). Hoboken, NJ: John Wiley & Sons Ltd.

Prochaska, J. O. and DiClemente, C. C. (1983) Stages and processes of self-change of smoking: Toward an integrative model of change. *Journal of Consulting and Clinical Psychology*, 51(3): 390–395.

Rittell, H. and Webber, M. (1973) Dilemmas in a general theory of planning. *Policy Sciences*, 4: 155–169.

Tilson, E. C. (2018) Adverse childhood experiences (ACEs): An important element of a comprehensive approach to the opioid crisis. *North Carolina Medical Journal*, 79(3): 166–169.

Tourish, D. (2020) Introduction to the special issue: Why the coronavirus crisis is also a crisis of leadership. *Leadership*, 16(3): 261–272.

Von Bülow, C. and Simpson, P. (2020) Negative capability and care of the self. In L. Tomkins (Ed.), *Paradoxes of Leadership and Care: Critical and Philosophical Reflection* (pp. 131–141). Cheltenham: Edward Elgar.

Vosoughi, S. and Roy, D. (2018). The spread of true and false news online. *Science*, 359(6380) (9 March).

West, M., Eckert, R., Collins, B. and Chowla, R. (2017) *Caring to Change: How Compassionate Leadership Can Stimulate Innovation in Health Care*. London: Kings Fund.

Whicker, M.L. (1996) *Toxic Leaders: When Organizations Go Bad*. New York: Praeger.

Williamson, T. (2006) Must do better. In P. Greenough and Michael P. Lynch (Eds.), *Truth and Realism*. Oxford: Oxford University Press.

12 The power of humble

Re-imagining the power of leaders after COVID-19

Morgen Witzel

***

'I don't like the idea of power', someone in a position of senior leadership said to me recently. 'The idea that I have power over other people sits very uncomfortably with me. I don't think I have power at all.' In my experience, this view is not uncommon. There is an assumption that with power come other less attractive traits like arrogance, greed or the desire for domination over others. Our view of power has been shaped in part by historical events – the blunders, errors and outright atrocities committed by people who misuse their power – and in part by a philosophical framework which sees power primarily in terms of power *over* people or things. Power has connotations of abuse, and that does not sit well with anyone with a strong sense of moral purpose.

This chapter argues that we need to shed some of this past baggage and reconceptualise power, not as control or dominion, but as the ability to ensure that things get done. As servants of the organisations we lead, power makes us useful; if we do not have the power to make things happen, then we are unable to fulfil our purpose. Leaders themselves are not always the active agents; Mary Parker Follett (1924) argued that 'management is the art of getting things done through other people', and I contend that this is true of leadership as well. But there is still a need for power on the part of leaders, the power to influence, the ability to make their voice heard and their views known, or even just the symbolic power that comes from existence, in the way that Nelson Mandela was viewed as a leader by millions of South Africans during his long and virtually silent imprisonment on Robben Island.

Power has many shapes and takes many forms. For too long, we have concentrated on the most visible and structured forms of power, power *over* things and people, believing that exercising this power is how we lead. But the COVID pandemic has exposed this as a myth. It is time now to look into the shadows at the quieter, humbler, more subtle forms of power that underpin how most successful leaders get things done.

Authoritarian power

Much writing about power and leadership assumes that the purpose of power is to help us claw our way to the top. For Jeffrey Pfeffer, in the unambiguously titled *Power: Why Some People Have It and Others Don't*, our purpose in life is to build up our personal power so that we can gain control over ourselves and over other people (Pfeffer 2010). This neo-Darwinist approach can be found in many popular management books on the 1990s and the early twenty-first century, which assert that the only way to survive is to become the apex predator. *Playing to Win* by A.J. Lafley, former chair of Procter & Gamble, is a relatively

DOI: 10.4324/9781003171737-14

gentle take on the subject, but still suggests that the primary purpose of business is to beat the competition and gain the largest market share and largest profits (Lafley and Martin 2014). At the other end of the spectrum are testosterone-fuelled rants like Peter Nabarro's *The Coming China Wars* which argued that the United States had duty to retain its dominant position in the world economy, if necessary by engaging in trade wars with China (a policy Nabarro did his best to put into practice during his years as an advisor to US president Donald Trump) (Nabarro 2008).

The notion of power as control also has intellectual roots. The sociologist Max Weber, who cast a long shadow over twentieth-century thinking on organisation and leadership, defined power precisely as the ability to control people, things and events, and even more specifically, to make things happen in the face of opposition, to overcome obstacles (Weber 2013, 2015). This ability to triumph over disaster is a key part of many modern leadership narratives, whether it be rags-to-riches stories or the ability to beat and break tough competitors. Success is all that matters. A Weberian leader is not unlike Nietzche's *Übermensch*: self-created, self-referential, knowing or admitting to no weakness, largely amoral in the pursuit of power, and of course male (and by implication, white).

Weber believed that power came from one of three sources: *traditional*, for example through inheritance (and which, although Weber didn't say so, is another way of reinforcing inequality); *legal*, though formal authority derived ultimately from the state; and *charismatic*, essentially leadership through force of personality, another version of the Great Man theory of leadership. Traditional and legal forms of power are binary and inflexible; some people are given power, others have it withheld from them, and that is that. If you don't have power, tough; there is no right of appeal. Charismatic leaders, on the other hand, are able to break the boundaries, step up and take power from the traditional and legal authorities. Revolutionary leaders were often held up as examples, as were 'strong men' like Napoleon Bonaparte. However, once charismatic leaders take power they usually, like Napoleon, entrench their position by recourse to traditional and legal forms of power, as well.

But Darwin himself famously said that survival depended not on strength or speed or even intelligence, but the ability to adapt to the environment. Is the traditional conception of power earlier described one that enables us to adapt? If we depend largely or solely on our ability to control others, does this not mean that we are neglecting other important aspects of leadership, such as the ability to develop ourselves? There is a strand of thought in leadership writing that says we cannot even pretend to be able to lead others unless we are first able to lead ourselves, and that one of the key lessons we need to learn as individuals is how to adapt. This need for self-mastery and personal adaptability and learning is particularly strong in Japanese thinking, visible as far back as the early eighteenth century in the works of the *samurai* philosopher Yamamoto Tsunetomo and running forward to the late twentieth century and Kenichi Ohmae's *The Mind of the Strategist* (Yamamoto 1979; Ohmae 1991).

That element has been sadly lacking in most Western thinking about leadership where models of domination and control have largely prevailed, despite the efforts of scholars like John Adair, Robert Greenleaf and others to advance more collective, collaborative models (Adair 2009; Gosling *et al*. 2007; Greenleaf 1998. Despite the efforts of these scholars, conceptualisations of leadership remain largely focused on the leader as individual person-centred, as Allan Leighton's collection of interviews with leaders demonstrates (Leighton 2008). And of course, implicit in this concept of person-centred leadership is the notion that the person – the leader – has power over others.

We should not assume that this attitude was universal. The lived experience of many leaders was the exact opposite; many felt there were distinct limits to their power and were, as the quote at the head of the chapter suggests, deeply uncomfortable with the notion that they should exercise leadership by attempting to control others. They were – and are – right to feel uneasy, because this is a fundamentally flawed model of leadership. We all know what happened to Napoleon in the end; less well known are the 3.5 million civilians and soldiers who died during his wars.

And Napoleon is just one example. The failings of other military leaders were brilliantly examined by Norman Dixon (1976), and in the corporate world many books have been written about why companies fail (Finkelstein 2003; Sheth 2007; Oliver and Goodwin 2010; Furnham 2010; Witzel 2015). In the vast majority of cases, the failure that broke the company was a failure of leadership, caused when leaders did not attend to their own development and were unable to adapt to changing circumstances and environments.

Bases of power

In the late 1950s, the psychologists John French and Bertram Raven laid out what remains one of the best known typologies of the bases of power (French and Raven 1959), an expanded and somewhat more humanised version of Weber's original triad. French and Raven originally posited five sources of power, with a sixth added later:

- *coercive*, based on the ability to force others to do what we want them to do;
- *reward*, the flip side of coercive power, the ability to reward others for doing what we want them to do;
- *legitimate*, power that comes from the formal positions we hold with the organisation or society;
- *expert*, power that comes from what we know or the skills we possess;
- *referent*, power that comes from who we are as individuals;
- *informational*, power that comes from our ability to control and direct information.

The conventional 'power-over' model of leadership tends to emphasise the first three bases of power. Legitimate power is the bedrock of this kind of leadership. If the prime minister lays down a set of rules, we are expected to abide by these rules – even if the prime minister themselves does not. If the sign on my office door says BOSS, then I am entitled to give orders and you are expected to obey them. Coupled with these come coercive and reward power. The Prime Minister controls access to the cabinet, and can promote or demote their favourites on a whim. The boss can decree who gets a bonus and who gets made redundant. It is expected that people will adjust their behaviours in order to seek reward and avoid punishment, and in fairness, by and large they do, at least in the short term.

As I have described elsewhere, this model of power based on legitimate authority and the ability to reward and punish has endured for millennia. In ancient China, the Legalist philosopher Han Fei argued that this was a natural state of affairs, and that obedience to legitimate authority was in accordance with natural law (Witzel 2012, 2019). The divine right of monarchy, promulgated in early modern Europe, was another attempt to entrench legitimate authority and make it the only acceptable base of power, as was the twentieth-century totalitarianism of Giovanni Gentile and Carl Schmitt. Gentile argued that even criminal gangs should be subject to the authority of the state; and to some extent, in Mussolini's Italy, they were (Gregor 2001).

The challenge to this legitimate–reward–coercion axis has always come from the second three bases of power: expert, referent and informational. Anti-authoritarian movements inevitably drew on at least one, and often all three. Expertise could mean particular skills such as the ability to organise people or set up networks; the organisers of the Underground Railroad that helped escaped slaves flee the American South is an example. Informational power meant the ability transmit information to people who wanted to hear it, sometimes in defiance of the authorities; Diderot and the publishers of the *Encyclopédie* who helped kickstart the movement that ultimately led to the American and French revolutions are examples. Referent power meant simply the ability to draw people to a cause and convince them to join it; Camille Desmoulins, the orator who inspired a mob to attack the Bastille in 1789, is as good an example as any.

The problem is that anti-authoritarian movements, once they overthrow the existing authority, usually revert to type and become authoritarian themselves. As Crane Brinton remarked in *The Anatomy of Revolution*, 'All [revolutions] are begun in hope and moderation, all reach a crisis in a reign of terror, and all end in something like a dictatorship' (Brinton 1965: 24). New anti-authoritarian movements arise and the cycle begins again, leading to yet more destruction. We can only speculate as to why this happens, but one reason could well be that the authoritarian model based on legitimate power is so entrenched in our thinking that we struggle to conceive of anything else. Yet that is exactly what we must do.

Alternatives

There are alternatives to the authoritarian–reward–coercive axis, and this has long been known. Opposing the Legalist school of thought, Chinese Daoism argues that authoritarian leadership is itself contrary to the natural order. People know what they need to do, and a good leader lets them get on with it, interfering only when they need assistance. Authority is 'the merest husk of faith and loyalty . . . the beginning of all confusion and disorder', and 'the highest type of ruler is one of whose existence the people are barely aware' (Wu 1990, p. 42). Mary Parker Follett (1924, 1928) similarly argues that the notion of control is itself an illusion; what leaders think of as control is in fact coordination, bringing people together so they can perform the task rather than directing the task themselves (again, very much in line with the later thinking of John Adair).

More recently, John Lawler and Jeff Gold (2015) argued that the notion of leadership by control is a paradox; the more leaders strive for control, the less effective they actually are. Most leaders operate in a 'fog', whereby they cannot see clearly what is going on around them and have no idea whether the orders they have given will be obeyed. In *War and Peace*, Tolstoy argued that Napoleon had absolutely no control over the battles he fought, as he was anything up to a mile from the front line and his view was obscured by clouds of gunsmoke (Tolstoy 1957). Ask any business leader whether this chimes with their own experience, and they will nearly always – after glancing around to make sure no one is listening – say this is true.

One person who was absolutely candid about this was the former chair of the Tata Group in India, Ratan Tata. During an interview, when I asked him to describe his leadership style, he insisted that he had absolutely no right to give orders to the CEOs of companies within the group. Instead, he said, he 'cajoles' them, putting his point of view forward, listening to them in turn and coming to a decision based on mutual discussion (Witzel 2009). That, I submit, is far closer to the lived experience of most leaders than the authoritarian model described previously.

Power in the pandemic

During the COVID pandemic, I was fortunate enough to work with a large number of leaders from a wide range of sectors – businesses large and small, the National Health Service, local governments, charities, educational institutions and the police, and including a number of people with military backgrounds – enrolled on a master's degree programme as part of the Degree Apprenticeship department at the University of Exeter Business School. These were front-line leaders, not right at the top of their organisations but in positions of considerable authority and sometimes with very large teams under them.

Their experiences of the pandemic, and in particular of their own leaders, were enlightening and sometimes horrifying. I should begin by pointing out that in many cases, the official, legitimate leaders of the organisations really did step up and guide their people through the crisis. But there were other cases – too many – when the person with BOSS written on their office door did not live up to their responsibilities. We heard stories of top leaders who refused to come out of their offices, or who simply could not cope and did not know what to do. Their organisations were left rudderless.

There is a concept known as eminent leadership, often associated with the thinking of the anarchist Rosa Luxemburg, which suggests that in times of crisis, leaders will emerge and come forward (Luxemburg 2006). Over and over again, our front-line leaders described how this happened; in some cases, it was they themselves who stepped up and assumed the mantle of leadership when the legitimate, authoritarian leaders failed to emerge. This experience happened elsewhere, too, in government and in communities, as other chapters in this book will attest. When leadership was needed, it came forth.

What were the features of these eminent leaders? First, they had specific skills and knowledge that were needed in a crisis. They knew how to get the right technology to people working remotely, or how to run an oxygen line into a hospital COVID ward; or if they didn't know themselves, they knew where to find the expertise. Second, they had access to information, and they made sure it got to the right people so everyone knew what they had to do. Third, they had the will and the courage to come forward. Finally, they were respected and trusted by their colleagues, meaning that people were willing to follow their lead. They did not offer rewards – in many cases, they had no power to do so – and given the highly stressful and often dangerous conditions in which they worked, attempts at coercion tended to end in failure. They did not appeal to legitimate authority because effectively, they had none. But they transformed their organisations and helped them get through the grimmest crisis most people could remember.

When the crisis came, leadership based on legitimate–coercive–reward power often – not always, but often enough – failed to adapt to changing circumstances. The power-over model of leadership did not have the capacity to adapt, because it was based on two premises: 1) that an order once given will always be obeyed, and 2) that in a crisis, the leader knows what orders to give. But having a sign on one's door that says BOSS does not confer any special skills or knowledge. The assumption often is that one has been made boss because one *does* have special skills and knowledge; but, promotion and reward systems being flawed as they are, there is no guarantee this is so. Authority *can* adapt, given time; but when crises come, there is never enough time to sit back and wait for the systems to reset. Adaptation has to happen now.

The expert–information–referent model, on the other hand, could and did adapt because it focused not on power relationships, but on what the leader could bring to the table and what they could contribute to the team. The task–individual–team nexus described by Adair became fully visible. The new, eminent leaders were humble enough to know they did not know everything; they were not yet sufficiently senior in their organisations to have been corrupted by the possession of high authority. Leaders brought their own form of power to their teams, but they also asked questions and involved their teams in key decisions. Skills, knowledge, information and most of all, trust and respect, where shared. These interactions with team members became themselves a form of power generation, in which not one person but the entire team had power. By forming the team, by listening to the team, the leader empowered the team, and both team and leader adapted to each other and to the situation, and pushed forward.

The power we need

Expert power

Expert power means knowing how to get things done, and even more importantly, the ability to show others how to get things done. Used well, expert power enables the rest of the team to learn and grow, and ultimately develop their own leadership capability. Coaches of sports teams are a good example of expert power; they enable experienced players and athletes to develop their skills, while at the same time bringing on younger people and helping them to learn. In this sort of scenario, the leader must be willing at times to be hands-on, in order to show other people what to do. 'I would love to be the kind of leader who stands back and lets others get on with it', one leader told me before the pandemic, 'but right now I can't. I have a young team who lack experience, and they are looking to me to show them what to do.'

Danger comes when the team becomes so dependent on the leader that they stop learning, and in effect sit back and let the expert leader do all the work. It can be tempting for leaders to fall into this trap, too – 'if you want something done right, you have to do it yourself' – but the priority must always be the passing on of expertise and knowledge. It could be argued that the expert leader's job is to make themselves redundant; eventually, the team will have soaked up all their skills and be able to do the job themselves. However, if the expert leader continues to update their own skills and knowledge, adapting to changes in the environment and passing the new knowledge on, then the process becomes one of continuous improvement.

Ernst Abbé, physicist turned entrepreneur and managing director of Carl Zeiss Jena, which for six decades was the leading maker of optical instruments in the world, is a good example. Abbé recruited other physicists, including graduate students, and oversaw their training, but he also retained his own interest in experimental optics and remained at the head of his field. Abbé was a very hands-off manager – rather than giving orders, he asked his teams to tell him what they were working on and what resources they needed – but he was always present to help his teams solve problems, sharing his own knowledge whenever needed.

Information power

Information power overlaps to some extent with referent power; as Polanyi (1966) pointed out, the unlocking of tacit knowledge and the sharing of that knowledge with others is critical. The work of Max Boisot (1995) also shows how important communication is. Boisot describes some organisation cultures as information bureaucracies, where information is something to be hoarded and collected, not shared, or 'fiefs', where gatekeepers deliberately control information for their own ends. This leads to deliberate information asymmetries and power over others; if I know something you don't know, that potentially gives me power over you. This reminds us that there are ethical dimensions to information power, just as there are to all forms of power.

But Boisot also identifies other cultures, which he calls 'markets' and 'clans', where information circulates freely, and it is these kinds of cultures that leaders need to cultivate. Information and knowledge are the lifeblood of organisations; when they circulate freely, the organisation flourishes and is healthy, but when circulation stops, arteriosclerosis sets in and the organisation begins to wither and die. People need information, not just to do their jobs but to keep them informed about the bigger picture and to reassure them that all is going well – or, if it is not going well, to help them deal with threats when they come. Studies of motivation and organisation behaviour such as Herzberg (2003) and Schein (2016) suggest that lack of information is closely linked to lack of trust, which can quickly cause people to lose faith in their leaders. 'Without trust, there is nothing', says Ratan Tata. 'Everything gets thrown away' (Witzel 2009, p. 117).

Referent power

Referent power can also be problematic. At its worst, referent power becomes an unhealthy attraction by followers to narcissistic leaders who secretly manipulate them for their own ends. Religious cults are an extreme example of this, but messianic leaders can be found in most walks of life. We said earlier that referent power is based on the trust and respect that people have for each other, but that trust can be illusory; idols really do sometimes turn out to have feet of clay.

Again, the ethical dimension comes into play. The ends that leaders serve will determine whether referent power is used for good or for bad. If the leaders are genuinely committed to servant leadership, to using their power to help other people achieve their aims, then that can be a very positive force; the trust and reassurance the leader gives will help people to coalesce and form into high-functioning teams. In some cases, as Goffee and Jones (2007) point out, the team already knows what it needs to do; what it needs from the leader is reassurance, trust and sometimes protection while the team goes about its work.

The expert–information–referent power base, used properly, makes leaders more flexible and adaptable and puts them at the service of their teams, rather than the other way around. However, this is not a good that comes about automatically. All three of these forms of power are open to abuse, just as legitimate–reward–coercive power is. I have argued the case for the former system because I believe the evidence shows that it is more effective, especially in times of crisis. And when are we not in times of crisis? The effects of the COVID pandemic are likely to rumble on, the climate crisis is worsening and global inequality remains rampant. Authoritarian, legitimate-power leadership has not solved any of these crises. It is time – past time – to start looking at alternatives.

The humble leader

The notion of service requires, of course, a degree of humility from leaders, and as Furnham (2010) and others have pointed out, our systems for identifying and promoting leaders are not naturally geared towards humble people; instead, they tend to single out narcissists and high-performing psychopaths. (A separate chapter could have been written about how we need to think about recruitment and training of future leaders.)

But the pandemic also left these self-centred leaders badly exposed. Their lack of empathy and understanding of their team led to some serious breakdowns of trust between them. On the other hand, my own students also talked about how they found that the focus of their job shifted, especially during the first lockdown. Productivity was no longer the primary focus;

the health and well-being of their teams became their first priority. Some estimated that 50 per cent of their job was now pastoral care rather than team management.

And is that not how it should be? In Chapter 13 of this volume, my colleague Tanmoy Goswami has written an excellent account of the activities of psychotherapists during the pandemic. One of the lessons is surely that our leaders need to learn some of the skills of psychotherapists in order to look after their teams, and they should put the team's interests before their own.

Even the smallest symbols of humility can help to create trust. When Tomás Baťa built his five-storey state-of-the-art shoe factory in the Czech town of Zlín, he installed his own office in a lift. When any worker in the factory wanted to see the boss, all they had to do was send him a signal by pager and he brought his lift down to their floor. Employees didn't go see the boss, the boss came to them. Baťa was known for his fierce loyalty to his employees, and they rewarded him with their own trust and loyalty in turn – and together, they took the company from a small provincial firm to the largest shoe manufacturer in the world.

The moral choice

Finally, we come back again to the notion of moral purpose. As I mentioned at the outset, power for some people has connotations of abuse and immorality. However, there is a counter-argument that says that we need to recognise when we do have power, and then put that power to good use. Some years ago, I interviewed another senior member of the Tata Group, R.K. Krishna Kumar, the chair of Tata Global Beverages, and began by asking a question about Tata's brand values (Witzel 2009). His response was startling. 'This is not a brand story', he said. 'This is a story about the struggle between good and evil.'

His reasoning, heavily paraphrased, went as follows. There are many things in the world – disease, hunger, war, violence, the climate disaster – which by any moral standard must be considered bad things. As leaders, said Krishna Kumar, we have power – not much, but a little bit – to do something about these. Therefore, we have a moral choice. Do we ignore our power and turn our back on the situation, or do we use that power as best we can to try and make the world a marginally better place?

The choice, of course, is our own; no one else can make it for us. Do we want to be part of the problem, or part of the solution? We have to decide – and given the state of the world, we probably have to make that decision quite soon. And when we have decided, as leaders we need to stop and take a long look at ourselves and decide what power we have and how we will use it. The rest is up to us.

References

Adair, John (2009) *The Inspirational Leader: How to Motivate, Encourage and Achieve Success*, London: Kogan Page.

Boisot, Max (1995) *Information Space: A Framework for Learning in Organizations, Institutions and Culture*, London: Routledge.

Brinton, Crane (1965) *The Anatomy of Revolution*, New York: Vintage.

Dixon, Norman (1976) *On the Psychology of Military Incompetence*, London: Pimlico.

Finkelstein, Sydney (2003) *Why Smart Executives Fail*, New York: Penguin.

Follett, Mary Parker (1924) *Creative Experience*, New York: Longmans, Green.

Follett, Mary Parker (1928) 'Leadership', Rowntree Management Conference paper, 28 September.

French, John R.P. and Raven, Bertram (1959) 'The Bases of Social Power', in Dorwin Cartwright and Alvin Zander (eds), *Group Dynamics*, New York: Harper & Row.

Furnham, Adrian (2010) *The Elephant in the Boardroom: The Causes of Leadership Derailment*, Basingstoke: Palgrave Macmillan.

Goffee, Rob and Jones, Gareth (2007) 'Leading Clever People', *Harvard Business Review*, March.

Gosling, Jonathan, Case, Peter and Witzel, Morgen (eds) (2007) *John Adair: Fundamentals of Leadership*, Basingstoke: Palgrave Macmillan.

Greenleaf, Ronald K. (1998) *The Power of Servant Leadership*, San Francisco: Barrett-Koehler.

Gregor, A. James (2001) *Giovanni Gentile: Philosopher of Fascism*, Piscatawa: Transaction.

Herzberg, Frederick (2003) 'One More Time: How Do You Motivate Employees?' *Harvard Business Review*, January.

Lafley, A.G. and Martin, Roger L. (2014) *Playing to Win: How Strategy Really Works*, Boston: Harvard Business Review Press.

Lawler, John and Gold, Jeff (2015) 'The Leader's Conundrum', in Morgen Witzel, Richard Bolden and Nigel Linacre (eds), *Leadership Paradoxes*, London: Routledge.

Leighton, Allan (2008) *On Leadership*, London: Random House.

Luxemburg, Rosa (2006) *Reform or Revolution and Other Writings*, Mineola, NY: Dover.

Nabarro, Peter (2008) *The Coming China Wars: Where They Will Be Fought and How They Can Be Won*, Engelwood Cliffs: FT-Prentice Hall.

Ohmae, Kenichi (1991) *The Mind of the Strategist: The Art of Japanese Business*, New York: McGraw-Hill.

Oliver, Jamie and Goodwin, Tony (2010) *How They Blew It: The CEOs and Entrepreneurs Behind Some of the World's Most Catastrophic Business Failures*, London: Kogan Page.

Pfeffer, Jeffrey (2010) *Power: Why Some People Have It and Others Don't*, New York: HarperCollins.

Polanyi, Michael (1966) *The Tacit Dimension*, New York: Doubleday.

Schein, Edgar H. (2016) *Organizational Culture and Leadership*, San Francisco: Jossey-Bass, 5th edn.

Sheth, Jagdish (2007) *The Self-Destructive Habits of Good Companies*, Upper Saddle River: Wharton School Publishing.

Tolstoy, Leo (1957) *War and Peace*, trans. Rosemary Edmonds, London: Penguin.

Weber, Max (2013) *Economy and Society*, Berkeley: University of California Press.

Weber, Max (2015) *Rationalism and Modern Society*, trans. Tony Waters and Dagmar Waters, New York: AIAA.

Witzel, Morgen (2009) *Tata: The Evolution of a Corporate Brand*, New Delhi: Penguin India.

Witzel, Morgen (2012) 'The Leadership Philosophy of Han Fei', *Asia Pacific Business Review* 18(4): 1–15.

Witzel, Morgen (2015) *Managing for Success: Spotting Danger Signals and Fixing Them Before They Happen*, London: Bloomsbury.

Witzel, Morgen (2019) *A History of Leadership*, London: Routledge.

Wu, John C.H. (trans.) (1990) *Tao Teh Ching (Daodejing)*, Boston and London: Shambhala.

Yamamoto Tsunetomo (1979) *Hagakure: The Book of the Samurai*, trans. William Scott Wilson, Tokyo: Kodansha International.

13 How Therapists Became the Unlikely Face of Leadership During the Pandemic

Tanmoy Goswami

Anamika's[1] inbox is full of messages from dead people. "Take care of our children," they plead. Anamika is my therapist. She is also these children's therapist – children whose parents died of COVID, leaving her the only constant figure in their lives.

Recently, Anamika had a health emergency in her own family. She spent all her time in the hospital and had to stop seeing clients for a few weeks. At the time of writing, she is still the primary caregiver to her ailing kin.

"If I take a day off now, I start getting anxious messages from the kids," she tells me during one of our sessions. "'Have you taken the vaccine? Are you alive?' They are terrified they might lose their therapist, too."

When Anamika tries to talk to her own therapist, an Australian man, about the emotional burden of the new surrogate role thrust on her, he reminds her of the limitations of her job:

"You are *not* their parent. You are *only* their shrink."

"It is difficult for me to strictly follow this rule," Anamika says. Therapists are trained to be neutral and maintain emotional distance from clients, but the cataclysmic nature of the pandemic, especially in low- and middle-income countries like India, has made such a hands-off approach unviable. COVID has led to a deadly collapse of systems and institutions, and unleashed a mental health crisis that has no parallels in our cultural memory, forcing professionals like Anamika to step up in radically new ways, even as they grapple with loss and grief in their own lives.

Just how grave is the pandemic's mental health impact? According to a large study in the United States, one in five COVID patients develop psychiatric disorders with 90 days after their diagnosis (Taquet 2021). Another study spanning multiple countries revealed increased anxiety, depression and stress in the non-infected population (Xiong et al. 2020). There is also evidence of a rise in suicidal behaviour among the youth (Ryan et al. 2020).

Large-scale disasters in the past have been followed by sharp spikes in mental health issues and suicides. Right after the 2008 global recession, for instance, Europe and North America saw nearly 5,000 additional suicides compared with the norm as a result of mass unemployment and financial insecurity (CNN Business 2013).

According to the World Health Organisation, before the pandemic, depression and anxiety already cost the world a trillion dollars in lost productivity (WHO 2013). Healing the psychological scars from the pandemic will be essential for rebuilding battered economies.

In India, mental health challenges were an acute crisis long before the pandemic. According to a study in *The Lancet* (2019), the proportional contribution of mental disorders to the total disease burden in India had almost doubled between 1990 and 2017. One out of seven Indians experiences some form of mental disorder over their lifetime (Banega Swasth India 2020). The country's mental health infrastructure is woefully inadequate, with services

DOI: 10.4324/9781003171737-15

concentrated in a handful of cities. As per a 2019 analysis in the *Indian Journal of Psychiatry* (Math et al. 2019), India would need another 42 years to bridge the supply deficit for psychiatrists, 74 years for psychiatric nurses, 76 years for psychiatric social workers and 76 years for clinical psychologists.

Historically, psychotherapy has kept a low profile in the mental health ecosystem, playing second fiddle to psychiatry. In India, where talking about mental health remains deeply stigmatised, therapy is seen as an obscure luxury. But the pandemic and a concerted public awareness campaign by therapists as well as mental health advocates with lived experience, has pulled therapy out of the shadows, fundamentally transforming the profession as well as society's relationship with it.

"For starters, demand for therapy has gone through the roof. And it's not a rigid professional transaction anymore because there's so much shared trauma between therapists and clients," Anamika says.

> Many of my colleagues fell seriously ill themselves or lost family members, but they had to return to work before they could fully recover because their clients desperately needed help. The switch to online sessions caught us off-guard. We had to get used to an alien modality, rapidly learn new habits and unlearn old ones. Then there's the sudden spotlight on mental health in the media and social media. Of course, growing mental health awareness in the public is great, but because so many big changes are happening simultaneously and in real time, we have to make sense of them on the fly. Nothing could have prepared us for this.

Exploding caseloads and relentless stress over the past 18 months have extracted a heavy toll from therapists. In May 2021, at the peak of the pandemic's deadly second wave in India, journalist Shephali Bhatt interviewed over 30 mental health professionals from 21 cities (Bhatt 2021). She discovered a community struggling with exhaustion and burnout. Some therapists were forced to take long, unplanned breaks, while a few even dropped out of the profession. Considering the country's massive mental health treatment gap, this intensified the burden on the therapists who were still accepting clients.

"All my colleagues are overwhelmed with a huge surge in cases, including pro bono support for those who cannot afford to pay for help," Anamika says. "My own calendar is booked solid for months. There's simply no respite."

Listening to Anamika reminds me of a watershed from the recent history of capitalism that I often encountered in my earlier career as a business journalist. In 1987, the US Army War College coined a term to describe the new, post–Cold War multilateral world order based on the work of leadership researchers Warren Bennis and Burt Nanus. They called it VUCA – volatile, uncertain, complex and ambiguous.

In the following decades, VUCA outgrew its military roots and established itself as a staple of business management. In a rapidly globalising marketplace shot through with unprecedented challenges, mastering volatility, uncertainty, complexity, and ambiguity became the ultimate test of leadership.

COVID has dramatically accelerated the evolution of the VUCA world. We are living through a moment when an idea originally meant for battlegrounds, business schools and boardrooms is becoming hyper-real for society at large. The chaos unleashed by the pandemic in a compressed time period has led to the birth of a new grammar of leadership, and therapists – seldom seen as anything more than society's quiet secret keepers – have emerged as its unlikely face.

"Who knows how long the aftershocks from this tragedy will last?" Anamika says when I ask her to sum up the disruption in her profession. "We have no rulebook to deal with this. It's by far the greatest challenge in the history of our profession."

Therapy was my safe space during the pandemic

I am quite an introvert, but the loneliness during lockdown was hard to deal with. The fact that I am practically unemployed and broke is a heavy burden to bear, especially when the gig economy is seriously bad. I started therapy around this time last year. I knew I had a lot to talk about, but didn't expect to gain so much self awareness in such a short time. It helped me put a lot of things into perspective, including my severe anxiety issues. My therapist listened without prejudice, didn't judge, didn't dismiss or diminish my views. You face a lot of this when you have ADHD, and it adds to your self-doubt and lack of confidence. Therapy for me was a comfortable and safe space.

– Kurt Bento, independent writer

Therapy's Leadership Journey During the Pandemic

Step 1: Shedding 'Neutrality'

During my research for this chapter, I repeatedly heard the same sentiment: Therapists are an unusual choice for a book on leadership. Born as a formal discipline towards the end of the 19th century, psychotherapy demands neutrality and inertness on the therapist's part. Let alone leadership, in the orthodox scheme of things, therapists aren't even supposed to demonstrate much of a personality. They are expected to function as blank slates on whom clients can project their own emotions.

Also germane to therapy's public image is a lack of awareness about how it works, contributing to its fuzzy position between science and art, medicine and placebo. Despite strong empirical evidence of its efficacy in treating a wide range of mental health conditions, therapists are rarely seen as 'healthcare' workers.

Psychiatry, by contrast, derives its authority from its identity as a medical discipline. Despite growing criticism of its overdependence on pharmaceutical solutions to biopsychosocial problems, psychiatry has dominated the mental health discourse with its putative scientific claims about mental illnesses being the result of chemical imbalances in the brain.

But the pandemic and its attendant socioeconomic crises – India's GDP plummeted to a historic low and the unemployment rate reportedly soared to its highest in three decades, pushing 75 million citizens below the poverty line – have laid bare that human distress isn't just a matter of this or that hormone (*Hindustan Times* 2020; Pew Research Center 2021).[2] Much of it is the product of broken systems and institutional failure. Pills are, at best, a fix for the symptoms and not the root causes of our malaise. Exclusively medical interventions have a limited role to play in helping people with post-traumatic stress or acute stress disorder, two of the most common psychological fallouts from the pandemic, Mumbai-based psychotherapist Hvovi Bhagwagar told me.

Complimenting this zeitgeist is a critical shift within the profession of therapy itself. Therapists have begun to venture beyond the client's private life and acknowledge the importance of addressing societal stressors – racism, sexism, inequality, discrimination, political polarisation, climate change – that are beyond the individual's control. In this schema, mental health is deeply intersectional and influenced as much (or even more) by our environment as by our biology.

This reframing is empowering for people, especially from marginalised groups, who have long suspected that their suffering doesn't lie purely 'in their head.'

In India's therapist community, a move away from neutrality towards activism began to take shape towards the end of 2019, just before the pandemic erupted, with the country bitterly divided around a citizenship law that was criticised for being anti-Muslim. In the ensuing melee of citizen-led protests and state crackdown, therapists stepped forward as allies to those affected, offering pro bono sessions and campaigning for justice and accountability.

Many of them, like Anna, vocally opposed the law as discriminatory and were keenly aware that their stance was challenging the very foundations of therapy.

"Not just in India, even in London I have seen that bringing politics into therapy sessions is frowned upon," Anna had then told me.

> Prominent therapists have this attitude: "Oh so you are a *feminist*, you are *bisexual*, let's indulge you." It's wonderful that things are changing, that more and more therapists are getting involved with political issues. What we need now is some investment in shared ethics, in the idea of greater good.

To be sure, the changing DNA of therapy isn't without its critics. There is a strong pushback that it isn't the job of a therapist to be their client's comrade or ideological ally, or influence their client's political choices with their own. Abandoning neutrality could pollute the therapeutic space and make clients wary of being judged for their beliefs. However, the pandemic has imparted decisive momentum to therapy's turn towards the structural and systemic influences on people's lives.

"When you practise therapy from a trauma-informed perspective, which has become urgent after the pandemic, you look not just at the biological component of mental health but also the environmental one," Bhagwagar explains.

> The role of a therapist cannot be limited to changing the client's perception about the world. COVID has brought to the surface that we cannot just tell people, "You need 12 sessions of therapy and you're done." We have to go much deeper. Where was this person before? What is their story? What brought them here? We are learning to make therapy less rigid and more open, taking into account the larger ecosystem our clients are part of.

How does one supply hope during a seemingly never-ending nightmare? Therapist after therapist told me that their only recourse has been embracing empathy and vulnerability in their communication with their clients.

"My clients would ask me for answers, something concrete, something they could rely on, to soothe their anxieties," says Smriti Joshi. Joshi is a tele-mental health specialist and lead psychologist at Wysa, a mental health platform that offers a combination of a free, artificial intelligence (AI)-driven chatbot and paid human therapists. "All my clients' stories felt like my story," she says. "I wanted to [tell] them, 'How can I offer you any certainty when I am just as lost?'"

The therapist circa 2021 can't afford to be a distant, oracular figure, hiding behind the therapeutic wall and projecting an aura of invincibility. And this has changed the traditional therapist-client dynamic.

Megha, a service user, says she was worried about her therapist's well-being during the worst months of the pandemic in India and felt guilty about burdening her with her problems.

> When I shared my feelings with her and asked her if she was OK, if her family was OK, she told me that while she was touched by my care towards her, our session was my safe space where both of us talk about me. She assured me that she has her own therapist and her support circle. We do talk about systemic failures and the anxiety and helplessness that results from it. She was almost 20 minutes late for the session once because she was trying to find a vaccine slot for her family members and we spoke about how difficult it was. I think instead of her telling me that it was her job as a professional, I felt solidarity when she shared her struggles, too, in a very weird, twisted 'we're all in this together' way, while reminding me that her needs are being taken care of, as well.

Therapy gave me hope in a hopeless time

I was on a break from therapy for the last few years, but the emotional toll of the pandemic got me to a point where I couldn't manage my anxiety on my own anymore. Anxiety gets exacerbated due to loss of control. Therapy gave me hope in what seemed like a helpless situation. My therapist helped me recognise that what I was going through was grief – and that grief isn't just about losing your close ones, but also about losing the world you had before the pandemic changed it, instantly and irrevocably. And that grieving is OK, even necessary, in a situation like this. Therapy provided me with the tools to understand that even though some things are not in your control, other things still are; for instance, a small routine you can follow every day that does not depend on anything or anyone else. It could be reading, going for a walk, journaling, painting. If you centre yourself through that one activity every single day, it becomes easier to make peace with everything you cannot control. I'm still struggling in some ways, but therapy is helping me heal with every single session.

– Nikhil Taneja, founder, Yuvaa, a youth-focused media platform

---

Step 2: Building a Supportive Work Environment

In popular imagination, therapists are mysterious figures who work alone. But with the rapid expansion in the market for therapy and the rise of mental health entrepreneurs, it has emerged as a legitimate business, with workplace and team dynamics just like any other business.

In June 2020, The Alternative Story, a Bengaluru-based therapy services provider, employed a team of six to eight full time staff. A year on, they are poised to grow to three times that size. Last year, the company offered 500 consultations a month. Now, with their listening circles, seminars, group therapy sessions, and corporate clients, The Alternative Story caters to over 10,000 people in a month, claims founder Paras Sharma. But this exponential growth in business has been bittersweet, with Sharma's team operating under severe stress.

"In the past six months, at any given time, we've had at least one third of the team either falling ill themselves or caregiving for somebody," Sharma says. "While some clients have been patient and understanding, others have not and understandably so." Managing the team and the clients' interests has required a delicate balancing act.

At Wysa, Smriti Joshi noticed that as the lockdown lengthened, she was getting jumpy and edgy and frustrated.

> I already had a decade's experience of working from home, but even I was struggling with my moods. It made me very empathetic about what could be happening with my team members. On the face of it, everything was OK. Therapists were showing up for their sessions. It was work as usual. But I felt there was a silence within the team. So what I started doing was, every time something upset me, I'd reach out to my team and tell them, hey this is how I feel. Are you also experiencing something similar? It really encouraged people to open up about their struggles.

Joshi credits Wysa's founders, Jo Aggarwal and Ramakant Vempati, with creating an open culture in the team.

"I've been honest with my feelings. I tell my team when I am tired and can't be present for a meeting or a session – just allowing myself to be vulnerable has made a big difference," she adds.

Joshi also started weekly check-in sessions where the goal was simply sharing about each other's week and understanding if anyone needs additional support.

"My team members are scattered in different cities. I live with my family, but everybody else doesn't. We tried to help people who were in the same city connect with each other."

In October 2020, Wysa ran compassion fatigue and burnout tests within the team and picked up some worrying signs.

"I checked in with the team if they were getting therapy for themselves. Many of our freelancers said they couldn't afford therapy because their other jobs were affected by the pandemic," Joshi says. "I took this to my founders and we decided to make therapy reimbursable up to a certain amount."

In a profession like this, where you are dealing with extreme sensitivities, senior colleagues could be tempted to try to monitor and control their less experienced colleagues. "I had decided that I will never be that kind of leader," Joshi says.

> I cannot dictate to them what they should or shouldn't do because they're all professionals. And I have hired them following a rigorous training process, so I need to trust them with doing their jobs. During the training for our team leads as well, I make sure we all agree that we will always put in a meeting request if we want to speak to a colleague, even if they are a part-time employee. We want to be respectful of everyone's time and space.

Making work a safe experience

Recently, a Wysa therapist, who doubled up as a content writer, told the company's lead psychologist Smriti Joshi that writing and engaging with readers was making them anxious. They wanted to get back to one-on-one work with clients. "They said they felt like a failure because they'd volunteered to do content work," Joshi says. "I told them I completely understood and that they could come back to therapy if that's where they felt safe."

Step 3: Pivoting to Technology

Before the pandemic, technology was already being talked up as the solution to the mental health sector's human resources crunch. Despite legitimate concerns about the safety and efficacy of technology as a proxy for human support, venture capital had started flowing into mental health apps and websites that promised to make care accessible to a wider population, but the pandemic complicated therapy's nascent romance with technology. With lockdown, the therapist's clinic – the heart of the profession since Freud – had to be replaced overnight by the computer or mobile screen, upending many sacred rules of the profession.

"If you told me two years ago that I'd be meeting my clients via video conferencing on a daily basis, I would have laughed," says Bhagwagar. "I didn't believe that conditions such as complex trauma could be handled sitting across a screen."

In the early days of lockdown, Bhagwagar felt disoriented in the new setting. "I had to break through those barriers in my mind. So I began taking a few courses to understand how to manage more complex clients via telehealth. It helped that therapists across the world were facing the same challenges, so we could exchange notes and learn from each other."

When Joshi started advocating for tele-mental health nearly a decade ago after a stint in the United States, her colleagues in India would look down upon it. "They would say this is not real therapeutic work," Joshi says.

> What can you do without seeing a person or being in the same room? You have to understand that in psychology textbooks, there are entire chapters on setting up the therapy room, where you place a desk or how you place a chair. Therapists were confused when this familiar world was taken away from them.

Eventually, with the realisation that the world isn't returning to its familiar shape in a hurry, acceptance seeped in. "There has been a big jump in demand for training," Joshi says. "I alone have given about 60 webinars and workshops on delivering tele-psychology."

As an organisation, Wysa has invested in improved online onboarding and training for new therapists, adding more emphasis to data privacy, information security and compliance to international standards.

> Since Wysa has clients all across the world, we need to follow telehealth regulations pertinent to multiple geographies, such as obtaining informed consent, transparently sharing the limitations of the platform, disclosing what user data we collect and how we plan to use it. We have had a lot of discussions around the right thing to do if somebody shares very sensitive information about themselves via text messaging, which is one of the modalities we offer clients. We now have a system where any sensitive, personally identifiable information shows up as highlighted, and the therapist who is reading through these messages can mask or redact the information after review.

Joshi is mindful that the switch to therapy from home is a fraught one for many of her clients who don't feel safe at home. Bhagawagar adds that she had to become comfortable with the fact that some clients might have to attend the sessions from their car, bathroom or basement.

Something as basic as access to a decent internet connection is beyond the reach of many. Poor connectivity can not only derail a crucial conversation – it can also worsen the client's feelings of distress and helplessness.

Then there are the economics of online therapy. Service users from India's socially and economically oppressed Dalit-Bahujan-Adivasi community had to discontinue therapy because they fell on the wrong side of the digital divide, wrote Bhatt in her report (Bhatt 2020). Once again, therapists had to take responsibility for something that ought not to be their domain.

"We had to [take care of] some of the phone bills for those who had access to the internet on their mobiles but no means to pay for it," Divya Kandukuri, founder of The Blue Dawn, a facilitator of mental health services and support to Bahujan communities, told Bhatt.

An underappreciated aspect of therapy's pivot to technology is how it has transformed business operations. Sharma of The Alternative Story says the app-ification of everyday life has blurred the lines between Uber or Amazon and healthcare.

The Alternative Story always thought of itself as an online-first organisation. "However, clients now see you as just another website or piece of software, where they place an order and expect smooth delivery," Sharma says. Most healthcare providers are at sea here, owing to poor telehealth infrastructure and systems.

"The other day, I was trying to get an appointment with a doctor at a big hospital," Sharma says.

> The system was a nightmare. You go to a website to fill out a form. Then somebody calls you. If you miss that call, you don't get an appointment. Then they send you a payment link. You make that payment and show the proof to them. Only then they enter you into the system.

Sharma's firm had to change its technology infrastructure three times during the pandemic, revamping everything from appointment booking to payments to invoicing to sending clients automated reminders about their sessions. "We also have a 'pay what you want' model. So we had to figure out a way in order to let somebody choose a variable amount," he adds.

In all these sweeping changes, the margin of error remains slender. "Because everything is online, a lot of our clients will never see us in person," Sharma says.

> We don't get a chance to establish a rapport with them. Besides, everyone's patience is running thin. The number of calls we get for failed payments etc. has shot up, so we've had to invest a lot on the administrative and logistics side.

Fixing the system

Among The Alternative Story's key missions is improving affordability and accessibility for service users and opening up the profession of therapy to people from marginalised groups. There's a lot of homogeneity among the mental health professionals graduating from our elite institutions that focus on a certain kind of exclusivist, Westernised pedagogy, says founder Paras Sharma. It is still difficult to find the LGBTQIA+ community or people from non-English-speaking backgrounds represented in the profession. This in turn discourages people from these communities from seeking help.

"We decided to run our own certificate course in counselling skills, which would be open to people with a bachelor's degree in any discipline and an interest and a commitment to working on ground-level issues," Sharma said "We also wanted to incentivise people who couldn't afford to drop whatever they were doing and go back to school."

To meet its goals, The Alternative Story has been running a crowdfunding campaign. The funds will be used to provide support for people with common mental health concerns, queer people and people dealing with grief; cover the cost of scholarships to people from marginalised communities to attend its counselling course; and deliver self-care workshops. It is also creating content around mental health in various Indian languages to reduce stigma and increase awareness.

Through these initiatives, the company hopes to directly benefit more than 2,000 mental health user-survivors and create ten new mental health professionals. It estimates that cumulatively, this work will touch over 10,000 lives.

Perhaps the most polarising technology-related trend in mental health is the rise of 'mental health influencers' (Bhatt 2020) on social media, mostly targeting the youth. They use memes, emojis, song and dance, or whatever else is in vogue to offer home remedies or explainers on mental health topics – quick grounding techniques to deal with anxiety or introductions to much more complex conditions like schizophrenia or dissociative identity disorder.

Seasoned professionals such as Joshi and Bhagwagar acknowledge the power of TikTok, YouTube, and Instagram in democratising the mental health conversation and busting stigma. Until recently, traditionalists in the profession would take extreme care not to have even their images circulate on the internet. Such orthodoxies are now passé, with young professionals – as well as lay people with lived experience – unabashedly putting themselves out there on social media and gaining tens of thousands of followers. "I have learnt that complex mental health concepts can be turned into creative posters that everyone can easily understand," Bhagwagar says. "This is great and we need more of it."

Given therapy is still a loosely regulated space in India, the mushrooming of influencers and the push to what some describe as packaging and marketing mental health care as infotainment has raised questions around quality and ethics. However, Bhagwagar believes the marriage of technology and therapy will outlast the pandemic.

"One is not a replacement for the other, but the blended model is here to stay," she says. "And if we therapists can embrace technology and become flexible in how we organise our work, I'm sure everybody can."

Conclusion: A Call for Compassionate Leadership

We don't know how deep and long the psychological damage caused by the pandemic will run. Memories of people scrambling for hospital beds, dying without oxygen, or carrying dead family members in their arms cannot be given the closure they deserve without meaningful systemic reforms, accountability and justice. Therapy is far from a magic salve for the devastation that is still unfolding in vast swathes of the developing world. If anything, perhaps this was a wake-up call for a profession that was at risk of becoming too insular and cut off from reality.

"Psychologists and psychotherapists spend time in their laboratories and classrooms or in their clinics," Bhagwagar says. "They don't really interact with the real world. The pandemic has forced us to [re-examine the way we work] and be compassionate with others as well as ourselves."

One of the most durable legacies of this time could be the honest contract between therapists and society that the former – often caricatured as mind readers who can simply look at us and tell us 'what's wrong with us' and offer a quick fix – are far from knowing all the answers. The best they can do is help us navigate a complicated time with empathy and a few time-tested tools.

For leaders in other fields, too, giving up the fantasy of omnipotence ought to be an essential life hack. Leaders in 2022 cannot posture as Iron Man-esque figures who always manage to get everything under control and wow the world with their charisma and resourcefulness. The greatest example leaders can, in fact, set for their team members today is by junking this old, black tie rulebook of leader-appropriate behaviour and normalising real human behaviour – and that includes the licence to get things wrong from time to time – and laugh about it if one can.

To demonstrate how, Bhagwagar shares a story from one of her recent sessions.

"I showed up for the session wearing a T-shirt that said, 'This llama doesn't like your drama.' My client saw it and burst out laughing." In a different time and a different world, this could have been a mortifying episode for a therapist. Not now.

" I posted the story of what happened on Facebook," Bhagwagar says.

> Things have changed for me. I have been in this profession for 22 years and never experienced the kind of validation for my work as I have in these 18 months. It has given me the confidence and belief that a lot of us – no matter what our job – need to learn that many of the so-called rules we tie ourselves to exist only in our mind.

Notes

1 Some names have been changed to protect the speaker's identity.
2 The economy has since strongly rebounded.

References

Banega Swasth India (2020) 'World mental health day 2020: in numbers, the burden of mental disorders in India', https://swachhindia.ndtv.com/world-mental-health-day-2020-in-numbers-the-burden-of-mental-disorders-in-india-51627/

Bhatt, Shephali (2020) 'The rise of mental health influencers', *The Economic Times*, https://economictimes.indiatimes.com/tech/tech-bytes/the-rise-of-mental-health-influencers/articleshow/79604272.cms

Bhatt, Shephali (2021) 'The year your therapist broke down', *The Economic Times*, https://economictimes.indiatimes.com/tech/tech-bytes/the-year-your-therapist-broke-down/articleshow/82811094.cms?utm_source=contentofinterest&utm_medium=text&utm_campaign=cppst

CNN Business (2013) 'Financial crisis caused 5,000 suicides', https://money.cnn.com/2013/09/18/news/economy/financial-crisis-suicide/index.html

Hill, Ryan F. et al. (2020) 'Suicide ideation and attempts in a pediatric emergency department before and during Covid-19', *Pediatrics*, https://pediatrics.aappublications.org/content/147/3/e2020029280

Hindustan Times (2020) 'Historic GDP contraction shows India among worst-affected by Covid-19 pandemic', https://www.hindustantimes.com/business-news/historic-gdp-contraction-shows-india-among-the-worst-affected-by-covid-19-pandemic/story-wOhzrKa66Di0aVhDiilBOP.html

The Lancet (2019) 'The burden of mental disorders across the states of India', www.thelancet.com/journals/lanpsy/article/PIIS2215-0366(19)30475-4/fulltext

Math, Suresh Bada et al. (2019) 'Cost estimation for the implementation of the mental healthcare act 2017)', *Indian Journal of Psychiatry*, www.ncbi.nlm.nih.gov/pmc/articles/PMC6482705/

Pew Research Center 2021, https://www.pewresearch.org/fact-tank/2021/03/18/in-the-pandemic-indias-middle-class-shrinks-and-poverty-spreads-while-china-sees-smaller-changes/

Taquet, Maxine (2021) 'Bidirectional associations between Covid-19 and psychiatric disorder', *The Lancet*, www.thelancet.com/journals/lanpsy/article/PIIS2215-0366(20)30462-4/fulltext.

WHO (2013) 'Mental health in the workplace', www.who.int/teams/mental-health-and-substance-use/mental-health-in-the-workplace

Xiong, Jiaqi et al. (2020) 'Impact of Covid-19 pandemic on mental health in the general population: a systematic review', www.sciencedirect.com/science/article/abs/pii/S0165032720325891

14 Why and How Leaders Can Navigate Reputation Among Multiple Stakeholders

William S. Harvey

Stakeholder Engagement

In the last few decades, there has been a slow shift away from agency theory to stakeholder capitalism. Agency theory stems from the 1970s, when some information economists referred to the agency relationship between one party (the principal) who delegates work to another party (the agent) (Eisenhardt, 1989), using the example of a contract to illustrate problems of cooperative effort (Ross, 1973; Jensen and Meckling, 1976). This body of literature has morphed into debates around the relationship between leaders and shareholders (Hill and Jones, 1992), and has been applied more broadly to the argument that leaders and boards should primarily focus on shareholder value (Bower and Paine, 2017).

There has been a wider acknowledgement of the contractual relationships that organisations have with a broader group of stakeholders such as employees, customers, suppliers, creditors, communities and the wider public (Hill and Jones, 1992). Each stakeholder provides the organisation with some kind of resource, and in exchange, they expect their interests to be satisfied (March and Simon, 1958). Shareholders, for example, provide the organisation with capital through buying shares, and in return, they expect a favourable return on their investment. Employees, on the other hand, provide organisations with their time, skills and expertise, and in return, they expect a fair wage, good working conditions and positive career prospects. Hence, organisations need to carefully consider their exchange relationship with multiple groups.

Stakeholders differ in the size of their stake in the organisation (Hill and Jones, 1992). Each person within a stakeholder category holds a unique exchange relationship with the organisation, depending on their investment in specific assets (Williamson, 1984). The stake of employees, for example, is high when their skills are not easily transferred to another organisation (e.g. a manager developing a niche product or a consultant working with a specific client base), compared to employees whose skills are more easily transferable (e.g. a factory worker on an assembly line or a receptionist in an office). Leaders play a particularly important role in exchange relationships because they are connected with all stakeholders (e.g. board members, senior managers, employees, investors, regulators and unions) and have strong control over the decisions of the organisation. The consequence of this is the actions and behaviours of leaders have a major impact on the reputation of the organisation, which I define as:

> The multiple perceptions of an organisation made by different stakeholders, based on their evaluations of the past capabilities and character of the organisation, and their assessment of its ability to provide future contributions.

DOI: 10.4324/9781003171737-16

In short, while agency theory is important for explaining the agency relationship, leaders must recognise why and how they can manage a wider set of relationships.

Purpose

The recent historical primacy towards the corporate shareholder has started to receive significant attention. The Business Roundtable (2019), an influential body that represents the chief executives of 181 of the largest companies in the United States, modified its principles on the purpose of the corporation in 2019, in particular moving away from shareholder primacy to a commitment to all of its stakeholders. The year before, across the Atlantic, the British Academy (2018) published an influential report *Reforming Business for the 21st Century*, which called for a re-emphasis towards the purpose of the corporation, which should come before discussions of profit:

> Corporate purpose is the reason why a corporation exists, what it seeks to do and what it aspires to become. Profit is a product of the corporate purpose. It is not the corporate purpose.
>
> (British Academy, 2018, p. 8)

The emphasis on purpose has been emphasised in a wide-range of outlets, from Gast et al.'s (2020) article in *McKinsey Quarterly* on a "company's core reason for being", to Malnight et al.'s (2019) article in *Harvard Business Review* highlighting the importance of businesses placing purpose at the core of their strategies, to *The Economist* (2019) asking "what companies are for." These articles – and many more that are too numerous to cover here – are questioning what the purpose of organisations is, how this should be decided and by whom.

However, let us assume that organisations have identified a noble purpose; how can this translate into desirable values and behaviours? The purpose may be something that is determined by the structure of an organisation, its governance code or its membership in a formal network. This may make it more difficult, but not impossible, as the example of the previously mentioned Business Roundtable statement shows, to change the attitude of organisations. However, uplifting statements are not the same as action on the ground, to which I now turn.

What Are Businesses Doing on Purpose?

The Triple Bottom Line (TBL) is a fashionable concept that was allegedly coined by John Elkington in 1994. Elkington (1997) argues that the TBL agenda is not only about the economic value, but also the environmental and social value that organisations add or destroy. This is not new and has similarities to stakeholder theory (Freeman et al., 2010). Norman and MacDonald (2004, p. 247) argue that many people who talk about the TBL are essentially referring to corporate social responsibility (CSR) because the emphasis is taking environmental, social and financial issues seriously, rather than measuring, calculating and reporting on the social bottom line. The authors suggest that there is an absence of using data to calculate a social bottom line and question whether it is even possible to calculate a meaningful social bottom line for an organisation. They recognise that however flawed its inclusion, drawing on accountancy language has been important for gaining legitimacy among certain business circles compared to the perceived fuzziness of other concepts such as CSR and sustainability. Notwithstanding some scepticism around the TBL, prominent events such as the #MeToo movement, Black Lives Matter, UN Climate Change Conferences (known as COP), extreme weather events, new patterns of living and working during the coronavirus pandemic have started to bring into question the actions of organisations and to formalise and codify a commitment towards economic, environmental and social issues.

Certified B Corporations (B Corps) are arguably an example of how people, planet and profit are starting to work in tandem. B Corps are a community of purpose-driven certified businesses. B Corps are expected to meet the "highest standards of verified social and environmental performance, public transparency, and legal accountability to balance profit and purpose" (B Corporation, 2021, n.p.). B Corps consider profits and growth as important vehicles for supporting a wider group of stakeholders, including employees and members of the community. There are many prominent examples of B Corps, with perhaps the most notable being Patagonia, the outdoors company, which in the 1980s imposed a 1% earth tax on itself to donate to grassroots environmental organisations; 70% of its products are made from recyclable materials, with the goal to be using 100% renewable or recycled materials by 2025. In 2019, the company received a UN Champion of the Earth award, which is awarded by the United Nations Environment Programme for putting sustainability at the heart of its successful business model (UN Environment Programme, 2019). While the B Corps movement and the example of Patagonia are positive steps, they need to be placed within a wider sector context of some questionable labour practices, including Boohoo's supply chain malpractices (Eley and Provan, 2020).

Another example of people, planet and profit coming together is through the UN's 17 sustainable development goals (SDGs). These SDGs are a call for action for countries and organisations to work in global partnership to address some of the world's largest challenges (UN, 2021). Importantly, businesses are starting to engage in the SDGs, from the coffee and tea producer Grosche funding safe water in developing countries through basic and natural bio-sand filters, to the telecommunications giant Telus creating a network of outreach clinics and affordable internet and mobile phone plans for marginalised and vulnerable Canadian communities (Klar, 2019). While cynics may just cite such examples as greenwashing, whereby businesses are providing false or misleading information to manage external impressions around their operations and products, there are examples of where the rhetoric is transforming into action. PwC (2018: 3), for example, found that of the 700 global companies surveyed, 72% of them mentioned SDGs, 27% included them in their business strategy and 19% were mentioned in CEO or chair statements around business strategy, performance or outlook. This shows that although there is a huge amount of improvement required to ensure more of the larger corporations are engaging meaningfully, big businesses have at least started to engage more deeply with the SDG agenda. Given the climate and biodiversity emergency, clearly this needs to gain rapid momentum. One way of achieving this is to demonstrate that business models that invest in social and environmental good can in fact lead to significant financial value generation, which has been a hallmark of the Ellen MacArthur Foundation and the circular economy movement.

A final example of where businesses are focusing more on purpose is the circular economy (CE). The CE aims to redefine growth, focusing on positive societal benefits, with three core principles: designing out waste and pollution, keeping products and materials in use, and regenerating natural systems (Ellen MacArthur Foundation, 2021). The CE movement has gained significant traction among business in the last decade because of four factors (Hopkinson and Harvey, 2019, p. 69). First, the strong vision of the benefits of moving from a linear economy to a circular economy that can bring economic, natural and social value. Second, a prominent and influential leader (Ellen MacArthur) who has gained respect and legitimacy among business and political leaders. MacArthur's accomplishments as a world-record breaking sailor, leading to a Dame Commander of the Order of the British Empire (DBE) and a Chevalier of the French Legion of Honour, has provided her with a solid mandate to launch the Ellen MacArthur Foundation. This, combined with her strong oratory skills, from talks for TED to the World Economic Forum, have helped her to gain further notoriety and to engage with wider sets of stakeholders. Third, partnering with key organisations from different sectors (e.g. BlackRock, Google, Ikea, Unilever and Renault) and with organisations that have significant influence with the business and political elite (e.g. McKinsey & Company, and the World Economic Forum). Fourth, visualising the movement through the Ellen MacArthur Butterfly has helped organisations to understand the concept and see how other businesses are applying it in their own contexts. One organisation that is seemingly embracing the CE is BioPak, a packaging company whose mission is to "produce packaging that puts the planet first and our ultimate goal is a waste-free world" (BioPak, 2020). BioPak makes foodservice packaging from renewable plant-based materials, alongside providing a collection and composting service, ensuring that its packaging and food is composted to produce healthy soils (Ellen MacArthur Foundation Case studies, 2021). This illustrates an organisation that has a clear purpose which is supported by its actions.

In order to understand how an organisation's purpose can translate into actions and behaviours, we need to look at how values are created, communicated and enacted. Leaders play a central role in connecting the higher level purpose of an organisation, with its values and behaviours. The following case study from research I conducted with colleagues in a Malaysian hospital (Harvey et al., 2021) explains the important process of internalising values. A leader who fails to embed meaningful values within their organisation is likely to face a disconnect between their organisation's purpose and the behaviours of its employees.

Case study: creating values in a hospital

We researched a hospital that was setup in the mid-1990s in Malaysia. Initially, the founder and CEO played an instrumental role in creating the hospital values, which stemmed from its purpose of delivering premium quality healthcare with a personalised experience. It was thought by communicating and rationalising these values that hospital staff would buy in to them and use them to guide their behaviour. As an aside, Malaysia scores 100 on power distance by Hofstede Insights (2021, n.p.), meaning that "people accept a hierarchical order in which everybody has a place and which needs no further justification." However, it was telling that hospital staff did not initially accept these values imposed on them by the CEO and senior leadership team. The reason was because they did not understand how the values related to them and their work. This rejection of values led to the leadership team recognising that they needed to truly engage and consult with their employees around the hospital's values. This is an important lesson for leaders who consider creating organisational values as a tokenistic exercise.

The engagement of employees included workshops, consultations and working groups to ensure that there was alignment between the purpose and strategy of the organisation and the identities and behaviours that were required by staff to carry out their duties in the hospital. This was neither top-down or bottom-up, but a diffused approach that engaged with staff at all hierarchical levels and across different functions of the hospital. The values that were co-produced included care and respect, passion, accountability, service excellence, anticipation, team spirit, change and growth, quality and safety, and social responsibility. Each value also had a set of corresponding value-based behaviours. Here it is less important understanding *what* the values are because every organisation has its own set of relevant values. More important is understanding the process of *how* values can be internalised because this determines whether they are for show or for real.

The engagement of staff at all levels was essential for empowering them to create these values. In addition to *creating* values, there were two further important steps: *communicating* and *enacting* the values. With communicating the values, leaders took an open office approach and also ensured that they were visible around the hospital to answer any questions around the values and to role model their own behaviours in relation to the values. With enacting values, line managers reinforced positive behaviours in huddles, meetings and events so that individuals and groups were aware and praised for behaviours that reinforced the values.

The outcome of this extensive process of internalising values was a positive impact on the reputation of the hospital among internal and external stakeholders. Internally, staff told us that they thought the values were both relevant and important, and recognised how their behaviours were aligning with their actions. Externally, when we spoke to in-patients and out-patients, they not only spoke highly of the hospital, but gave many examples of how they had personally experienced and benefited from behaviours that aligned to the values.

Recognising that every organisation has its own unique structure and culture, how can others learn from this case study? We created a model to help guide organisations to internalise values to build their reputation. We find that leaders, managers and employees all play a role in internalising the values of an organisation. Leaders are important for role modelling behaviour and engaging others, managers are important for embedding and reinforcing behaviours, and employees are important for empowering and promoting reciprocal behaviours. As I have discussed previously, the process of internalisation has three parts: creating, communicating and enacting those values. This diffusion process of people at all levels within the organisation internalising the values is essential for generating positive beliefs about the organisation's values, employee behaviours that correspond to those values, and ultimately positive perceptions internally and externally of the organisation. Hence, when internalised effectively, values can be an important point of connection between the purpose of an organisation that a leader identifies and the desirable behaviours that are expected from employees. This has important implications for the reputation of the organisation which is another major consideration for leaders.

How Can Leaders Manage Reputation?

I started out by arguing that we are witnessing a slow but steady trend towards stakeholder capitalism, which Schwab and Vanham (2021, n.p.) from the World Economic Forum define as: "a form of capitalism in which companies do not only optimize short-term profits for shareholders, but seek long term value creation, by taking into account the needs of all their stakeholders, and society at large." This is important for leaders to be aware of because it requires them individually and their wider leadership teams collectively to engage with a broader set of stakeholders. This creates added complexity for managing internal activities and for how to present themselves externally. Apple Inc., for example, in the last decade has witnessed strong iPhone sales and 13-fold growth in its share price. It is considered a good place to work by recruitment agents such as GlassDoor and Reed. However, with such large volumes of electronic products being sold, this has also raised questions around the data privacy of the users of its products. Critics have also argued that Apple needs to address its environmental footprint in both the production and disposal of its products. Finally, some poor labour practices have been well documented by certain suppliers. With these examples, there are different stakeholders to consider: investors, analysts, customers, employees, recruiters, unions, NGOs and governments, to name only a few, all of whom Apple need to engage with around multiple issues. The growing pressure for all organisations to take wider responsibility for their actions on people, society and the environment, which links back to my starting point around the growing salience of stakeholder capitalism, means that it is more difficult for them to ignore or brush off.

Leaders need to ensure that the purpose and values of their organisations are mirrored through both *what* products and services they provide and through the process of *how* they deliver them to different groups. This is why identifying purpose and values is so important and why they need to be reflected for wider groups in their products and services. Social influencers and other intermediaries have an uncanny ability to make large populations aware of any dissonance between what organisations are claiming (the rhetoric) versus what other groups experience (the reality). If the gulf between an organisation's identity (how it sees itself) and its reputation (how others perceive the organisation) is so large, then the organisation has a crisis (Harvey et al., 2017). Fortunately, most leaders do not face such crises, although there are plenty of examples, from Boeing's 737 Max disaster to Facebook's management of fake news. However, many more leaders who are seeking to build or change their businesses will experience large gulfs between the claims they make and the reception of those claims by others, without them necessarily being a crisis. Political leaders face a similar challenge with public reports, speeches and interviews being closely interrogated before intermediaries and the wider population are satisfied that the rhetoric is sufficiently aligned with the reality. Typically, if that gulf continues, then this will force leaders to U-turn on their policies, which undermines their credibility. This is why meaningful engagement with multiple stakeholders is so important for the long-term reputation of organisations of all shapes and sizes. This is heightened further because of the role of social media.

Social Media and Social Influencers

Multiple stakeholders and wider expectations mean more noise for organisations to address. In the past, leaders could influence their reputation in the media through pre-packaged stories, corporate communications and the threat of lawsuit. However, content today is now being created online at breakneck speeds by a much wider group of people, including social media users, which can be posted, shared, refracted and subverted to unprecedented numbers of people (Etter et al., 2019, p. 59). The implications are that good and – more often – negative news stories about organisations can spread very quickly to large volumes of people. In addition, social media influencers place further pressure on organisations through their reach.

Most sectors have social media influencers who work across many platforms, including Instagram, YouTube and TikTok, regularly commenting on daily life and experiences, and providing insights on products, services and societal issues. Anna O'Brien, for example, is known as @glitterandlazers on social media and has 7.5 million followers on TikTok, as well as operating across other social media platforms such as YouTube and Instagram. She has quickly become popular for posting fun and funny clothing videos which have captured the interest of large audiences. This fame has meant she has gained brand deals with organisations such as Target and Kool-Aid. Through regular posts, social influencers such as O'Brien can capture the attention of large audiences, impacting on how people perceive not only individual products and services, but also their organisations and leaders. This is significant because whether leaders like what social influencers say or not, they need to be aware of their wider influence. In other words, they are another kind of intermediary (see Deephouse, 2000; Harvey et al., 2018) that shape the reputations of leaders and organisations.

Conclusions

I started this chapter by highlighting the emerging importance of stakeholder capitalism. Leaders are particularly important to consider in this context because unlike other organisational members, they hold relationships with multiple stakeholders, which will have significant implications on their own reputations as well as the reputations of the organisations they lead.

We have witnessed a strong movement towards the purpose of organisations, from the Business Roundtable to the British Academy, with coverage from influential outlets such as Harvard Business Review, McKinsey Quarterly, The Economist and the World Economic Forum. In the words of Mayer (2020, n.p.), corporate purpose should be: "to produce profitable solutions to the problems of people and planet, and not to profit from producing problems for people or planet." But if purpose is a function of stakeholder capitalism, then how does it translate into action? I have given some examples of wider movements and organisational action that relate to – but are not entirely the same as – stakeholder capitalism. Although far from an exhaustive list, the TBL, the B Corps, SDGs and the CE illustrate that organisations are starting to act even if some of their actions are still at a nascent stage.

To understand how an organisation's purpose can translate into actions and behaviours, we need to look at how values are embedded. I have shown through an example from a Malaysian hospital of how purpose can be internalised in organisations. This is a difficult and timely process, and requires acceptance from people at all levels.

In summary, stakeholder capitalism is a phenomenon that leaders of organisations cannot and should not ignore. The proliferation of social media and social influencers is shining an even brighter spotlight on the wider activities of organisations. What products and services organisations provide, and how they are presented to multiple stakeholder groups, needs to align with the purpose and values of those organisations. There also needs to be alignment between what organisations say (the rhetoric) and what they do (the reality). If a gulf persists, then leaders will likely be forced to change direction, undermining their credibility. Coming back to the premise of the chapter, this is why leaders must navigate the reputations of their organisations among multiple stakeholders with adeptness.

References

B Corporation (2021). About B corps. Url: https://bcorporation.net/about-b-corps

BioPak (2020). Why choose BioPak. Packaging that puts the planet first. Url: www.biopak.com/uk/about/why-choose-biopak

Bower, J. L., & Paine, L. S. (2017). The error at the heart of corporate leadership. *Harvard Business Review*, 95(3), 50–60.

British Academy (2018). *Reforming Business for the 21st Century. A Framework for the Future of the Corporation*. The British Academy, London.

Business Roundtable (2019). Our commitment. Url: https://opportunity.businessroundtable.org/ourcommitment/

Deephouse, D. L. (2000). Media reputation as a strategic resource: An integration of mass communication and resource-based theories. *Journal of Management*, 26(6), 1091–1112.

The Economist (2019). What companies are for. Competition, not corporatism, is the answer to capitalism's problems. Url: www.economist.com/leaders/2019/08/22/what-companies-are-for

Eisenhardt, K. M. (1989). Agency theory: An assessment and review. *Academy of Management Review*, 14(1), 57–74.

Eley, J., & Provan, S. (2020). Boohoo has 'significant issues' in its supply chain, review finds. *Financial Times*. Url: www.ft.com/content/3cc4acc9-3f8a-4fb8-90e5-9a70116df7d4

Elkington, J. (1997). *Cannibals with Forks: The Triple Bottom Line of 21st Century Business*. Capstone, Oxford.

Ellen MacArthur Foundation (2021). Concept. What is a circular economy? A framework for an economy that is restorative and regenerative by design. Url: www.ellenmacarthurfoundation.org/circular-economy/concept

Ellen MacArthur Foundation Case studies (2021). Biopak. Closing the loop on single-use food packaging. Url: www.ellenmacarthurfoundation.org/case-studies/closing-the-loop-on-single-use-food-packaging

Etter, M., Ravasi, D., & Colleoni, E. (2019). Social media and the formation of organizational reputation. *Academy of Management Review*, 44(1), 28–52.

Freeman, R. E., Harrison, J. S., Wicks, A. C., Parmar, B. L., & De Colle, S. (2010). *Stakeholder Theory: The State of the Art*. Cambridge University Press, Cambridge.

Gast, A., Illanes, P., Probst, N., Schaninger, B., & Simpson, B. (2020). Purpose: Shifting from why to how. *McKinsey Quarterly*. Url: www.mckinsey.com/business-functions/organization/our-insights/purpose-shifting-from-why-to-how

Harvey, W. S., Groutsis, D., & van den Broek, D. (2018). Intermediaries and destination reputations: Explaining flows of skilled migration. *Journal of Ethnic and Migration Studies*, 44(4), 644–662.

Harvey, W. S., Morris, T., & Müller Santos, M. (2017). Reputation and identity conflict in management consulting. *Human Relations*, 70(1), 92–118.

Harvey, W. S., Osman, S., & Tourky, M. (2021). Building internal reputation from organisational values. *Corporate Reputation Review*. https://doi.org/10.1057/s41299-021-00115-7

Hill, C. W., & Jones, T. M. (1992). Stakeholder-agency theory. *Journal of Management Studies*, 29(2), 131–154.

Hofstede Insights (2021). What about Malaysia? Url: www.hofstede-insights.com/country/malaysia/

Hopkinson, P., & Harvey, W. S. (2019). Lessons from Ellen MacArthur and the circular economy on how leaders can build and sustain transformation? *The European Business Review*, March–April, 65–69.

Jensen, M., & Meckling, W. (1976). Theory of the firm: Managerial behavior, agency costs, and ownership structure. *Journal of Financial Economics*, 11, 5–50.

Klar, D. (2019). Corporate knights. The voice for clean capitalism. 50+ Real world examples of private sector SDG leadership. Url: www.corporateknights.com/?sponsors_post=50-real-world-examples-private-sector-sdg-leadership

Malnight, T. W., Buche, I., & Dhanaraj, C. (2019). Put purpose at the core of your strategy. *Harvard Business Review*, 97(5), 70–78.

March, J. G., & Simon, H. A. (1958). *Organizations*. New York: Wiley.

Mayer, C. (2020). It's time to redefine the purpose of business. Here's a roadmap. *World Economic Forum*. Url: www.weforum.org/agenda/2020/01/its-time-for-a-radical-rethink-of-corporate-purpose/

Norman, W., & MacDonald, C. (2004). Getting to the bottom of "triple bottom line". *Business Ethics Quarterly*, 14(12), 243–262.

PwC (2018). From promise to reality: Does business really care about the SDGs? And what needs to happen to turn words into action? Url: www.pwc.com/gx/en/sustainability/SDG/sdg-reporting-2018.pdf

Ross, S. A. (1973). The economic theory of agency: The principal's problem. *American Economic Review*, 63(2), 134–139.

Schwab, K., & Vanham, P. (2021). What is stakeholder capitalism? Url: www.weforum.org/agenda/2021/01/klaus-schwab-on-what-is-stakeholder-capitalism-history-relevance/?utm_source=sfmc&utm_medium=email&utm_campaign=2740992_Agenda_weekly-29January2021&utm_term=&emailType=Newsletter

UN (2021). Department of economic and social affairs. Sustainable development. The 17 goals. Url: https://sdgs.un.org/goals

UN Environment Programme (2019). US outdoor clothing brand Patagonia wins UN champions of the earth award. Url: www.unenvironment.org/news-and-stories/press-release/us-outdoor-clothing-brand-patagonia-wins-un-champions-earth-award#:~:text=US%20outdoor%20clothing%20brand%20Patagonia%20wins%20UN%20Champions%20of%20the%20Earth%20award,-Pixabay%20%2F%2024%20Sep&text=24%20September%202019%20%2D%2D%20US,of%20its%20successful%20business%20model

Williamson, O. E. (1984). Corporate governance. *Yale Law Review*, 93, 1197–230.

15 The Future of Cultural Leadership

Ciara Eastell

***

Introduction

The UK's arts and cultural sector has been amongst the hardest hit by the COVID pandemic. Theatres have been closed, exhibitions put on hold, buildings closed then re-opened and then closed again; finances have fundamentally destabilised in even the biggest and most established of our national institutions, and corporate plans have been written and rewritten multiple times as circumstances and national government guidance has shifted and changed in response to the pandemic. Artists and freelancers have seen their incomes radically reduced almost overnight, and there are understandable fears that huge artistic and professional talent will be lost to the sector.

As of July 2020, the Government has made more than £1.57 billion available to the arts, culture and heritage sectors through the Cultural Recovery Fund, the largest single investment the sector has ever seen.[1] The aim has been simple: to keep theatres, music venues and galleries afloat at a time when they have seen almost all of their commercial income disappear.

In parallel, the Black Lives Matter movement has catalysed a huge response within the arts and cultural sector with an understandable demand from many quarters for much more diverse leadership and new voices within our national cultural institutions. And, if all that was not enough, Brexit has affected the ability to tour beyond the UK, as well as to bring artistic talent into the country.

As a consultant and executive coach with a long track record of leading ambitious programmes of change within the arts and culture sector, I'm interested in what it's felt like to lead these organisations when so much is at stake – how have our country's arts leaders coped with this unprecedented time of change and uncertainty? And, as we begin to face a very different future for the arts and cultural sector, what we can learn from this past 14 months to enable us to lead our institutions in the future in ways that support our local communities and our wider civic society to rebuild and reshape with inspiration, creativity and hope?

This chapter draws on interviews I carried out in Spring 2021 with some of the country's leading figures within the UK arts and cultural sector. All have generously shared their honest reflections – on what has gone well, on what they could have done better and how they see the nature of cultural leadership developing in the future.

DOI: 10.4324/9781003171737-17

Approach and Methodology

This chapter comprises insights from:

- Interviews with eight chief executives and/or artistic directors of leading UK arts and cultural organisations.
- An interview with the chair of a major national arts organisation.
- Presentations from two chief executives of national cultural organisations given as part of the Oxford Cultural Leaders programme in March 2021.

Of the 11 leaders featured, six are women and five men. Three are leaders of colour. Leaders from across theatre and the performing arts, museums and libraries were interviewed. Interviews took place between March and May 2021. All quotes have been provided anonymously to enable respondents to share their honest insights.

As well as the direct observations of the respondents, I bring to this chapter my own insights having worked with, and coached, leaders across the arts and cultural sector during this past 14 months.

Themes that have emerged from the interviews which form the structure of this chapter include:

- Finding an 'emergency leadership mode'.
- The challenge of sustaining a new form of leadership.
- The power (and limitations) of shared leadership.
- The value of networks.
- New approaches to supporting health and wellbeing.
- Transparency, openness and involvement.
- The challenge of furlough.
- Handling the tough times as a leader.
- Governance opportunities and challenges.
- Looking to the future of cultural leadership.

Finding an 'Emergency Leadership Mode'

Asked about how their leadership has shifted over the 14 months of dealing with the pandemic, almost all leaders identified the initial days and weeks of the pandemic as a period when they needed to move into a directive model of leadership – one that focused on the operational challenges of closing venues and moving their organisations to remote and online working. Several leaders highlighted the singular focus they knew was required of them at that point, and went into a very different mode of leadership from their typical, often more consensual, style – there was a job to do and they knew they needed to give direction and instructions to close venues and enable home working in short order:

> It's so interesting to reflect back . . . 13 months – that very first phase was about instantly digging deep to find an emergency leadership mode. . . . I remember that first 10 days, I was trying to find a calm which didn't reflect my inner feelings. So much uncertainty – I was trying to make decisions quickly.
>
> Library leader

My leadership at that point became quite focused and quite singular. I definitely knew I had a job to do. In normal times, your spotlight swings from thing to thing – getting drawn into different directions but [with the pandemic] everything was paused for the singularity of the task which was about survival.

Theatre leader

Others reflected on some very early work they did (often with their executive teams) to agree – from the outset – how they would tackle the challenge ahead:

Early on, X [artistic director] and I both identified our values and what's important during this phase. The theatre had to survive – the institution we are custodians of must survive. [The] second thing was how to support and keep as many people [employees, freelancers] as we can through this process. [These were] our two guiding principles – long term security but with as little collateral damage as possible. The commercial imperative to sustain must always be balanced by the emotional.

Theatre leader

For others, learning how to deploy technology in new ways was a fundamental shift they needed to make in order to keep their organisations going and to build a new communications model across their organisations. Few arts and cultural organisations appear to have had much experience of remote working and collaborating, so the move to this way of working and communicating proved challenging for some. One leader talked about the first call with his wider (and rather large) leadership team of more than 30 managers taking place via audio conferencing. Others talked about their previous experience of connecting across disparate locations as being centred on use of a spiderphone – an object that now, 14 months into the pandemic, feels rather quaint and old-fashioned in the light of the ubiquity of Zoom and MS Teams.

Talking to these leaders, you sense that it wasn't just the technological challenges associated with moving into leading from a distance that challenged them; more fundamentally, it was also the enormous challenge of attempting to build and sustain closeness and affinity with their wider teams at a time when you are – as a leader – physically distant from your team. This was particularly true for one of the leaders interviewed who had only joined her organisation a few months before the pandemic:

Then Covid happened. That idea of fact finding and intelligence finding [when you're new in a role] just ground to a halt. I really felt cut adrift from the organisation and suddenly I had to go from someone who was learning into action mode. It was really hard – I suddenly have to be this person who was really decisive with a leadership team who had really high expectations [of me]. I had to become this more visible leader from a distance; I had to develop an online persona.

Museum leader

So, in those early days and weeks of the pandemic, our leaders – by and large – found a way to move into an emergency leadership mode; one that was more decisive and directive; one that was enabled and supported by using technologies in new ways but one that was not without its challenges. Once the shock of those initial weeks ebbed away, how did our leaders develop their leadership to sustain them and their organisations into – what turned out to be – a much longer and more challenging period than anyone ever really anticipated?

The Power (and Limitations) of Shared Leadership

Whilst all the leaders interviewed had to adapt their own leadership during COVID to deal with the particular challenges of leading their organisations through the pandemic, many highlighted that they were not alone in shouldering the leadership challenge:

> When the sun is shining, you gather around people who are at the top of their game and give them every reason to get them to stay so when the chips are down (as they were in the pandemic), you can leave them to get on with it.
>
> Theatre leader

> What I observed most was people really rising to the occasion and doing everything to make things work and being creative in response. . . . We had our most successful year for individual fundraising because our teams were really creative about maintaining the connection [with donors].
>
> Performing arts leader

Not all, though, found their colleagues able to cope with the enormity of the crisis. Several reflected that members of their senior teams, especially those whose work is focused on the artistic direction of the organisation, found the pandemic hugely challenging:

> There were chunks during that period of time when it was clear to me that this was the job I had to do. Compare X – he just couldn't do anything and was deeply traumatised by the whole thing. It's an interesting thing that although on the face of it, I had the problem to solve, it was – in some ways – easier for me. . . .
>
> Performing arts leader

> We've seen the best and the worst and that doesn't surprise me. X was completely use-less at the beginning . . . in his own panic – He's calmer now, that's for sure. He thinks it [the pandemic] is something to be endured. That he has very little agency over. He's become very short term in his thinking.
>
> Museum leader

In my wider coaching work over the past 14 months, I've noticed growing interest in new models of shared leadership emerging across the sector. Several male CEOs I've been work-ing with, for example, have increasingly been reflecting that they no longer feel comfortable with their female deputies, who have – during the pandemic – put as much effort, commit-ment and leadership into their organisations whilst being paid less and having less status and institutional power than them. Several are now exploring co-CEO relationships with women who were previously their deputies. The example of Sara Wajid and Zak Mensah who, in September 2020, took on the shared role of CEO at Birmingham Museums Trust,[2] is a timely example of a duo working together to take on the CEO role in a cultural organisation on the cusp of significant transformational change. As we move forward, it will be interesting to see whether these new models – that begin to tackle systemic racial and gender inequalities within established leadership hierarchies – begin to take a hold within the wider sector.

The Value of Networks

When asked what has sustained them during the pandemic, all our leaders highlighted the enormous value of their professional networks. For almost all, it has proved the single most important way of sustaining their own leadership and resilience – simply by having a regular opportunity to connect online with trusted peers who can relate to the particular leadership challenges of their peers and colleagues:

> The peer support from other leaders – it's just been epic. Every Friday, we have met at 9. It's such a valuable support structure. We rarely talk about anything other than work; it's the camaraderie to see the people at the very top of other organisations and realising you're not alone. No one knows the answer to this. The peer support and the value of it was a big surprise.
>
> Theatre leader

For a sector that can be competitive, the power of networks has proved a revelation for some. Many of those within the theatre industry, for example, found themselves in weekly online meetings with people they previously would have considered their competitors. For others working in less competitive sectors, the regular catch ups with their peers has seen increased openness, trust and candour than was there previously.

On a strategic level, national museum leaders have found value in sharing their respective financial challenges; developed strategies for liaising with, and sometimes lobbying, central government; and the more personal challenges of being at the forefront of often painful and controversial changes within their institutions. This, too, has helped deepen trust and increase openness amongst peers:

> We've developed new friendships during adversity . . . [arising from] trying to lead through a pandemic whilst simultaneously being vilified on social media.
>
> Museum leader

For leaders of colour, there has been particular value in building networks with other peers:

> We have a Black Cultural Leaders lunch . . . [there are] five of us, men and women. The challenge will be to keep these going once we start to re-open.
>
> Museum leader

These new networks have not only provided regular mutual support benefits; they have also had benefits that were never anticipated. Several theatre leaders now realise that their new-found collaboration will help them negotiate much more effectively in the future with commercial producers, who previously – unbeknownst to them – played one of them off against each other. For black women leaders, they now have more insight into the work they were collectively doing – unpaid – for headhunters looking for diverse candidates for their clients.

At the time of our interviews, most leaders were anticipating a return to their venues with re-opening plans well advanced in many instances. As things begin to get back to [some kind of] normal, there appears to be an inevitable risk that these new networks – that have proved so valuable during the pandemic – will ebb away. Sustaining them into the future will take time, energy and commitment, with perhaps an element of 'curation' or, at the very least, one or two people willing to take a lead in sustaining the respective networks.

The Challenge of Sustaining a New Form of Leadership

What emerged from the discussions with our leaders was a sense that, though those initial days and weeks of the pandemic were incredibly challenging and gruelling and required a much more decisive leadership style than they would ordinarily adopt, it was in many ways a more straightforward leadership response than what emerged subsequently. Most reflect that they – like most of the general public – had little sense of the length or severity of the pandemic and how it might affect their organisations. As the months have worn on, the impact on them has been significant and highly personal:

[I've] very openly said this is the biggest personal leadership challenge I've ever found myself facing. I've felt in a constant state of improvisation and self-questioning through it. If I'm honest, it's been cyclical. There have been periods when because outside circumstances have stabilised for a while, I've found a language of leading through this distanced uncertainty. But then there have been moments of deep exhaustion and anxiety. I've not felt any of the usual levers of control.

Library leader

I've had to become more emotionally vulnerable because anything else would be lying. I've had to be much more audibly and visibly emotional.

Museum leader

Though the response has been deeply personal and caused several of the leaders interviewed to reflect on a lack of inner confidence and emotional vulnerability at times during the past 14 months, most highlighted that it was important for them – as the ultimate leaders of their organisation – to balance demonstrating their own vulnerability with giving confidence to their wider teams that they were still resolutely 'in charge':

The leadership that's helpful is not heroic; it's more like stoic. And I think consistently across the 12 months, when I've felt very, very far from this, I've known I needed to be calm and reassuring but also very honest either about what I don't know or what we can't do much about.

Museum leader

Adaptability has been the watch word for most leaders interviewed; with rapidly changing plans evolving – often overnight – as Government guidance and advice on re-opening venues and social distancing shifted and changed:

My leadership has had to become more tech, more agile, more responsive to something that might change at 10pm at night to be delivered at 7am the next morning.

Museum leader

For leaders of colour facing the dual challenges of both the impact of the pandemic and responding to the issues raised by the Black Lives Matter movement, the pressure – at times – has been even more intense than their white counterparts:

I do think they [my team] want to hear what I think; take a position on things. I've probably done more public speaking on what my views are on social justice [than I ever have done before]. My team want more and more from me . . . so much expectation on me. That has made me nervous. Am I allowed to fail? Am I allowed to get stuff wrong because I'm just human? [I have a] Sense of being elevated [as a person of colour].

Museum leader

The burden on leaders of colour during this period feels immense and, for some, potentially overwhelming, with such a high level of expectation falling onto their shoulders without – arguably – adequate acknowledgement or support from the rest of the organisation. That's a huge issue for the sector (and wider society) to consider and respond to as we move forward.

New Approaches to Supporting Health and Wellbeing

The single biggest leadership shift highlighted during the interviews has been the increasing focus on the wellbeing of staff teams in ways that are far more profound than pre-pandemic days. Though wellbeing has been an increasingly hot topic in leadership circles in recent years, our leaders reflected that there has been a real gear shift in their need to reflect on – and respond to – the mental health challenges facing their teams:

> I would say that the major acceleration or amplification is the amount of attention I've had to pay to my colleagues. That has meant sometimes things that I would do – programmes, shows I would have produced, I've deliberately not – due to trying to look after the mental health of the organisation. . . . That's been an empathy muscle I've had to exercise. It's a muscle that has grown in strength [during the pandemic].
>
> Theatre leader

> The extremity of colleagues' needs and worries was unprecedented. In stepping into that, 'we know you're feeling very worried', it has built a trust that didn't exist before.
>
> Museum leader

Leaders cited extensive additional investment in a variety of wellbeing services, from increased counselling services available to all members of staff to a psychologist brought in to support senior managers deal with trauma within the organisation through to coaching available to staff at different levels of the organisation. One organisation has brought in 'Wellbeing Wednesday', with new resources commissioned and increased training and support. Several have supported their teams to become Mental Health First Aiders and others highlighted increased flexibility offered to staff with caring responsibilities as an important mechanism for supporting their staff teams.

One major arts funder is pursuing We Invest in Wellbeing accreditation (part of the wider Investors in People accreditation) as a result of their increasing awareness of the importance of employee wellbeing generated through the pandemic. That same organisation has – for some time pre-pandemic – been investing in training their managers to become accredited coaches as a way to develop more meaningful conversations between line managers and their teams. They plan to sustain and develop their commitment to their internal coaching culture in the future, having seen the benefit of that growing coaching culture within the organisation.

In their leadership around health and wellbeing, it has proved crucial that the leader models good practice on this topic:

> Visible signs to make sure that people are clear we care about them. We launched our values during this period [one of which is focused on care]. . . . Now we've been able to live our values. If you're the ultimate leader, there is a real expectation that your behaviour is being checked on – you become a lynchpin for the organisation.
>
> Arts leader

For many of our leaders, this need to shift into a much more emotionally engaged leadership position at a time of significant personal pressure has been incredibly challenging. Almost all of our leaders cited their own personal stress levels as something they were concerned about, and though many have their own strategies to support their personal wellbeing, there is a recognition of the irony of trying to support others when you don't always feel on stable and solid ground yourself.

Transparency, Openness and Involvement

A consistent theme for all our leaders was the fundamental shift they have had to make in communicating with, and involving, their staff teams during the pandemic. Several lead large and dispersed teams such that they would previously have used standard internal communications tools – such as newsletters, occasional set pieces and conventional line management structures – to communicate with their wider staff teams. Almost all leaders have found themselves much more visible and available to their wider workforce than previously. Using technology more extensively and effectively has been key to making this shift. Many of our leaders have become more adept at online town hall–style meetings, and most have relished the opportunity to speak to very large numbers of staff members simultaneously, opening up access to senior management to everyone, regardless of role or seniority:

> There's been great democratisation – everyone's got the same kit. Staff feel much more able to send me an email now in a way they didn't before. I've probably had more one-to-one meetings with people across the organisation than I ever did before.
>
> Arts leader

One leader explained that he has instituted fortnightly sessions where members of staff could ask him anything:

> We've definitely learned that digital does enable us to improve our internal comms in a way that's been transformational. . . . It's reinforced how important that extreme transparency is. I wouldn't have had the confidence to embrace it otherwise. My 'ask me anything' sessions – you can ask any question, total visibility to everyone. Every question has to be answered. Sharing what I don't know and the rationale – at a level I wouldn't have done before.
>
> Performing arts leader

All our leaders recognise that it will now be essential to retain this much more open and transparent approach with their staff teams in the longer term, reflecting that – in the main – it is no longer expected that leaders will be all-knowing and all-seeing. Whilst most acknowledge that the pandemic has helped them realise that it is OK to admit you don't have all the answers as a leader, there is recognition, too, that in times of uncertainty, employees understandably have a thirst for clarity and certainty on financial and strategic issues. Balancing the twin challenges of being both authentic and open, and admitting when you don't have the answers, whilst also sustaining your credibility as a senior strategic leader is a challenge for most of our leaders.

In taking on this much more proactive and visible role for organisation-wide communication, our leaders have inevitably set the tone for communication within their respective organisations. Many have adopted a much more personal and emotional communications style than they would typically have done, often as an instinctive response that recognises that this is the only mode that will build trust across the organisation:

> [The large staff meetings have] . . . built a network of trust there. If I'd stayed aloof, it would never have happened. Aloof isn't a mode in this time.
>
> Museum leader

For others, it's been important for them to be an ambassador for hope and recovery within their organisation:

> We wanted to talk about recovery – things that people could look forward to. . . . Work on visioning future audiences, learning strategy, digital strategy, horizon scanning. . . . There was a fear that they were going to lose their jobs – so having a forward looking statement so you can see your place in the future to try to take the sting out of the very real fear of worrying about the future [was important].
>
> Museum Leader

Beyond communication, our leaders have found themselves thinking profoundly about how employees can have greater influence over decision making within the organisation. Pressure in the summer of 2020 arising out of the Black Lives Matter movement from – typically – younger, more junior employees has focused on pushing leaders to make a bigger and more radical difference around social and racial justice and to make that change faster than previous action plans or commitments. For one of our leaders, the impact of this pressure has been transformational, with membership of the organisation's senior leadership team being opened up to staff at much more junior levels:

> Suddenly the idea of bringing staff voices into the top table – shifted from feeling experimental to feeling urgent and natural. . . . By Sept we'd expanded SLT with reps of our trade unions and chairs of our staff networks. They have full rights and full access to all documents. . . . It was an experiment – we collectively realised that summer that we needed to go further in terms of listening and openness, otherwise we were in danger of taking really bad decisions.
>
> Library leader

Other leaders are following suit, building their organisations' staff networks into a force for change within the organisations and giving increased power and influence to younger, more diverse employees. In the coming months and years, we will all begin to see the impact of this increased involvement and influence. In my view, it will need ongoing commitment, careful support and genuine opportunities for influence if such initiatives are to result in meaningful and systemic changes within organisations.

The Challenge of Furlough

One of the particular challenges that many of the CEOs faced was in shaping a 'one team' narrative in their communications at a time when some of their teams were on furlough whilst others were still at work. This has proved hugely challenging for many leaders as they sought to find an authentic way of thanking both those on furlough (for the financial assistance that their furlough status was giving to the organisation), as well as to those still at work and often doing long hours to keep the organisation going:

> It was important to have empathy for both. [It was] natural to get a sense of resentment. But we need to remember there's a tax associated with being at home – am I going to get a job? . . . But equally it's been important to shine a light on the teams who haven't stopped working.
>
> Theatre leader

Beyond employees, most arts leaders have also had the huge challenge of recognising the impact of the pandemic on the artists and freelancers they work closely with and have historically relied on. Whilst the government's Cultural Recovery Fund has provided much-needed assistance to organisations, it has not focused on the needs of individual artists and freelancers, which has understandably generated significant frustration and concern. For our leaders, there was a keen awareness that their responsibilities do not only lie with their employees but also with the wider eco-system that enables them to operate their museums, theatres and arts venues. Rebuilding that eco-system is likely to be one of the biggest challenges for arts leaders going forward.

Handling the Tough Times as a Leader

'Resilience' has become a by-word during the pandemic for simply keeping going. For the leaders interviewed for this chapter, simply keeping going has been very tough at times:

> It was a shit storm. It's easy to feel sorry for oneself and I did at some points but it's happened to so many organisations: big universities, theatres and museums. I think there was a period in the summer, especially in the younger generations who felt cultural anger about lots of things. . . . That was very, very difficult. It was difficult in a way that I think lots of leaders have felt during this time.
>
> Museum leader

When asked how they have coped during this period, most leaders cited the simple pleasures of daily walks, yoga, new pets, discovering more about the place where they live and having older children back home again as providing respite from long and stressful working days.

Others have found that they have learned over the course of the past 14 months how to schedule their day:

> The final third lockdown has been the one where I've worked out how to do it ultimately. I don't have 6–8 Zooms in a day – it rapidly makes you exhausted and not able to think or get on with your work.
>
> Museum leader

For others, working closely with their colleagues has been an important part of what has sustained them:

> My relationship with X [artistic director]. . . . If I hadn't had that, it would have been awful – the release from black humour has helped us both. And my relationship with the Senior Management team – they all pulled together in a way that was extraordinary.
>
> Theatre leader

Governance Opportunities and Challenges

All of the organisations featured in this chapter have non-executive boards, who themselves play a significant leadership role in the strategic direction of their individual cultural organisations and collectively the sector as a whole. Our leaders reflected on a mixed picture in terms of the support and direction of their boards during the pandemic:

> Board leadership? They've not responded well. There's a lot of – 'where is your plan?'. My response? 'There was a plan last week [but things have changed] so we're re-writing'. There's been a remarkable lack of insight into the strain of running the business which is changing every day – but a desire to run the Board in a way that seems the same as ever.
>
> Museum leader

The chair interviewed for this chapter highlighted the challenge facing boards, many of whom are not used to leading at a time of huge instability:

> Many of these Boards have got into the habit of running organisations who are fundamentally stable. The Board meets four/eight times a year; they know that the business is going to be OK. They know their personal liability is limited but they've never had to worry about it before but quite suddenly they're facing having to make large numbers of people redundant and do it humanely.
>
> Chair

Others have had much more positive experiences with their boards:

> Our board stepped up in different ways. A finance oversight committee [was set up] and they were really good at holding the financial risk with us. They could have been nervous but they weren't. That was really important.
>
> Performing arts leader

In my wider work with CEOs and leaders during the pandemic, it appears that there is a variable picture about the effectiveness of governance during this time. Understandably, many boards have felt ill-prepared for the challenge of steering an organisation through an unprecedented period of change. Some have provided incredible support to their CEOs and senior teams, putting in place ad hoc committees to help steer the organisation's finances through and being flexible and understanding the need for constant review and change of corporate plans and providing moral support to the CEO as they take the organisation through redundancy or restructuring processes. However, others appear to have fallen short of what was needed, leaving their CEOs without the support they have needed to implement often very painful changes and often not alive to the wider societal issues around race and equality and how those have been manifesting within the organisations whose boards they sit on. Pre-pandemic, good governance was already an important topic for the arts and cultural sector; now it appears that there is even greater need to reflect on the governance challenges that have emerged during the past 14 months and consider how to build on what's gone well and begin to remedy what needs to change.

Where to Now? The Future for Cultural Leadership

So what can we all learn about the future for cultural leadership in this country from this extraordinary period?

Most of the leaders interviewed felt that they had had little time or space to reflect on their leadership over the past 14 months – their interviews for this chapter were, for many, the first time they had spoken about how they had responded as leaders. Most expressed a desire for more time and headspace for further reflection. There is clearly huge scope to provide more opportunities in the coming months and years to analyse and develop resources to help cultural leaders manage and lead their institutions out of the pandemic. Sadly, the challenge of leading the sector through the impact of the pandemic is almost certainly at the start rather than at the end – the legacy of this period in the arts and cultural sector will be felt for many years to come as the sector has to adapt to reduced operating models, new (and often exciting) ways of reaching existing and wider audiences through digital content, emerging forms of artistic expression and creation, and a revitalised approach to enabling employees, artists and freelancers to influence the future direction of our national arts institutions.

One leader anticipates that there will be an exodus of individuals in their 50s and 60s leaving senior roles in the cultural sector in the next year or two when faced with the prospect of large-scale and painful transformation. Others reflect on a generational shift that has emerged both from the pandemic and particularly from Black Lives Matter that will profoundly impact the type of leadership that will be needed:

> Lots of leaders are going to have a really difficult time in the next 12 months as they don't fully appreciate the gap that has grown between senior leadership and younger members of staff. There's a really big generation gap now . . . they will face an impatience for change in cultures that they can't quite fully anticipate. It's going to be really testing.
>
> Arts leader

> There's an awful lot of feedback from the smaller groups feeling really disempowered and disenfranchised – we need to rebuild [over the next 12 months] without being defensive.
>
> Performing arts leader

Others point to a new leadership style based on kindness and empathy:

> I have re-emphasised my belief in kindness – thinking in a kind way should be our starting point as we go forward as an organisation.
>
> Museum leader

An increased sense of the ability to be much more agile was identified by several of our leaders as having huge potential for the future:

> There's probably something that's changed around urgency. We managed to do all that in a nine-month period. I'm wondering if I'm carrying a bit of impatience – we all responded that way in September; why can't we do it now?
>
> Performing arts leader

For several leaders, there is the beginning of a sense that cultural leadership in the future will need to be focused on anticipating and synthesising some of the most challenging issues of our time – whether that be social or racial justice or climate change:

> What does the future look like? It's a difficult question. . . . After having to live in the moment so much. It's harder rather than easier [to think] about what the future

might look like because of the humbling we've all been through. Based on the scale of the wake up call that we've all individually and collectively experienced, I'm probably thinking there of the pandemic as not something isolated but a long expected symptom of the other kinds of profound system or ecological shift of the natural world. . . . . That sense of humility in the face of forces that are really big.

Library leader

For me, the lessons from these and other leaders I've worked with in the cultural sector point to a new model of cultural leadership emerging. In many ways, it is not likely to be vastly different from models of leadership emerging in different sectors and countries, but the profound shift that will be needed in order to sustain a viable and creative arts and cultural sector will place a huge expectation on the current and future leaders of our arts institutions in the months and years to come. What the interviews tell me is that our future model of cultural leadership is likely to be characterised by the following

- *New models of shared leadership* that recognise that one invincible leader at the top of an organisation is unsustainable for the future. We're likely to see more shared CEO (and potentially shared chair roles) emerging, bringing different skills and perspectives into the most senior roles of organisations with a parallel shift towards increased employee influence and engagement in answering and shaping the very big questions that many of our long-standing arts and cultural institutions face; not least how to build legitimacy and an enduring mission for the organisation that speaks to, and authentically responds to, the clamour for greater openness, transparency and radicalism around social and racial justice.
- Those models supported by *energetic and curated professional networks* that build sustained trust and openness across different parts of the cultural sector. It will be easy for these networks, so valued during the early weeks and months of the pandemic, to ebb away as leaders return to their theatres and museums, but it is vital that that bedrock of new professional friendships are cultivated and sustained.
- Increased support and insight into *mental health support* for senior leaders and their teams. We need to go beyond the initial response, which was a patchwork of different support and initiatives, to a more evidence-based and co-ordinated approach to supporting leaders, their teams and the wider ecology of artists and freelancers to emerge from the trauma and uncertainty of this terrible period. Careful attention should be given around the particular pressures and issues faced by leaders of colour within the arts sector.
- Investment in, and recognition of, *new leadership capabilities and competencies* that are needed not only at CEO level but also amongst the boards of arts and cultural organisations. These include horizon scanning skills – increased confidence and capability around digital leadership, and support for reflecting on leadership styles that may need to adapt to reflect a more honest and emotionally engaged environment.

Our arts and cultural sector is an incredible one making a huge contribution to the social and economic fabric of our communities and our civic life. Investing in – and supporting – its leaders is an absolutely vital part of helping to rebuild and refocus our nation's cultural and civic life.

Notes

1 www.artscouncil.org.uk/blog/delivering-governments-culture-recovery-fund
2 www.museumsassociation.org/museums-journal/news/2020/09/sara-wajid-and-zak-mensah-to-share-ceo-role-at-birmingham-museums-trust/#

16   Creating Certainty Out of Chaos

School Leadership in the UK During COVID-19

Mike Cladingbowl and Alison Hooper

***

When referring to growing competition faced by the United States because of rising levels of education in other countries, Stanford economist Paul Romer quipped recently that 'a crisis is a terrible thing to waste'.[1]

In this chapter, we explore how school leaders in a small group of UK schools set out to create certainty in otherwise chaotic times.[2] Above all, we argue that the most successful leadership during the COVID crisis recognised the importance of building confidence and leadership capacity in others. We also reflect on how the crisis has changed us and the lessons that we have learned.

As the initial wave of COVID swelled in the UK in early March 2020, school leaders were in the spotlight. They faced the greatest educational challenge of their generation as, almost overnight, the status quo was upended. Daily news coverage in the UK reported soaring infection, hospitalisation and fatality rates. Schools remained open as the COVID crisis grew with little public understanding of how children might contribute to its spread.

It was apparent in mid-March, to many school leaders at least, that the UK response to COVID was inadequate. More believed more urgent action was needed. At the time, a national headteacher association prevailed on the Department for Education (DfE) to provide more and better advice. They also warned that schools were likely to close very soon because of staff shortages.[3]

Daily news coverage in the UK began to report that schools were partially or fully closed, usually because of a lack of staff. The UK government responded on 18th March 2020 by ordering the immediate closure of schools in England for all but children of key workers and those in vulnerable circumstances.[4]

During those frantic days, it seemed to many school leaders that the UK government was following rather than leading the news. By this time, the United Nations Educational, Scientific and Cultural Organisation (UNESCO) estimated that 107 countries had closed their schools already, affecting 862 million children or roughly half the global student population.[5] All this fostered unease in an uncertain climate and a sense that events were rapidly running out of control.

In the face of this critical uncertainty, it was essential for school leaders to show strong leadership by seizing initiative and creating surety. But in doing so, and in order to win trust, our school leaders had to be painstakingly honest and quick to acknowledge the fears of those around them.[6]

DOI: 10.4324/9781003171737-18

A primary headteacher writes:

> In my experience, it was critical to take the time to make sure people felt truly seen, heard and valued. Lead by example and be honest about your own fears and those of others. Remember, too, that while small things matter, they can matter differently so personalise your approaches. Generate enthusiasm, raise the profile of what others do and reward any positive engagement you see. There are times when you have to be tough, mostly with yourself, but find time for compassion as that's where real strength lies. Give yourself time, too, to reflect and be strategic, to think how it is going overall.

In our case, we identified the key principles needed to guide our thinking, support immediate decision-making and underpin communications: protect children, protect staff, protect education. This simple framework allowed us to recognise and focus on priorities. Instinctively, these priorities felt right. Looking back on those difficult days, and at our instinctive reflexes, those priorities reflected the very strong emphasis placed in all our schools on caring for our children and our workforce. The values of The Learning Alliance, our Trust, were reflected in the behaviour of school leaders and served as a powerful lever to further strengthen the collective leadership and of that in individual schools while continuing to work under strict protocols throughout the new academic year of 2020–2021.

A headteacher in one of our primary schools relives those difficult times:

> A national lockdown was imminent. School leaders were faced with huge uncertainty. Our school community was genuinely frightened and looked to us for reassurance and guidance.
>
> As it became clear to me that we were facing a national lockdown, I had to consider what that meant for our school practically, strategically and emotionally.
>
> From the outset, I was brutally honest in all my communications to all stakeholders but particularly parents. I had never dealt with a critical incident on this scale but was determined to provide clear information about safety for children and staff and about how education could continue.
>
> From mid-February, COVID was a regular feature of my weekly letter to parents. A page on our school website was dedicated to COVID. I was very careful about the information I gave, repeating specific messages especially regarding COVID symptoms. I had to make sense of the speculation in the press and be clear through the noise around me. My letter to parents and families on the 15 March 2020 had to make clear that we were not closed.
>
> Once the announcement was finally made, I put into action a plan we had been working on for remote learning, which involved distribution of learning packs and information about how to use our online learning platforms. Parents were already very familiar with these as children post their work daily from school. Now the tables were turned and children would be posting from home to their teachers.

In their handling of the crisis, our school leaders utilised the strong relationships they had built up over time to create confidence in staff, parents and children.

Inevitably, underneath apparently calm exteriors, most school leaders had the same doubts and worries that plagued everyone else. The challenge of interpreting last-minute and often vague guidance led to fear of missing information or getting things wrong. At the time, government guidance came in the form of a lengthy online document, updated daily, with an almost unmanageable number of links to additional documents. Alterations to the guidance were rarely highlighted and, as a result, leaders found themselves scrutinising the document daily to spot anything of significance. In one week alone during the month of May in 2020, there were more than 40 changes. Even with the support of fellow headteachers and others locally, this created significant stress and fear among school leaders.

Despite this, by the end of the initial lockdown in June 2020, school leaders had recognised that being honest with staff and other stakeholders – including by sharing some of their own doubts and worries – was building resilience among other school staff. In return, the support given by teachers and administrators to school leaders was almost universally strong. Leaders were able to draw on the expertise of staff, and their professional associations, to interact with ideas and practical solutions to what had once seemed intractable problems.

Within a very short period, this helped our schools to move to effective online education, care and guidance. Daily online meetings with teachers and others ensured that the best ideas were generated and assimilated quickly. Experts in using technology, including online meetings and learning platforms, rose to the challenge and taught other, often more senior, colleagues. In retrospect, without the emergence of such leadership from different quarters and across our different schools, it is very unlikely that robust online education would have been delivered so well.

Such willingness to encourage leadership from different levels in the organisation helped to provide the best education in difficult circumstances. More broadly, it reflects the argument of Macbeath and colleagues that such cooperation leads to greater learning, leadership and professionalism among school staff.[7]

Cooperating across the wider school system in the UK is not always straightforward. There are many different types of schools, even within particular age ranges, and different ways of organising them. Some state-funded schools have charitable status and are accountable to independent trustees. Others report into local government authorities. Although cooperation does exist between schools, it is often patchy or spasmodic. Moreover, many schools compete routinely and actively with each other to attract new children into their own school.

Moreover, after decades of reforms, the UK education system has yet to strike a agreed balance between acquiring knowledge, personal growth and skills development. There is often disagreement about the benefits of vocational education. Different initiatives, over many years, have sought to improve educational outcomes, including for those most disadvantaged children, but without striking or significant success. Other initiatives, such as character education, have sought to equip children with the tools to navigate life. Although there is an outline national curriculum, there is no legal requirement for all schools to follow it.

Since 1992, DfE has used Office for Standards in Education, Children's Services and Skills (Ofsted) guidelines[8] to evaluate and report on school performance. An unfavourable inspection report can lead to significant reputational damage. Fear of this, and compliance with particular approaches to pedagogy thought to be favoured by the inspectorate, and narrow accountability measures, can foster compliance rather than invention or creativity. As such, the suspension of routine inspection and examinations during COVID eased pressure on schools. Doing things differently became the norm rather than the exception. It also increased cooperation between schools and sharing of new ideas and great practice. In our experience, most school leaders argue that while the burden of COVID leadership was heavy, it was lightened considerably by the sharing with others. It will be interesting to see if the cooperation, innovation and trust between schools that developed during COVID is sustained as society becomes more normalised.

In our particular case, our eight schools were not in direct competition with each other. As such, there are fewer disincentives to cooperate. It is more straightforward for school leaders to work with others across the Trust. Doing this gives them access to more resources, greater contacts, a wider range of ideas and specialist support services.

During COVID, for example, regular keeping-in-touch meetings between Trust executives and headteachers made sure that all were in step with guidance formulating our own where needed, and we devised and helped with risk assessments, facilitated remote learning and equipment, and liaised with relevant government agencies. Trust leaders helped to set the pace across all schools, working with school leaders, and kept a sharp focus on what mattered most. As Stephen Covey (1992) famously wrote, 'keep the main thing the main thing'.[9] Even before the first school closures were announced, the Trust team of human resource, finance, governance and communication experts worked to support schools in managing the crisis though well-rehearsed critical incident management procedures. Studies of different types of schools in England during COVID[10] has encouraged the DfE to recommend that more schools adopt similar structures to our own.[11]

Much of our Trust's success is linked to the way we interact around shared and agreed values. As in other schools across the world, we want to provide the best possible education for all. But we are careful to balance the benefits of joint working towards shared aims, and the support this can bring, with preservation of the unique characteristics of each school in our Trust.

The same primary school leader writes about some of the things that matter most to her school:

> Throughout 15 years of Headship, what matters most to me is the value I place on the people who make up our unique school. Investing time in growing strong and positive relationships with children, staff, parents and others connected with the school has helped establish a shared vision and common culture.
>
> Four years ago, we set about the challenge of reflecting on our vision and the values underpinning it. This was a transforming experience for all and was a turning point for the school. We were resolute in wanting a creative, research-led and rich curriculum, which placed emphasis on global learning and empowered children to know themselves and thrive academically.
>
> Our school embeds the UN Convention on the Rights of the Child[12] into its policy, practice and culture. Children see themselves as global citizens and advocate for fairness and children's rights locally and globally. A strong partnership with a 'sister' school of the same name in Njoro, Kenya, also founded by Lord Egerton of Tatton Park in Cheshire was forged in 2005. This living historical legacy helps children in both schools learn about their different daily lives, exploring together what it means to be a global citizen today. We want children to grow the knowledge, skills and values they need to fulfil their potential as global citizens in an ever-changing world. Most important of all, we do this in an exciting and consistent way.[13]

Having a consistent approach to delivering an educational vision was a further feature of successful school leadership during the COVID crisis. Children adapted quickest to remote learning when they experienced familiar approaches to teaching. As far as possible, the remote reproduction of the usual learning experience helped children to flourish. In the same way, schools with a focused and well-organised curriculum found it easier to set work and help children make progress. Some national initiatives offered a variety of 'off-the-shelf' online lessons, which could be used to bolster teachers' own efforts, but they were not an adequate substitute for well-planned and sequenced programmes of subject work.

In this context, an important determinant in helping children to learn well was the tremendous effort made by hard-working staff. In practical terms, staff flew into action once leaders had set initial direction. Books for home; recording of videos; allocation of new responsibilities; sourcing of laptops from local business; distributing desks, pens, paper and textbooks; volunteering in the local community; preparing distance learning materials; making home visits to see children; organising food parcels; setting up home work-stations; running meetings virtually; attending virtual training; regular safe and well checks; and so on – all this and much more helped to transform the way education was delivered within 48 hours. In one primary school, the headteacher visited every family during one week to make sure they had everything they required. Subsequent visits were made to support families who were experiencing difficulties in supporting their children while working full time from home. The most vulnerable families and those with children with special educational needs benefited from bespoke support and weekly welfare checks. This approach was hugely appreciated by parents.

The dedication and innovation shown by school leaders and their staff – including by keeping schools partially open – was remarkable. It was only possible because school leaders and their staff drew on their compassion and commitment to social justice. They went above and beyond the expected – not because they were told to do so, but because they were determined to. Our analysis, over 18 months after the initial lockdown, is that learning loss among children was not as great as many had feared. For example, although there are discrepancies between children from different socio-economic backgrounds, levels of reading and numeracy have not been significantly adversely affected by remote learning. Younger children's writing is more of a problem as teachers were often unable to intervene at the point of composition. Children's writing resilience and stamina suffered in many cases, too. In secondary schools, children may have missed elements of the curriculum, including practical work. But we know this and it is being tackled over the coming months.

School leaders were careful to applaud their staff for this very great effort. Showing insight and appreciation of the challenges staff faced built optimism, energy and a 'can do' attitude in what became a physically distant but emotionally close school community. Stephen Covey again:

> When you show deep empathy toward others, their defensive energy goes down, and positive energy replaces it. That's when you can get more creative in solving problems.[14]

Like elsewhere in other schools, our leaders took particular interest in staff and children's wellbeing. Regular virtual coffee mornings and social events for staff kept levels of energy high while more formal arrangements were introduced to keep staff fit and well at home. These built on surveys and suggestions from staff, which allowed all involved to contribute to the greater good.

In most schools, children were helped from the very first reports of the virus to understand what it might mean. As it escalated, support grew to include lively discussion and children's research, including by exploring issues in one school in routine Philosophy for Children sessions. Once it became clear there would no early return, school leaders and staff involved children in videos in lieu of end-of-term concerts and events. They produced virtual school tours for prospective parents and children. Schools reached out regularly into the wider community using newsletters, social and print media. In response to a school survey of parents and carers in July 2020, a parent wrote the following, which typifies the views of most:

> Communication has been great! It has been timely, open, honest, supportive, clear and factual. We have been kept up to date in every aspect, which has been brilliant.

Visible leadership in schools, and across communities, helped to stabilise uncertainty and lessen fear as children returned to school in early Autumn 2020. The negative narrative about the impact of COVID on learning generated by many,[15] widely reported in the press, was challenged by our school leaders. As Professor Barry Carpenter argues,

> Recovery curriculum is a construct, it is not a written curriculum or accountability to government. It is a series of signposts as to where we might go with children when they return to school based on sound hypothesis of what their lived experience might have been during these weeks of lockdown.[16]

The quality of remote learning and high level of engagement, combined with measured and supportive communication to families, generated a positive approach to developing a recovery curriculum. One headteacher reported:

> We put the child's well-being at the centre of our thinking and planning. We acknowledged that the children will have had different experiences during that time and we ensured that our values, represented by our school's vision, continued to be at the centre of our work.

Our schools adopted a three-tier approach, encompassing universal and targeted recovery. All subject and class teachers identified any misconceptions or gaps in learning, and modified the curriculum so that this was dealt with over time. For many children, this first stage was all that was necessary. Through their routine activities with children, staff were also able to identify those who needed greater and more personalised support. This involved support for individual wellbeing, as well as for learning, helping children to feel safe and valued, and building their confidence. For a small number of children, including those who had experienced trauma and bereavement, specialist support was made available.

This structure provided a stable framework for recovery. It was underpinned by the hard work of staff as they paid careful attention to the emotional and academic needs of each child. In those early weeks after the return to school at the start of September 2020, staff built a recovery curriculum at the same time as making daily diagnostic assessments. Within days, it was clear that the majority of children were eager to return to full and familiar curriculum.

As the weeks progressed, all of our schools remained open, although guidelines on reducing the spread of infection meant that some staff and groups of children were sent home to self-isolate for short periods. Most children were only ever at home for a handful of days. Moreover, new approaches to distance teaching and learning, developed earlier in the year, were deployed quickly and seamlessly for any child being taught at home. All schools used information from surveys of children and their families to improve the remote learning experience and the wider support they provided to children.

Sadly, this success in maintaining children's learning and wellbeing was not fully repeated when schools closed again in early 2021, just one day after the term started following the winter break.

The 'Spring lockdown' from January to around mid-March in 2021 was more challenging for everyone. Despite high levels of communication between home and school, and better online assessment of progress, maintaining motivation in children at home was more of a struggle. The weather was very cold and the rain seemed relentless. An increased number of children experienced a lack of focus and, at times, anxiety. While we made regular welfare and learning checks, and gave full support to parents, some children returned from 8 March 2021 onwards less settled. This had some impact on learning, which is being remedied, but it had also an impact on the attitudes, concentration and behaviour of some children, most notably those from more disadvantaged backgrounds, as they struggled to adapt back into the routines of school life.

This was most evident in secondary schools. It was also not helped by the large-scale COVID testing of children that schools were asked to carry out. Large or communal spaces such as sport halls were turned into testing centres, for example, and this disrupted the timetable and daily school life.

As if this was not difficult enough, the steep rise in infection rates after the emergence of the 'Delta variant' in Spring 2021, and the lifting of some social restrictions, led to more children and staff having to self-isolate. By mid-July 2021, school leaders were increasingly concerned by the growth in the number of children and families needing to self-isolate. Some schools even had to close early. All this was compounded by the announcement that a wider 're-opening' of society would occur from 19 July 2021. The rationale behind this decision lay in the successful vaccination of the great majority of the adult population. However, many health professionals cautioned against the relaxation of measures, not least as they could lead to the emergence of new, and vaccine-immune, variants, which emerged with the Omicron variant in late November 2021.

The announcements made in July 2021 also made it clear that all earlier preventative measures would be removed after the return to school in September 2021, aside from onsite testing in secondary schools. School leaders and their staff felt further and sustained uncertainty during July and August 2021 not least as they believed that infection rates would be high when children and staff returned to schools in September 2021. This proved to be the case.

It is clear that COVID has presented a high level of challenge to school leaders not just in the UK but across the globe. In our experience of the crisis, leaders who lived by a set of clear principles and who were ready to learn have met these challenges best. The last 2 years, or so, have taught us that we can build confidence and certainty in chaotic times, and do this best by focusing on compassion, empathy and care for social justice. Our leaders, like many others, were able to stand firm in an unsure context because of their commitment to these values. Like beacons, these values helped leaders to illuminate the road ahead for them and others when all else was unclear.

None of us really knew what we faced in the early days of COVID, but we did rapidly recognise that we needed to create a foothold of certainty. In doing so, leaders found opportunities to embrace the unexplored and exploit the potential in those around them, which built greater confidence. Our leaders needed staff to find ways of managing new and often complex tasks. Talented administrators in one school, for example, took on the task of managing routine communications with parents, leaving the headteacher to focus on more immediate aspects of each day. In the same school, teaching assistants' creativity spiralled as they made videos of creative activities and recorded children's stories for use at bedtime.

Taken together, these experiences have strengthened our understanding of what constitutes strong and sustainable leadership. It does not reside in any one individual or their successors.

Instead, it is built on integrity and a resolute desire to act as one for children and families. It rests in the collective ability of all in an institution to step up, and make contributions, in what is always a new or changing environment.

We know we are still learning from the COVID experience. One of the benefits of this global pandemic is that it has served to ignite debate on the organisation and delivery of education, its assessment and purpose. This debate is not new. Arguments for 'traditional' and knowledge-based education, modelled largely on a curriculum and pedagogy that our own great grandparents would have recognised, contrast with more progressive voices. Both sides argue that their approaches are rooted in evidence, although we, and many other UK educators, remain unconvinced that the evidence is overwhelming on either side. We do know that the usual approaches to assessment were abandoned by the UK government during the pandemic. No formal or externally assessed data, on which school performance is usually judged, exists for 2020 and 2021. Of course, most schools continued to assess the progress of their children and can provide evidence of this, begging the question of whether formal statutory assessments need to be reinstated, particularly in primary schools.

As school leaders, we also fear that too little will be done to exploit the new ways of working that emerged during the pandemic. Instead, as the usual systems return, school leaders will revert to competition over cooperation, focusing on a narrow range of outcomes as measured by external assessment, and making changes to their school curriculum and methods of teaching to suit the prevailing views of changing governments and their arms-length bodies.

The global crisis has stirred many school leaders into being braver and resolute regarding what is best for their children. It has led to school and Trust leaders demonstrating civic leadership in their communities, collaboration between schools and trusts being central to the work of local communities.

Whether they will be able to continue to do so if the education system returns to the previous status quo is questionable. In our case, we very much hope that current and successive governments will foster a climate that allows for educational innovation, cooperation and civic leadership. Without this, we are in real danger of 'wasting the crisis'. If we simply return to what we had before, with its many imperfections and failings, we may even exacerbate existing problems – such as teacher and headteacher supply – further. We already know, for example, that many teachers and school leaders are choosing to leave the profession early as a direct result of the pressure resulting from this pandemic.

As yet, sadly, we do not see much that signifies any change in the direction of educational policy. There appears to be little appetite for learning from the crisis. Many of the gains made during COVID, for example, the greater confidence in tackling what appear to be intractable or unsurmountable issues, civic leadership and the growing culture of innovation, may be lost. As it did during the earlier stages of the pandemic, successful leadership now must recognise the importance of building confidence and wider leadership capacity throughout schools and be more ready to consider all the lessons that can be learned.

Notes

1 *The New York Times Magazine*, 'A terrible thing to waste', www.nytimes.com/2009/08/02/magazine/02FOB-onlanguage-t.html.
2 All of these schools are now part of The Learning Alliance (TLA). This is a publicly funded organisation that is responsible for three primary and six secondary schools in the UK.
3 SecEd, 'Coronavirus: Staff shortage will force schools to close, ministers are warned', www.sec-ed.co.uk/news/coronavirus-dfe-williamson-ascl-naht-closures-staff-shortage-covid-19/.

4 Department for Education, 'Guidance for critical works and vulnerable children who can access schools or educational settings', www.gov.uk/government/publications/coronavirus-covid-19-maintaining-educational-provision.

5 *The Lancet Child & Adolescent Health*, 'School closure and management practices during coronavirus outbreaks including Covid-19: A rapid systematic review', www.thelancet.com/journals/lanchi/article/PIIS2352-4642(20)30095-X/fulltext#:~:text=On%20March%2018%2C%202020%2C%20the%20UN%20Educational%2C%20Scientific,young%20people%2C%20roughly%20half%20the%20global%20student%20population.

6 Nancy Koehn, 'Real leaders are forged in crisis', *Harvard Business Review*, 3 April 2020, https://hbr.org/2020/04/real-leaders-are-forged-in-crisis.

7 John Macbeath et al., *Strengthening the connections between leadership and learning* (Routledge, 2018).

8 Ofsted 2021, www.gov.uk/government/organisations/ofsted.

9 Stephen Cover, *The 7 habits of highly effective people,* Simon and Schuster (1989).

10 Daniel Muijs and Karl Sampson, 'The trust in testing times: The role of multi-academy trusts during the pandemic', *Ofsted blog*, 2021, https://educationinspection.blog.gov.uk/2021/01/19/the-trust-in-testing-times-the-role-of-multi-academy-trusts-during-the-pandemic/.

11 Freddie Whittaker, 'Williamson: Government "looking at" how to get more schools into multi-academy trusts', *Schools Week*, https://schoolsweek.co.uk/williamson-government-looking-at-how-to-get-more-schools-into-multi-academy-trusts/.

12 UNICEF, 'The United Nations convention on the rights of the child: The children's version', www.unicef.org/child-rights-convention/convention-text-childrens-version.

13 This school's vision was influenced by the work of Professor Ken Robinson, a strong advocate of radical reforms. He proposed principles of education: personal, cultural, social and economic. He argues that 'the aims of education are to enable students to understand the world around them and the talents within them so that they can become fulfilled individual and active, compassionate citizens' (Robinson, 2015: xvi).

14 Stephen Covey, *The 7 habits of highly effective people,* Simon and Schuster (1992).

15 Alison Andrew et al., *Primary school closures created substantial inequality in time spent learning between pupils from poorer and better-off families – and re-opening schools may be the only remedy* (Institute for Fiscal Studies, 2020), https://ifs.org.uk/publications/14976.

16 Barry Carpenter and Matthew Carpenter, *A recovery curriculum: Loss and life for our children and schools post pandemic*, 2021, www.evidenceforlearning.net/recoverycurriculum/.

Reference

Covey, S. *Seven Habits of Highly Effective People*. Simon and Schuster, New York. 1992.

17 Leadership in Crisis

What Lessons Can be Learned From the NHS Response to the COVID-19 Pandemic in 2020–2021?

Simon Hollington

***

Under-funded, under-staffed, under-resourced, over-pressurised and taken for granted.

That would certainly be the outsiders' view of the UK National Health Service (NHS) if all they did was judge it by the media headlines in the last decade, but somehow, this supposedly broken, crisis-riven organisation has risen to the enormous challenge of the COVID pandemic. How? That is the root question that will be examined in this chapter. Although it will primarily examine leadership from an organisational point of view, lessons for leaders will undoubtedly emerge. It will also look at whether the lessons from the NHS can be applied to most (if not all) organisations.

Leadership, Vision and Values

If, as Daniel Goleman (1996) maintains, leadership is "is not a domination, but the art of persuading people to work towards a common goal" (p. 149), then the starting point for organisations is their common purpose. While, as we will see later, the NHS had a common purpose at its formation in 1948, it no longer has a clearly defined purpose. Trawl through the NHS England website and you will find a page with the words "Our Vision and Values." Click through and you will be disappointed. There is information there about the different boards' make up, its corporate publications and the regional teams, but there is no vision. As Nigel Crisp[1] maintains (2020, p. 201) in his seminal work Health is for Home, Hospitals are for Repair:

> There is also something missing. There is a long-term plan for the future, but, as yet, not truly compelling vision.

A similar situation exists around the NHS values. A simple online search reveals the seven core values of the NHS, the six nursing values of the NHS and the five values of caring. It is a recipe for confusion, as while some of the values are the same, there are different ones in each list. So, in simple leadership terms the NHS fails in its foremost, fundamental leadership tasks – its vision and values, or, as Simon Sinek (2009) maintains, the "Why" and the "How."

What the COVID pandemic provided was a common purpose (for purpose, read 'enemy') around which everyone in the NHS and beyond could unite – and in doing so, there was a common approach (read 'values') in which everyone was encouraged to do whatever they could do, without pressure to do more.

DOI: 10.4324/9781003171737-19

The NHS

The NHS was founded in 1948 by the then-Health Minister Aneurin Bevan, though discussions on a National Health Service had occurred throughout the first half of the 20th Century. The biochemist Benjamin Moore is credited with the first use of the phrase 'National Health Service' (in his book *The Dawn of the Health Age*, p. 178, which was first published in 1910), but it was nearly 40 years later that it became a reality. Prior to that, patients generally paid for any medical or dental treatment, though in some cases, local authorities ran hospitals for local ratepayers, an approach originating from the Poor Law.[2] During the 1930s, discussions and criticism of the existing system continued and there was a growing consensus that the health insurance system should be extended with voluntary hospitals integrated. The Second World War halted such discussions, but the creation of the Emergency Hospitals Service to care for wounded meant that care services were dependent on central government for the first time. By 1941, attention turned to post-war care provision and the Beveridge Report (Cmnd 6404, 1942) recommended "comprehensive health and rehabilitation services". In 1944, the government (a coalition, cross-party wartime government) issued a White Paper that set out the guidelines for the NHS that included how it was to be funded (general taxation) and who could access its services (everyone including visitors to the UK). The NHS was formally launched on 5 July 1948 and was based on three essential values: the services were available to everyone; healthcare was to be free; and care would be provided on the basis of need – not ability to pay.

There have been many changes to the NHS since 1948 but, as Nigel Crisp points out:

> this sense of common purpose, shared values and social justice still inspires healthcare professionals, is written into government policy and attracts wide public support.
>
> (ibid., p. 184)

We will return to the theme of common purpose and public support later in this chapter. "Free for all at point of contact" has been a mantra for the NHS since 1948, but it has placed a significant financial burden on the NHS and had been a political hot potato for successive governments, whatever their political philosophy. In fact, the concept of 'free' changed as early as 1952 when prescription charges were introduced to ease the growing cost of the NHS.[3]

The NHS in 1948 faced a totally different set of circumstances and challenges to the NHS 70 years later. Then the NHS faced the challenge of specific discrete illnesses and injuries, while now there are far more complex and long-lasting challenges, with treatment being similarly complex and expensive. In 1950–1951, NHS spending accounted for 3.5% of GDP, while it is estimated that in 2020–2021 it will be marginally over 7%.[4] Expenditure has therefore increased at twice the rate of GDP and public expenditure over the NHS's existence and there have only been decreases in five of those 73 years. On average, the NHS has enjoyed above-inflation annual increases of 3.9%, but despite that significant expenditure, commentators and healthcare professionals continue to bemoan the financial challenges faced by the NHS. In 2010, a Kings Fund analysis predicted a funding gap of £21 billion by 2013–2014, while in 2013, NHS England indicated that the savings target of £20 billion by 2015 would not stop the NHS from going into the red. Charlie Cooper writing for the *The Independent Online* on 15 April 2014, reported that the NHS faced a "financial disaster," while on 9 October 2015, writing for the *Telegraph Online*, Laura Donnelly suggested that the "NHS faces the biggest financial crisis in a generation."

Like finances, staff shortages have featured regularly in headlines. On 11 September 2018, Denis Campbell writing for the *Guardian Online* (UK needs £102Bn boost to NHS and social care) denounced the worst ever staff shortages in the NHS with 107,403 unfulfilled NHS posts at the end of June 2018, of which 41,722 were nurses. This represented 11.8% of all nursing posts, while shortages of equipment and beds have also been highlighted by mainstream media for a good number of years.

So, on the face of it, the NHS is an under-funded, under-resourced organisation, but that viewpoint is certainly challenged by Pradeep Madhavan, Clinical Director of Trauma and Orthopaedics and Ophthalmology at Musgrove Park Hospital in Taunton. While acknowledging that more money is of course helpful, he stated in an interview that the NHS is both very effective and also very inefficient, but it is far from broken. The NHS was designed to tackle very different challenges than those it now faces and at a different time and with a different culture. Even in its formation, it was shaped by political manoeuvrings of the day, with doctors and hospitals dominant and deep divides between primary and secondary care and between the NHS and social care. It carried enormous historical baggage and vested interests, and it appears that not much has changed in the intervening years.

Organisations set up for a specific purpose find it difficult to adapt to another (even more so if that new purpose is not clear) as almost everything needs to change. That means tackling professional demarcations, what services will need to be provided, funding streams, power bases, supply chains and job security, to name just a few – and for a publicly funded organisation like the NHS, significant political courage and willpower is needed. As James Hollington (Senior Lead Clinical Scientist at the Southeast Mobility and Rehabilitation Technology (SMART) Centre in NHS Lothian) stated in an interview, it is made more difficult because "the problem with the NHS is that everyone owns it."

Turning though to the NHS response to the COVID pandemic, it should have approached it prepared. Under the headline, "Swine Flu Could Overwhelm the NHS says Health Secretary" (26 July 2009), The Independent quoted Andy Burnham, the then-Health Secretary, saying that: "People should be assured that we have been planning our response to a pandemic for a long time," and in 2016, there was a major exercise – Exercise Cygnus – to test the preparedness of the UK in the event of a pandemic. But, by all accounts, the UK in general and the NHS in particular were not prepared and the lessons learned from Exercise Cygnus were not acted upon. The UK government did not react to the reports coming in during late 2019 from Wuhan, where the virus is commonly accepted to have originated, nor to the crisis in northern Italy in January/February 2020. It is, of course, easy in hindsight to be critical of the way that any crisis has been handled, but there was little or no understanding of the severity and complexity of the challenge. On 8 March 2020, Professor Martin Marshall, Chair of The Royal College of General Practitioners (and subsequently one of our interviewees) told Sophy Ridge of Sky News that while the outbreak was a "significant crisis" for the NHS, "estimates that 100,000 could die were a worst-case scenario,"[5] while a study by Ferguson et al. from Imperial College London, which largely informed governmental policy in the early days of the pandemic, suggested that, with a lockdown and social distancing, deaths could be hopefully kept to close to, or under, 50,000.

Unlike the scenario during Exercise Cygnus, whereby the plan was to tackle the exercise pandemic while still continuing to provide a normal NHS service, during 2020 (and to an extent during early 2021), the NHS stopped offering much of its traditional services. Elective surgery was halted, general practitioners (GPs) and NHS dentists closed their doors and as a result, staff and resources were available to be reallocated. Added to that, the NHS was helped by unlimited financial support from the UK and national governments. Previous medical protocols were streamlined as were decision-making processes, 'attend anywhere' clinics made significant use of video technology and many internal NHS inter-discipline barriers appear to have disappeared in the face of the enormous and unknown (at least initially) challenge the pandemic posed. Pradeep Madhavan described the allocation process of funding pre-pandemic as "bartering for resources and constantly competing" with over 200 Clinical Commissioning Groups (CCGs) allocating the local budgets depending upon local needs. As a result of 27 mergers in 2020–2021, that number of CCGs has dropped to just over 100, but the result has been that emotive, headline-catching services such as cancer and heart disease were better funded than less glamorous areas, while Martin Marshall said in his interview, "Public Health has been under-funded for years."

However, this chapter is not about the government's handling but an analysis of how this supposedly over-stretched organisation managed to rise to the greatest medical challenge since the Second World War and what other organisations can learn from its experience. The answers do not come from the media, however accurate their reporting might be, but from the experience of those working in the NHS during the crisis. Those interviewed were deliberately a cross-section not just those directly involved in fighting COVID at the front line because, as will become apparent, the COVID crisis affected everyone in the NHS and a good many associated organisations.

The most striking theme that emerged from the completed questionnaires and from the interviews (conducted from February to May 2021) was that there was complete agreement over the assessment of the NHS. Like Pradeep Madhavan, everyone agreed that it is very effective but at the same time very inefficient – two very different things. Once a patient is in front of a clinician, their treatment is as good as anywhere else in the world (a few headlines notwithstanding) but getting to that point is something of a lottery and, to a large extent, can depend upon the patient being proactive and resilient in the face of that inefficiency or at times simply shouting the loudest. The systems that operate in the NHS are tortuous and bureaucratic, communication between the patient and the NHS regularly fail, but that is down to the administrative process and the administrative staff, not the clinicians. Several respondents commented on how they had "learned to work round people" to get matters done, so it seems that the NHS performs *despite* the lack of effective, lean, simple processes. That it does is testament to the dedication of the clinicians and speaks wonders about their ethos. One is left wondering how amazing the care would be if the administrative processes matched their dedication.

That being the case, how did this ineffective organisation rise to the challenge, and what leadership lessons are there for other organisations? An analysis 15 months into the pandemic and of the completed questionnaires and interviews suggests that the NHS (and the leaders therein) needs to ensure that:

- There is clear sense of purpose – the 'Why?'.
- The organisational culture runs deep through its DNA.
- Resilience is built into the organisation.
- All leaders are role models.
- Decision making is delegated as close to the front line as possible.
- Leaders question, question, question and then listen, listen and listen again.
- Leadership styles are flexed: one size does not fit all.
- The focus is on key deliverables.
- Everyone knows they are appreciated.

While these points fall directly from research, the completed questionnaires and the interviews that were conducted, these aspects apply to all organisations.

A Clear Sense of Purpose – The 'Why?'

When the NHS was formed in 1948, there was a clear vision: free healthcare for all dependent on need. While this lofty ideal still inspires individual healthcare clinicians, there is no longer a clear vision, and clinicians work to their own idea of the organisational purpose. Ashok Subramanian (trauma consultant and orthopaedic spine surgeon at Musgrove Park Hospital in Taunton) spoke of a duty of care and being driven by the Hippocratic Oath, James Hollington said that he was in the NHS to improve society, while Debbie Williams (advanced clinical practitioner at University College Hospital Trust, London) simply said that she wanted to do something meaningful. While maintaining that there was a vision or purpose for the NHS, Pradeep Madhavan could not say what it was or where it was to be found. So there is a tremendous amount of goodwill within the individual clinicians and no doubt in the teams that they work with, but there is no overarching clearly stated vision or purpose. Individuals are therefore left to work to the best of their ability to a lofty but unwritten ideal. However, though no one person or body formally stated it, during the pandemic there was a clear purpose: stop the pandemic overwhelming the NHS and save lives. There was a common enemy – COVID – and a common sense of purpose. Despite the challenges, the fears and the unknown, everyone was in it together supported by the government and enormous public goodwill – of which more later. Everything else the NHS had done before became of secondary importance. In the words of Lisa Sadler (senior sister, mixed COVID and medical ward, University College Hospital Trust, London): "Everything else just stopped and the NHS reduced to just the essentials."

Buster Howes, in his paper "A Primer for Resilience & Leadership Through the Coronavirus Pandemic," (p. 5) wrote that "what most people want is a sense of identity, purpose and belonging" and quoted Nietzsche who observed that "he who has a why to live, can bear almost any how." So the principal role of any leader *and* any organisation is to ensure that everyone in their team or in the organisation has a clear sense of purpose. Why do we do what we do? It applies to any organisation, large or small, and to any team. Everyone, if they are to be as effective as they can be, must know how what they do helps the organisation and its purpose. That purpose was and is fundamental in uniting people across the NHS and in UK in rising to the pandemic challenge and going forward, Ashok Subramanian is clear that the NHS needs "a clear long-term vision."

Ensure That the Organisational Culture Runs Deep Through Its DNA

What was striking during the interviews that I conducted was how much of a cultural shift has happened during the pandemic. Staff were encouraged to do what they could and not feel guilty if they couldn't. Debbie Williams spoke of spending much more of her time providing pastoral care and listening to others; Ashok Subramanian spent more time training others rather than just doing the job; Martin Marshall said that his greatest challenge was maintaining energy and morale; and Pradeep Madhavan described the need to be more collaborative, a point reiterated by Hannah Cairns (Head of SMART Services, NHS Lothian) who said there was a need to combine a compassionate leadership style with strong direction where needed, while James Hollington stressed the need to empower and enable everyone to make decisions that are in the best interest of the patients – within the limits of budgets. Both he and Pradeep said that too often pre-pandemic, they had to work round people to get what was needed for the patient. Sadly, in the caring organisation that is the NHS, the culture is expected but is not demanded. As Buster Howes points out (2020, p. 2), "The NHS has a poor record for failing to deal with difficult or indeed toxic people, particularly in positions of power," and stories of whistle-blowers being ostracised and unable subsequently to work in the NHS are all too common. This is a failure both of leadership and culture. But during the pandemic, Lisa Sadler, Debbie Williams and Pradeep Madhavan all spoke of being conscious not to pressurise staff, merely encouraging them to do whatever they felt safe in doing. For some, that was helping out by doing extra shifts in the COVID wards if they were suitably qualified, but for others it was simply covering shortages of staff. Ashok Subramanian set up a 'proning team' of consultants and doctors who could not directly help in looking after COVID patients, but could help by proning (turning patients on ventilators – it takes six staff to turn one patient), thus freeing up COVID trained staff for other tasks.

What became apparent from the interviews is that the NHS has procedures and policies in place to ensure that nothing goes wrong, but no systems to empower, enable and encourage staff and support clinicians. As James Hollington points out, "it was the people who made it happen, not the organisation." So if the primary role of the organisation, department and leader is to set a clear purpose, the next step is to ensure that the culture is one that supports everyone to deliver that purpose and that all policies and procedures are similarly aligned and focused. The question to be asked of every policy is: 'does this policy help to deliver our purpose and is it aligned with our stated culture?'.

Building Resilience Into the Organisation

One of the clear messages coming from the pandemic has been how staff throughout the NHS and care sector have pushed themselves beyond normal expectations to provide care for those impacted by COVID. Staff have worked longer shifts, have worked in different areas to their normal expertise, have left families to live in care homes thus shielding residents, or have taken on additional roles to help those directly involved in the COVID wards. Yet, one wonders, how have they all found the energy to do so? Yes, there has been demonstrable public support, a point we will return to, but as Ashok Subramanian points out, "goodwill doesn't last forever," adding that "it (the pandemic) has been the biggest challenge of my life." Martin Marshall maintains that GPs are exhausted, and Debbie Williams said that at times she didn't know how she would be able to continue. Resilience, she maintains, "is the ability to reset after a particularly difficult day" and she commented on how valuable the breakout rooms with free teas and coffees have been to staff, something that – surprisingly – is not provided as a matter of course throughout the NHS.

Intensity needs downtime, even if just for a few minutes, to enable that reset and allow people to engage at a different level and on different topics. This downtime enables people to work at high intensity levels and it is this that builds individual resilience. The Royal Marines have a motto of "train hard, fight easy" and everyone is pushed to breaking point – or beyond – during basic training. The objective is not to weed out people, but to get them to understand where their limits are and enable them to go beyond those limits the next time. Everyone is carefully supported throughout this resilience building and most – if not all – Royal Marines would admit that they 'cracked' at some stage in training. They would also say they didn't know what their limits really were when they first joined up.

But, just as individuals need to build resilience, so to do organisations. Resilience can, to an extent, be built through organisational policies, procedures and training (testing contingency plans, etc.), but resilience can only really be built by experience. Leaders, though, have a direct role in building resilience by stretching individuals, promoting them into roles with greater responsibility (with appropriate support, of course) and ensuring that organisational contingency plans are regularly tested under challenging conditions. Interestingly, it would appear that most hospital contingency planning exercises tend to focus on a major trauma incident (train crash or terrorist bomb) such that emergency procedures last for a few days or a week. Nothing prepared government departments or the NHS for the long grind of the pandemic. Those involved will certainly have built up resilience, but there is a significant danger that a good proportion of them will have succumbed to feelings of anxiety or depression, or become burnt out – and sadly, many will suffer from post-traumatic stress disorder before the pandemic can truly said to be contained. Members of the armed forces who serve in conflict (such as in the Falklands, Northern Ireland, the Balkans, Kuwait, Iraq or Afghanistan) are given time off on return to recuperate and regenerate. This is not an option for NHS staff, who will face a significant backlog of patients understandably demanding treatment for trauma and illness that has been put on hold during the pandemic. The pressure of the pandemic will be replaced by the pressure of waiting times and targets.

Ensure All Leaders Are Role Models

The leaders of the NHS pre-pandemic were unknown to all but a handful of the British public, but they have been thrust into the limelight by the daily COVID briefings from Whitehall, Holyrood, Cardiff and Belfast. Those leaders – and indeed, leaders at all levels – have become more visual simply because of the pandemic and their behaviours, actions and words will have been seized upon and scrutinised as never before. They have been sending messages every day that have said – or at least ought to have said – this is how to behave and react to the pandemic. Professor Chris Whitty has been Chief Medical Officer for England throughout the pandemic, briefing the Prime Minister, regularly participating in the televised news briefings and giving evidence to parliamentary bodies. These onerous tasks did not, however, stop him from working shifts in his capacity as a practising doctor and consultant at University College Hospitals Trust and Debbie Williams described him as 'having no airs and graces', showing no arrogance or conceit. But being a role model is not just a necessity during a crisis; it is a fulltime occupation of a leaders all the time. Anytime a leader walks into a room of people, they will, consciously or unconsciously, be assessing that leader's mood and will take their cue from that almost instantaneous assessment. Leaders need, consciously and continuously, to ask themselves the questions "what message do I need to send?" and "how do I need to behave to send that message in the most effective way?"

Delegate Decision Making as Close to the Front Line as Possible

The NHS is well known for its bureaucracy and managerial oversight, both of which often get in the way of clinicians. As Lisa Sadler says:

> There is lots of bureaucracy and waste, and we've more project managers than we know what to do with.

Getting to see a clinician in the first place can be a challenge, and GP appointments are said by some commentators to be like gold dust. In some cases, technology has helped cut through red tape, with both Ashok Subramanian and Pradeep Madhavan saying that first appointments by video have risen considerably. Importantly, they both say that patients, their partners and their carers are more relaxed and less intimidated speaking from home than during a face-to-face in a clinic and, from a clinical perspective, Ashok and Pradeep both get a better insight into the patients' needs. In the case of GPs, it is the practice receptionist who acts as gatekeeper and it is they who decide – unless the patient is assertive and proactive – whether a patient's situation warrants a call back from a GP or even an appointment. But despite the challenges faced by many patients, decision making has rightly been devolved during the pandemic, a situation that needs to be maintained, as evidenced by this quote online from an un-named hospital doctor in the Midlands:

> The most important thing has been giving power to front line teams. . . . In the past, many barriers were in place to making changes, with centralised decision-making that stifled innovation. In COVID early stages, national oversight stepped back in response to the emergency, and clinical teams were able to self-govern, innovate and collaborate to implement changes that met the immediate needs of their patients. My main urge would be to remember that NHS staff have moved mountains to reply to the pandemic. Leaders please trust frontline staff to do what is needed and empower them to deliver the best for their own patients.

Steve Jobs is reported to have said that "It doesn't make sense to hire smart people and then tell them what to do. We hire smart people so they can tell us what to do." It is a sentiment that organisations – the NHS included – need to remember and act upon.

Leaders – Question, Question, Question, and Then Listen, Listen and Listen Again

In his book *Lessons from the Top*, Gavin Esler (p. 5) says:

> The indispensable skill for all leaders in business, politics, sport or any significant field of human endeavour is the ability to create followers and communicate effectively with them.

Creating followers depends upon creating relationships with them and for those relationships to be ones in which the follower has the trust and confidence to say what they truly think and feel, without worrying about negative consequences. It is perhaps glib to say that patients "need a damned good listening to," but that is a key aspect of any patient–clinician relationship. There remains (and not just in the older generation) a reverence for doctors and the old adage of "the doctor knows best" still prevails. But, to be fair to clinicians, they can only deal with what they are presented with. When busy and short of time, it is very easy to fall into the trap of treating the symptom, not the cause. Listening, therefore, can only be effective if clinicians create the atmosphere that encourages and allows patients to feel totally free to be *really* honest with the clinician: to dispense with the aura that surrounds clinicians. That atmosphere is best created by questioning: using more open than closed questions, and the clinician being focused on the cause not the symptoms. It is a point so beautifully and powerfully made by Nancy Kline in her book, *Time to Think* (1999) which should perhaps be made mandatory reading for all leaders.

Such an approach takes time – something that clinicians will say that they don't have enough of – but treating the cause will prevent repeat attendance, save money and save time.

Nigel Crisp continually discusses the need for a partnership based on equality, not one that, in Transactional Analysis terms, is parent/child. The one skill needed by all leaders – not just those in the NHS – is questioning. Without it, patients/clients/customers will not present the full picture of their illness/complaint/concern and clinicians will continue to treat the symptom, not the cause.

Flex Leadership Styles: One Size Does Not Fit All

Goleman, Boyatsis and McGee, in their book "Primal Leadership," postulate that there are six basic leadership styles: visionary, coaching, pacesetting, affiliative, democratic and commanding. Each has its strengths and weaknesses and is situationally and follower appropriate. Over the long term, research suggests that the visionary and coaching styles produce the best results: Churchill's "We will fight them on the beaches . . . we will never surrender" speech and Pep Guardiola's quiet encouragement of Raheem Sterling and Phil Foden at Manchester City are testament to those styles, but in a crisis, there is no doubt that a pacesetting style comes firmly to the fore. Pradeep Madhavan mentioned the formation of a 'surgical hub' with short regular meetings which have "made us a lot closer . . . and infighting is a lot less," an affiliative approach, while Hannah Cairns was clear that at times her leadership style had become more directive than usual – a point also made by Lisa Sadler, who said:

> A more dictatorial style was needed during the pandemic, changes had to be made quickly leaving little time for negotiation and discussion, which while necessary during the height of the crisis, it isn't something I will carry forward (until the next crisis).

Each of the respondents mentioned that they had needed to flex their leadership style during the pandemic. As examples, Martin Marshall said that he needed to be more empathetic and Hannah Cairns maintains that future leadership is about influence and has had to learn to delegate more and give up control. Perhaps the greatest leadership challenge post-pandemic will be to ensure that the cultural shift over the last two years does not fade and that the NHS does not revert to pre-pandemic norms and bureaucratic processes. It will need significant influence and a cumulative collaborative approach.

Focus on Key Deliverables

Simon Sinek maintains that there are three simple steps to an effective organisation: first focus on the 'Why?' – the purpose of the organisation; then the 'How?' – the culture; and finally the 'What?' – the product, the service or the deliverables. The NHS fails to articulate a common purpose, its internal culture is not defined but yet it is expected to deliver everything to everyone. What has been striking about the pandemic is just how spectacular the delivery has been *in terms of fighting COVID and saving lives*, but that has come at significant cost to the myriad of other services that the NHS has been expected to deliver. As Lisa Sadler said:

> we just downed tools is every other area to cope . . . and reduced to just the essentials. There was lots of support to do stuff that nurses normally do.

Debbie Williams spoke of dental nurses being deployed to ITU; engineers at the NHS Lothian SMART centre made face-masks instead of running clinics; for both Ashok

Subramanian and Pradeep Madhavan, routine (elective) operations came to a halt; while resources (including wards and beds) across the NHS were reallocated. So fundamentally the NHS – the supposedly broken, crisis-riven organisation – rose to the challenge of the COVID pandemic by doing almost nothing else, and the consequences are significant. According to Triggle and Jeavens (BBC News Online, 27 May 2021), the number of patients waiting for more than a year for routine treatments rose from just 1,600 in March 2020 to more than 436,000 at the end of March 2021. More than five million (9% of the population) people are now on the hospital waiting list in England alone – in Scotland, the percentage is similar; in Wales, it rises to 17%; while in Northern Ireland, it is a staggering 23%. So what? What can other organisations learn from these stark statistics? The NHS is over-stretched as much because it is expected to do too much, by too many, with too little. If the NHS is to recover from the pandemic, then there needs either to be a significant increase in funding and staffing, or there needs to be a serious, adult, non-political conversation about what it is expected to deliver. Organisations need to do the same: define what they offer and what they don't, in a clear unambiguous way, not hidden in the small print of their Terms and Conditions.

Make Sure That Everyone Knows They Are Appreciated

One of the most visually emotive images from the first spike of the pandemic in Europe was the explicit outpouring of gratitude towards health professionals. First noted in Italy, Spain and Portugal on 15 March 2020, the concept of 'Clap for Carers' went global by the beginning of April that year. At first it focused purely on healthcare professionals, but it was subsequently widened to include all key workers who continued to provide vital services during lockdown. It was a demonstrable show of gratitude to the NHS (and other) staff across the UK and it provoked both positive and negative reactions. On the positive side, NHS staff were given priority access to supermarkets so that staff did not have to queue for groceries and many restaurants, closed by the lockdown, turned their hands to providing free meals for NHS staff. On the negative side, many in the NHS felt that it was a hollow gesture with Gemma Mitchell (writing for *The Nursing Times* on 7 January 2021) suggesting that nurses would be happier if everyone concentrated on maintaining social distance, wearing face-masks and washing their hands. James Hollington spoke of a planned visit by a senior NHS Lothian manager who was coming specifically to thank the SMART employees who had produced 35,000 items of personal protective equipment, which helped to fill the gap in supply before commercial industries could react. At the last moment, the visit was cancelled – by the manager's secretary – with no explanation. James described it as "a real kicking."

But the concept of gratitude holds good – providing it is sincere. A Gallup survey of four million employees in 2004 found that:

> employees who receive regular praise are more productive, engaged and more likely to remain with the organisation than those who don't.

Peter Langton, writing for the Training Industry website (5 Before 5: The Importance of Praise at work), says that:

> Praise is one of the most underused and most powerful management tools that money just doesn't need to buy.

Whether public gratitude will survive the long waiting times and the inability to get a face-to-face remains to be seen, but people want and need to feel appreciated. Too often, organisations and organisational procedures focus on identifying mistakes, preventing repetition and making improvements. Important though that is, rewarding and publicising successes lifts spirits and improves morale.

Summary

In his book *Let My People Go Surfing: The Education of a Reluctant Businessman*, in which he describes the birth and growth of his retail company, Patagonia, Yvon Chouinard (2006, p. 168) says:

> Leaders take risks, have long-term vision, create the strategic plans, and instigate change.

He goes on to say:

> The key to confronting and truly solving any problem is to continue to ask enough questions to get past all the symptoms and reach the actual cause, a form of the Socratic method or what Toyota management calls asking the "five whys."
>
> (ibid., p. 172)

Chouinard concludes his chapter on his management philosophy by maintaining that:

> every organisation, business, government, or religion must be adaptive and resilient and constantly embrace new ideas and methods of operation. (ibid., p. 173)

Yvon Chouinard succinctly summarises the leadership lessons that have emerged during the analysis of the way that the NHS has faced the crisis of the COVID pandemic. The NHS, its leaders, the government and the British public should heed these words if they want the NHS to continue to be the iconic organisation that was so spectacularly founded in 1948 and was so central to the UK's success in fighting the COVID pandemic in 2020–2021. But so, too, should every organisation. That the NHS has been able to respond to the challenge of the COVID crisis has not been down to careful pre-planning, to smart systems and to inspirational leadership at the top. It has been because of the three following fundamental aspects.

- First, that the people who deliver the service to the patients are dedicated, talented and passionate about what they do and individually and collectively they rose the occasion, helped and supported by leadership at the local level.
- Second, many of the bureaucratic systems that have been put in place over the years were simply swept aside to ensure that care was provided as needed.
- Third, a great deal of what has habitually been delivered by the NHS was simply put on hold. It was a case of all hands to the pumps to fight COVID and almost everyone else had to wait.

There are certainly lessons to be learned from this: get great people and give them the freedom to deliver their objectives, make sure that all processes and procedures add value and help those great people, and ensure that delivery is focused on the key aspect of the business. Finally, ensure that the *'Why?'* and the *'How?'* are absolutely clear to everyone in the business – before focusing on the *'What?'*.

Notes

1 Nigel Crisp is a former Permanent Secretary in the UK Department of Health who was CEO of the English NHS between 2000 and 2006. He was made a Life Peer in the UK House of Lords in 2006 where he co-chairs the Al-Party Parliamentary Group on Global Health.
2 The Poor Laws were first introduced in 1349 (ironically, given the circumstances!) in response to the Black Death in England. Updated in 1601 and 1834, they were designed to provide a framework for support to the poor in each parish.
3 There are different charging systems for prescriptions across the four home nations.
4 Figures for 2020–2021 had not been confirmed at time of writing, but the estimate is based on the House of Commons Briefing Paper CBP 0724 dated 17 Jan 2019. NHS Funding and Expenditure.
5 At time of writing (29 November 2021), deaths within 28 days of a positive COVID-19 test were approaching 145,000; deaths with COVID-19 on the death certificate was marginally under 168,000.

References

Books

Beveredge, W. *Social Insurance and Allied Services (Cmd. 6404) (commonly known as the Beveridge Report)*. HMG, London. November 1942
Chouinard, Y. *Let My People Go Surfing. The Education of a Reluctant Businessman* (2nd Edition). Portfolio Penguin, New York. 2016
Crisp, N. *Health is Made at Home Hospitals Are for Repairs*. Salus, Billericay. 2020
Esler, G. *Lessons from the Top*. Profile, London. 2012
Goleman, Daniel. *Emotional Intelligence. Why it Matters More Than IQ*. Bloomsbury, London. 1996
Goleman, D, Boyatzis, R, & McKee, A. *Primal Leadership – Unleashing the Power of Emotional Intelligence*. HBR Press, Boston, MA. 2013
Kline, N. *Time to Think. Listening to Ignite the Human Mind*. Cassell, London. 1999
Moore, B. *The Dawn of the Health Age*. St Thomas Hospital, London. 1910. Report Volume 44. Reprinted 2019 by Forgotten Books, London
Northouse, P.G. *Leadership: Theory and Practice* (3rd Edition). Sage Publications Ltd, London. 2004
Sinek, S. *Start with Why*. Portfolio Penguin, New York. 2009

Articles

Howes, B. *A Primer for Resilience & Leadership Through the Coronavirus Pandemic*. 4 May 2020

Interviews (comments from the questionnaires and interviews occur throughout this chapter)

Cairns, Hannah. *Head of SMART Services*. NHS Lothian. 17 February 2021.
Hollington, James. *Lead Cliniscal Scientist, SMART Services*. NHS Lothian. 26 February 2021
Madhavan, Dr Pradeep. *Clinical Director Trauma and Orthopaedics and Ophthalmology*. Musgrove Park Hospital, Taunton. 10 March 2021
Marshall, Dr Martin. *Chairman*. Royal College of General Practitioners. 15 February 2021
Sadler, Lisa. *Senior Sister, Mixed COVID-19 and Medical Ward*. University College Hospital Trust, London. 19 March 2021
Subramanian, Dr Ashok. *Consultant Trauma & Orthopaedic Spine Surgeon*. Musgrove Park Hospital, Taunton. 17 March 2021
Williams, Debbie. *Advanced Clinical Practitioner*. University College Hospital Trust, London. 10 March 2021

Online Resources

Campbell, D. The guardian online. UK needs £102bn boost to NHS and social care. 6 March 2021. www.theguardian.com/society/2021/may/06/uk-needs-102bn-boost-to-nhs-and-social-care-says-major-report?utm_term=a57071096594209a03755ae2d17720fd&utm_campaign=GuardianTodayUK&utm_source=esp&utm_medium=Email&CMP=GTUK_email

Campbell, D. Record A&E waits show NHS is cracking under pressure. 12 December 2014. www.theguardian.com/society/2014/dec/12/nhs-crisis-record-patients-wait-more-four-hours-a-and-e

Cooper, C. Exclusive: NHS faces financial disaster in 2015 as politicians urged to find radical solution. The Independent Online. 15 April 2014. https://www.independent.co.uk/life-style/health-and-families/health-news/exclusive-nhs-faces-financial-disaster-in-2015-as-politicians-urged-to-find-radical-solution-9259915.html

CEMS Guide: Leadership in a post-COVID-19 world C EMS. December 2020. https://cems.app.box.com/s/6f72wtplz476t9sfc07r93ujd52kfiri

Donnelly, L. NHS faces biggest financial crisis 'in a generation', Telegraph Online. 9 October 2015. https://www.telegraph.co.uk/news/nhs/11921381/NHS-faces-biggest-financial-crisis-in-a-generation.html

Ferguson et al. (On behalf of the Imperial College COVID-19 Response Team). *Impact of non-pharmaceutical interventions (NPIs) to reduce COVID19 mortality and healthcare demand.* 16 March 2020; https://spiral.imperial.ac.uk/bitstream/10044/1/77482/14/2020-03-16-COVID19-Report-9.pdf

Fisher, Dr R. Today's figures highlight that the NHS in England is desperately struggling to stay afloat. *Health Foundation.* 14 November 2019. www.health.org.uk/news-and-comment/news/desperately-struggling-to-stay-afloat

Healthcare Leadership Model The nine dimensions of leadership behaviour NHS leadership academy. October 2013. www.leadershipacademy.nhs.uk/wp-content/uploads/2014/10/NHSLeadership-LeadershipModel-colour.pdf

Hinds, P. and Elliot, B. WFH doesn't have to dilute your corporate culture HBR. 1 February 2021. https://hbr-org.cdn.ampproject.org/c/s/hbr.org/amp/2021/02/wfh-doesnt-have-to-dilute-your-corporate-culture

Hougaard, R. Carter, Jacqueline and Hobson, Nick. Compassionate leadership is necessary – but not sufficient. 5 December 2020. https://hbr.org/2020/12/compassionate-leadership-is-necessary-but-not-sufficient?utm_medium=email&utm_source=newsletter_monthly&utm_campaign=leadership_not_activesubs&deliveryName=DM113690

Is the NHS crisis of our own making? NHS support federation. February 2021. https://nhsfunding.info/nhs-crisis-making/

ITV 12 March 2018 NHS under pressure: Crisis worse than last year, doctors warn. www.itv.com/news/2018-03-12/nhs-under-pressure-crisis-worse-than-last-year-doctors-warn

Langton, Dr P. Training industry. 5 Before 5: The importance of praise at work. 28 December 2018. https://trainingindustry.com/blog/performance-management/5-before-5-the-importance-of-praise-at-work/

Marone, M. Dale Carnegie. Why managers should praise their employees' good performance. 11 July 2020. www.dalecarnegie.com/blog/why-managers-should-celebrate-good-work/

Mitchell, G. Nursing Times clap for heroes: Nurses say they do not want return of applause. www.nursingtimes.net/news/coronavirus/clap-for-heroes-nurses-say-they-do-not-want-return-of-applause-07–01–2021/

Pa, L.M. Swine Flu could overwhelm the NHS says Health Secretary. Independent. 26 July 2009. https://www.independent.co.uk/life-style/health-and-families/health-news/swine-flu-could-overwhelm-nhs-says-health-secretary-5489417.html

Sinek, S. *Start with Why- how great leaders inspire action.* TED Talk. 29 September 2009, Pugot Sound USA https://www.youtube.com/watch?v=u4ZoJKF_VuA

Teuton, Paul. The secret of transformational leadership. 19 February 2021. www.prophet.com/2020/03/the-secret-to-transformational-leadership/

Training Journal. The power of praise and recognition. 18 February 2014. www.trainingjournal.com/articles/feature/power-praise-and-recognition

Triggle, N. and Jeavens, *The NHS Covid legacy – long waits and lives at risk BBC News Online*. 13 May 2021. https://www.bbc.co.uk/news/health-57092797

Zucker, R. and Rowell, D. 6 Strategies for leading through uncertainty. 26 April 2021. https://hbr.org/2021/04/6-strategies-for-leading-through-uncertainty?utm_medium=email&utm_source=newsletter_monthly&utm_campaign=leadership_not_activesubs&deliveryName=DM131180#

18 Leadership in Social Enterprises

Simon Hollington

***

One of the significant aspects of the 2020–2021 COVID pandemic has been the prevalence of comments in all media forms when discussing the socio-economic aspects of the crisis about the so-called new normal. Type 'new normal' into Google and the list is huge (about 2.430 billion in 0.59 seconds), though typing 'Leadership in the New Normal' brings the list down to a mere 560 million (Safari search, 2 December 2020). But what is new normal – indeed is it new – and what is its impact on leadership? This chapter will explore if and how leadership has (been forced to?) changed as a result of the COVID pandemic, specifically looking at the social housing sector in the UK. After first briefly exploring leadership, this chapter will explore the concept of the new normal as a backdrop before examining the changing leadership requirements, now and in the future.

Leadership

There is no universally accepted definition of leadership and many commentators choose not to define it. It is, however, safe to say that everyone, consciously or subconsciously, has a personal view of leadership. Northouse (2004)[1] identified the following four common themes in the way that leadership tends to be conceived.

- Leadership is a process.
- Leadership involves influence.
- Leadership occurs in a group context.
- Leadership involves goal achievement.

He defines leadership as a "process whereby an individual influences a group to achieve a common goal," while Daniel Goleman (1996) defines leadership stating that "it is not domination, but the art of persuading people to work towards a common goal" (p. 149). Goleman's definition, in my view, encapsulates the fundamental difficulty of leadership: it is an art and, as in the traditional world of art, what appeals to one person may not to the next. Leadership is in the eye of the receiver.

So, if leadership is persuading people to work towards a common goal, then how will leadership need to change to adapt to the new normal? It is, after all, difficult enough to lead in a group situation, but with the ever-changing face of work, how must leaders adapt to continue to influence their followers and what does that mean for the approach that they must adopt?

DOI: 10.4324/9781003171737-20

The pandemic has caused many – perhaps the majority – to change their operating models with online offerings soaring. As an example, John Lewis' online business rose from some 40% of its turnover in 2019 to 70% in 2020 (John Lewis Shop Online Report of 21 December 2020), while for some smaller retailers, online – at least for a time – became their only offering. Larger organisations have dispensed with call centres as staff have reverted to working from home (WFH) and offices have atrophied. But what has been intriguing has been the different leadership approaches at the national level to that displayed by many organisations. In the UK, government-supplied loans to support businesses were conditional on not paying bonuses or dividends, while the Canadian governmental support to its airline industry was conditional on buying Canadian and taking additional steps to tackle the industry's environmental impact. Both are examples of transactional leadership while, as will become apparent, the organisations in this case study display a remarkable degree of transformational leadership.

The New Normal?

Commentators have regularly used the word 'unprecedented' in an effort to describe the challenges that the pandemic has brought to the world, but at a macro level, the challenges are not unprecedented in scale. All governments, countries and communities are facing challenges and resultant questions that have been faced before, though admittedly the detail might be different. The pandemic has brought considerable uncertainty – How long will it last? What will be the impact on me/my friends/my family? What should my/our community's/our government's reaction be? – but these questions were all present during the 2008 financial crisis and during both world wars. It has been suggested that the level of complexity, both of the pandemic and the global supply chain, is unprecedented, as is the inter-connectedness of our current world, but I doubt that Winston Churchill and other leaders during the Second World War would agree. The pandemic has been fought against the backdrop of a US presidential election, Brexit and the global climate crisis, but former US President Barack Obama fought his successful 2008 election against the backdrop of the then–financial crisis and Winston Churchill's wartime coalition government had to face the challenges of the Luftwaffe and German U-Boats, the war in North Africa and latterly Europe, along with the war in the Far East, while at home they faced strikes by coal miners, dockers and bus drivers and conductors, with nearly four million working days lost in 1944 alone (TUC History Online, n.d.). The latter is something the UK government has not (at time of writing) had to deal with, despite trade union leaders expressing concern over the impact of lockdowns and restrictions. So, while the detail of the challenges are new, multiple complex interconnected ones are not. We may be in a VUCA (volatile, uncertain, changing and ambiguous) world, but, as those who lived through the last world war will surely testify, that is hardly new or unique. Interestingly, before COVID arrived in our consciousness, the then Chief of the Defence Staff (CDS), General Sir Nick Carter, said:

> I would suggest we are in a period of phenomenal change – more widespread, rapid and profound than humanity has experienced outside of world war. And it is more sustained than the two world wars of the last century combined – and it is still increasing. Our fundamental and long held assumptions are being disrupted on a daily basis.
>
> (RUSI, 5th December 2019)

But while WFH has for the first time been included in the 2020 *Oxford English Dictionary*, the concept of the new normal is certainly older. It can be traced back to the 1920s and was used more recently and extensively during both the avian flu crisis of 2005 and the financial crisis of 2008. It seems, therefore, that each period of significant change prompts the generation of the time to consider the impact of the new normal and either push back against it (as happened after the last world war when women were expected meekly to return home after working in factories) or to support the change as has happened with the call for racial equality after the death of George Floyd in Minneapolis on 25 May 2020. What perhaps is different to previous global crises is the degree of inter-connectedness in our current world, with technological advances allowing and encouraging organisations to adopt different working patterns (i.e., WFH) and to extend existing working patters such as flexible working patterns to a much greater extent.

So, what is the new normal and how, in post-pandemic (2023–2024?), might it differ from pre-pandemic 2019? The most obvious manifestation will be the prevalence of WFH, with Zoom, Microsoft Teams and similar technological offerings replacing office face-to-face meetings. For some organisations, WFH has been forced upon them by lockdowns, but others proactively adopted WFH as they anticipated the impact of the pandemic. As an example of the latter, Warner Music announced on 12 March 2020 that, worldwide, remote working would start on 16 March and mandatory WFH would start on 18 March. That was before the first lockdown was announced in the UK and before the then-US President Donald Trump announced his ban on flights from Europe. Despite the shock to many employees and contractors, there would appear to have been little diminishment of output or effectiveness in the short term and, apart from apparent virtual meeting overload, no long-term negative impact. In fact, Warner Music has saved significant travel and accommodation costs and, as office leases come up for renewal, can expect more savings in the future.

Some leaders will see WFH as a benefit, but for others, it comes with complications. In discussion with Richard Spencer (CEO of The Royal Marines Association – 30 October 2020), he mentioned that previous, brief, in-office conversations were now taking much longer and needed to be diarised, thus extending his working day, a sentiment confirmed by Jamie Saunderson (discussions, 4 December 2020), the Creative Director of X For Why? Design Consultancy. The latter suggested that in his ideal world, he would be in the office for a third of his time and WFH for the remainder. He also agreed with Richard that his diary was filled with virtual meetings, meetings that previously had occurred in a more spontaneous way "at the moment." Such diary filling might diminish as organisations and employees become more used to and adept at WFH, but at time of writing, that appears not yet to be the case. So, it appears that the future new normal will consist of a mix of WFH, remote working, office hot desking and flexible office/business location working. Full offices seem to have been consigned to history, as indeed has the concept that office size, location and grandeur is a measure of organisational success.

Although some organisations have been able to revert almost entirely to WFH, those organisations that have a personal interface with their clients have not been able to do so to the same extent. Some have looked to introduce more flexible working, while those with little or no direct customer contact (online retailers, delivery firms and financial organisations) appear to have introduced more digital barriers such as virtual assistants that seem designed to limit customer contact even more. That being the case, what are the implications for leadership?

Leadership in Social Housing

In examining leadership in social enterprises, I drew heavily on contacts within two social housing organisations: Wythenshawe Community Housing Group (WCHG) and Orbit Group. The former is a relatively small organisations (circa 530 employees) and is firmly centred on Wythenshawe, a small but deprived area of south Manchester. The latter operates across the Midlands, East and South East of England, and has some 1,200 employees. Orbit is therefore larger in terms of employees, but it is significantly larger in terms of turnover (£323 million compared to £64 million in 2019–2020), fixed assets (£2.7 billion compared to £353 million), and properties (42,000 compared to 14,000). However, while both organisations face similar leadership challenges, Orbit's leaders have the additional challenge of geographical spread unlike WCHG, which is concentrated in a relatively small area.

The social housing sector is not merely concerned with providing affordable housing. Social housing organisations regenerate areas, build communities, provide financial and well-being advice, and build, sell and rent houses, all the while being required to run effective and profitable businesses. They are on the receiving end of government policy and policy changes, are regularly caught up in local and national politics and yet, are the point of contact and complaint for their clients. They are landlords and estate agents, house builders and renovators, educators and social workers, environmentalists and agony aunts. Above all, their employees are passionate and dedicated and are driven by a deep sense of social justice.

If their talents are to be released, effective leadership of such employees is not – and cannot be – a transaction. Each employee will have a different perspective of the key aspects of their organisation's vision and a different view of the leadership required to achieve that vision. Added to that is the challenge that while some of their employees (call centre staff, support staff and similar) can WFH, there are others (gardeners, repair and maintenance team members) who cannot. So, leaders are faced with the challenge of leading remote and sometimes isolated employees with their individual challenges and anxieties, while also leading those who remain at the coalface, with different challenges and anxieties.

How therefore should leaders respond? Needless to say, there is plenty of advice available. On 26 June 2020, The *Harvard Business Review* article "Will the Pandemic reshape notions of female leadership?" suggested (p. 5) that: "Society at large may become less surprised and more accepting of leader(s) elected on their expertise, intelligence, curiosity, humility, empathy, and integrity," while only five days later, it published another article by Faigen, Wallach and Walendh (2020) that advised leaders to "Look to Military Leadership for Lessons in Crisis Leadership." In it, the authors suggest that leaders should:

- Be decisive.
- Be in the trenches.
- Be agile.
- Lead with confidence.
- Communicate to inspire.
- Move leaders and tasks rapidly.
- Rest the troops.

So much advice, and so much of it apparently conflicting.

The collective wisdom on leadership in the social housing sector came first from questionnaires sent to contacts in both WCHG and Orbit, and then follow-up conversations. My contacts were open and honest about the challenges that they have faced over the last year (early 2020–early 2021) and the lessons they have learnt. Their collective thoughts suggest that leaders should focus on a number of key aspects:

- Think very carefully about your leadership message.
- Create the environment and ensure that policies both support and embed that environment.

- Manage customer expectations and demands.
- Recognise and adapt to the challenge of leading remote workers.
- Look after yourself by carving out 'me time'.
- Consciously build relationships.
- Flex your leadership style – consciously – to meet the situation and people requirement.
- Prepare for the future – act when the storm clouds gather, not when the rain starts to fall.

The Leadership Message

Speaking at length to both Mark Hoyland (CEO of Orbit Group) and Nick Horne (CEO of WCHG), I was struck by how similar their views were, particularly around communications. Both stressed the need for a clear message about priorities during the crisis and both stressed that there was absolutely no change in their organisational visions.[2] Reacting to the crisis, Nick pushed the message 'work is what you do, not where you are', a point he reinforced regularly with his leaders and managers. Initially, this caused concern as a number of his managers were intent on ensuring that remote and WFH employees continued to work in a similar way to the way that they had worked when they were in the office, thus making oversight easier. But, by continuing to push his message about output rather than location, Nick Horne is confident that there has been no diminishment in the service that WCHG provides its clients. Realising that some members of his team were concerned about the viability of WCHG, he shared fully the financial position of the organisation so that everyone could see that it was financially secure.

Mark Hoyland took the decision, in a change from his normal style, to send out a whole-company message and speak directly to all of his staff, rather than rely of his usual chain of command. On 10 March 2020, 13 days before Prime Minister Boris Johnson announced the first UK-wide lockdown, Mark announced to the whole of Orbit that he had three priorities: to protect clients, to protect Orbit employees and to protect Orbit's finances. To protect finances, he was freezing recruitment. He subsequently also increased liquidity and banking facilities. At time of writing had not had to resort to their use, but, he added, there would be no redundancies and no-one would be put onto furlough. The result in Orbit was increased commitment. Mark received a number of unsolicited letters of appreciation from employees and that additional commitment from employees has, in part, resulted in a number of national awards. Orbit rose from No. 77 in 2019 to No. 46 in 2020 in the Times Best Companies list, its customer engagement platform won the Delegate's Choice Award at the National Housing Maintenance Forum Conference in January 2021 and Orbit was awarded the Royal Society for the Prevention of Accidents (RoSPA) Gold Award for Health and Safety, amongst other honours, while WCHG has been listed in the Certified Top Employers list for 2021 which recognises organisations "of the highest calibre who work hard to create, implement and progress their people strategies."

What is striking is that both leaders were clear in their expectations and they set boundaries. Both commented that this clarity helped to engender trust and confidence, which are key aspects of leadership. It was a point emphasised by Craig Wilcockson (Group Head of People and Strategy, Orbit Group) who said that more than ever, trust and integrity were absolute requirements in leadership. Without integrity, trust will not be engendered so relationships will not be built. Emma Jacobs in her article for *The Financial Times* "My wish list for the new normal after working from home" also commentated on the need for trust when she said: "I hope this experience has taught managers to trust their workers."

Corporate Culture

Trust and integrity are key to building a corporate culture. Leaders, like it or not, cast a shadow – and sadly, it is easier to inadvertently cast a negative shadow than a positive one. Our followers will, consciously or unconsciously, be aware of our actions, our tone of voice, our body language and our reactions to events. So, as leaders, we make or break the culture we espouse. As US President Joe Biden said on 21 January 2021 when he swore in around 1,000 appointed political aides during a virtual ceremony from The White House State Dining Room:

> I am not joking when I say this. If you're ever working with me and I hear you treat another colleague with disrespect or talk down to someone, I promise you I will fire you on the spot – on the spot. No ifs and buts. Everyone is entitled to be treated with decency and dignity.

In saying so, he set out his expectations for the culture that he expects to pervade The White House for the next four years, a culture that, by all accounts, will be very different from the culture set by his predecessor. It behoves leaders to provide absolute clarity about the culture of their organisation or department. Unless leaders are clear about their expectations, they cannot expect their followers to meet them.

But there is more to corporate culture than words in an annual report or on notice boards. Everything – from recruitment to departure, from appraisals to bonuses – must add value to that culture. In the words of Paul Richards (Group Director of Customer and Communities, Orbit Group), "we must ensure that policies and procedures are not *office centric*".

Managing Customer Expectations

The two aspects around expectations and culture are simply the starting gate for leaders within an organisation, but they also apply externally. Both Nick Horne and Mark Hoyland spoke about the challenge of managing customer expectations and demands. The COVID pandemic has led Orbit to close some of its offices and led, at least initially, to some customer disgruntlement. However, Orbit customer satisfaction improved in 2020, a testament to both the efforts that employees took to keep in touch with their customers and to some technological innovations. It took staff a great deal of extra effort to maintain those relationships, as they had to replace face-to-face interactions with voice and video calls. Face-to-face conversations provide valuable bring customer intelligence and this intelligence is hard to maintain when meetings are not possible. As Nick said, a couple of hours in Wythenshawe market (where some 30% of the market traders were clients) provided him with a real first-hand feel for WCHG's customer performance. Conversely, Louise Palese (Director of Customer Services, Orbit) maintains that it is not possible to have really informed conversations via technology, so has instituted walking conversations. These are simply catch up one-to-one sessions with her team, whereby both parties speak while out for a walk; Louise maintains that the atmosphere and environment created by walking gave her greater insight into her team members' states.

Leading Remote Workers

With employees WFH, leaders need to recognise and adapt to the challenge of leading remote workers. WFH will be a bigger challenge for some employees than the regularity of working in an office, but it will be an opportunity for others. Nick mentioned that his rent team manager asked to work permanently from home and from Nick's perspective, the manager's performance was better than ever. He then mentioned that the manager's home was in Galway, Éire; not just WFH in Wythenshawe but in a different country. But, Nick added, in the early days of the pandemic, there was considerable fear around: fear of going into the office; fear of going into houses to carry out repairs; fear of the organisation going bust; and fear of the outside world (WCHG is close to Manchester International Airport, where many of WCHG's clients work). Added to that there were personal anxieties around family members who were vulnerable and there has also been the considerable challenge of home schooling. These different personal fears and anxieties are exacerbated when people cannot more easily share them with friends and colleagues, so Nick instituted weekly team 'walks in the park'. These were so that teams could get together, bring spouses, partners, children and dogs, and – appropriately socially distanced – gave teams an opportunity to catch up. There were no rules on how long they were to take and no rules on discussions but, importantly, they were counted as work time. It is, he said, all about flexibility, a point reiterated by Paul Richards. It is important, Paul said, to recognise that some of his team had thrived by WFH, while others had not.

Look After Yourself

Paul also mentioned that he had started a new regime at the beginning of 2021 by consciously taking a lunch break and going for a walk. In his words, he needed "me time". Previously, he got that (and thinking time) during his 45–60 minute daily commute into the office, but he realised that he was missing that in 2020 while WFH. He has stressed to all members of his team that 'me time' is vital, but that it is not fixed to the traditional lunch time. For some, it might be a run after dropping children at school, but for others challenged by childcare at home, it might be in the evening. Flexibility is the key, and leaders need to recognise and adapt to whatever works best for the individuals – and for themselves.

Consciously Build Relationships

New normal will be very different for leaders than the normal pre-pandemic, but building relationships – both internal and external – will remain as important as it ever was, even if some of the social conventions might have changed. Jamie Saunderson maintains:

> The barriers have gone from client relationships. Instead of meeting across a table in a formal setting with client barriers in place (table, name badges, seating positions, etc.), conversations now occur with clients in their home, study and bedroom, where the barriers of corporate life have been replaced by background noise, children, dogs and cats. So relationships have become much more personal. It feels to me that both parties have benefitted from this change. We have found, though, that there can be a need to bring the conversation round to corporate matters, rather than, as before, trying to humanise conversations.

So, it appears that while it might take greater – or at least a conscious – effort to build relationships with employees WFH, leaders should be able to establish those relationships more easily at a deeper and more personal level, instead of simply allowing those relationships to develop gradually over time through contact in the office. Individual conversations at work are more likely to be constrained by the corporate culture and office atmosphere, aspects that will be missing in a FaceTime or 1–2–1 Zoom conversation. There is, however, one aspect of building relationships via technology that needs leaders' conscious attention: that of new employees. Paul Richards spoke of the son of close friends who had joined a global telecommunications organisation in August 2020. Five months later, when Paul and I spoke, the son had not yet met any of his colleagues and had not gone into the organisation's head office. Moreover, he was unlikely to do so until the summer of 2021 at the earliest. Building relationships with new employees, ensuring that they both understand and adapt to the organisational culture and confirming that they explicitly understand their leaders' expectations, will require leaders and organisations to examine critically their corporate induction schemes to ensure they are fit for purpose in the new normal.

Flex and Adapt Your Leadership Styles

All of this requires leaders, consciously, to know and adapt their style to the situation and their team members more than ever before, and to place greater emphasis on checking on the well-being of their team members. As Louise Palese said in her completed questionnaire:

> I need to focus more on communication and collaboration as we move to a more agile environment, and I need to increase my (digital) engagement when I am more used to meeting face-to-face.

As well as her walking meetings, Louise has instituted well-being meetings just to touch base with her immediate team and says that one of her challenges going forward is to approach the future with an "agile mindset." But perhaps the greatest challenge to those who are leaders is to change their approach. Those appointed to new leadership roles in 2022 and beyond will not be facing a 'new' normal. To them, it will simply be normal. But those who have been used to the pre-pandemic situation (offices, group meeting all in one room, private 1–2–1 conversations and chats in the office kitchen) could well face the painful task of reinventing (at worst) or adapting (at best) their leadership style.

Knowing themselves, their predominant leadership style and the impact of that style is a prerequisite for leaders, but it is only the starting point. As leaders, we need to be able to recognise our inner drives – those impulses that cause us to react to situations, to build relationships, and the desire to succeed. Tony Robbins, the American coach and motivator first presented his 'Six Human Needs' at the TED Conference in February 2006. All humans, he postulates, have four personality needs (certainty, uncertainty/variety, significance and love/connection), and two spiritual needs (growth and contribution). But, while we all share these needs, the unconscious rules we apply to get these needs fulfilled are shaped by our experiences, so while one leader might get their significance simply by being the leader, another might get their significance by developing others. One person might get their love/connection from family and friends, another might get it through membership of sports teams or clubs, and so on. The importance of these needs and why it is vital for leaders to recognise them, is that pre-pandemic, many employees would have all of these needs fulfilled at work: the certainty of the routine and the same office, but the variety of the tasks and customer interactions; the connection with colleagues and the significance from being the longest-serving person in the team; the challenge of the difficult task or learning a new skill and the contribution to helping a customer sort out debt or get their boiler fixed. All these needs are certainly met – and some – in the social housing sector.

But the pandemic and resulting WFH has changed the provision of those needs for many. Those driven by certainty will have found the unknown future a particularly worrying phenomena, so Nick Horne's decision to share WCHG's financials and Mark Hoyland's confirmation of no redundancies will have been very reassuring and met their need for certainty. But those who have a strong drive for variety are likely to have found WFH energy draining, as Paul Richards discovered. Those with a strong drive for love/connection could well have felt isolated by WFH. Those with a need for significance might have felt downbeat or out of the loop when not in the office. What Jamie Saunderson found was that while some of his team thrived while WFH, there were others for whom the office had been a lifeline. There is plenty of anecdotal evidence that the pandemic has had a great impact on employees' personality needs – hence, the fears and anxieties experienced in Orbit and WCHG – while the mental health impact of the pandemic has yet to be fully understood.

The impact of these human needs on leaders and leadership is explicit. A vital part of a leader's role and responsibilities is to create the environment that lets their team flourish and fully utilise their talents and potential. It is, as Simon Sinek (TED Conference 2014) would contend, "to create a circle of safety in which everyone knows and feels that they are protected," thus allowing them to focus all their energy and enthusiasm on their customers. Leaders must – if they are to be effective – provide both certainty and variety; allow for connection (well-being calls and walks in the park); recognise and publicly acknowledge tasks well done (hence meeting significance needs); find ways to challenge employees, thereby promoting individual and team growth; and emphasise the continued contribution to clients and communities. And here is the rub: if leaders are to create that environment and those conditions, they need those needs fulfilled for themselves so that they can play at the top of their game. To do so, they might need to rewrite some of their own unconscious rules.

Prepare for the Future

There is one final aspect from this research that leaders need to consider; they need to look forward rather than being immersed in the present. When Mark Hoyland joined Orbit in March 2017, there was no incident management process in place. It took some ten months to be fully introduced, though it was tested in the June of that year after the Grenfell Tower fire and refined thereafter. Since the pandemic hit in late February 2020, Orbit's incident management process has been continually tested, with three different cross-functional groups meeting as appropriate both to consider and act upon the different twists and turns of the pandemic and react to governmental and local authority decisions. The group most appropriate to the situation and subsequent impact has been charged with deciding what, if any, action is needed in Orbit. So far, the Orbit process has proved up to the task. As Paul Richards said, "Leadership is preparing the organisation in advance so that it is ready for the unknown."

Summary

From the research for this chapter, and particularly from the in-depth conversations that I have had with those in WCHG and Orbit, one clear leadership responsibility emerges: to lead consciously.

- *Consciously* consider your leadership message and consciously consider how best to communicate it.
- *Consciously* build, maintain and demand a corporate culture that supports the organisational vision and ensures that all policies are designed to support that culture.

- *Consciously* manage customer demands and expectations.
- *Consciously* consider the opportunities and the challenges of those WFH and those still in the office or the front line.
- *Consciously* carve out time to look after yourself.
- *Consciously* consider how best to develop internal and external relationships.
- *Consciously* recognise your own natural or preferred leadership style and consciously seek out and learn how to adapt and flex your style to suit different groups of people and situations.
- And finally, *consciously* prepare your organisation, your team and yourself to meet the unknown and the unexpected.

Notes

1 Northouse, P. G. (2004) *Leadership: Theory and Practice* (3rd ed., p. 3). London: Sage Publications Ltd. Quoted in Bolden, R. (2004) *What Is Leadership? Leadership South West Research Report 1* (p. 5). Exeter: Exeter University.
2 Orbit Group's vision is: "building thriving communities," while that of WCHG is "creating communities where people choose to live and work, having pride in their homes and services."

References

Books

Goleman, Daniel. *Emotional Intelligence. Why it Matters More Than IQ*. London: Bloomsbury. 1996
Northouse, P.G. *Leadership: Theory and Practice* (3rd Edition). London: Sage Publications Ltd. 2004

Articles

Fatania,Tejal. 'Workinginthenewnormal:Thefutureishereandthereisnogoingback.'*CMI*.24August2020. https://managers.org.uk/knowledge-and-insights/blog/working-in-the-new-normal-the-future-is-here-there-is-no-going-back/
Jacobs, Emma. 'My wish list for the new normal after working from home.' *The Financial Times*. 29 December 2020 www.ft.com/content/0974c953-e422-4586-818e-2063c0493af7
Feigen, M., Wallach, B., and Warendh, A. 'Look to military history for lessons in crisis leadership.' *Harvard Business Review*. 1 July 2020. https://hbr.org/2020/07/look-to-military-history-for-lessons-in-crisis-leadership
McWilliams, Douglas. 'Working from home completely will NOT be the new normal: Schools reopening will get parents back to their desks but at least half will mix home and office.' *This is Money*. 7 September 2020. https://thisismoney.co.uk/money/news/article-8706773/schools-opening-tipped-kick-start-return-office.html
'Why remote working will be the new normal, even after COVID-19.' *EY Belgium*. September 2020. www.ey.com/en_be/covid-19/why-remote-working-will-be-the-new-normal-even-after-covid-19
Chamorro-Premuzic, T., and Wittenberg-Cox, A. 'Will the Pandemic reshape notions of female leadership?' *Harvard Business Review*. 26 June 2020. https://hbr.org/2020/06/will-the-pandemic-reshape-notions-of-female-leadership

Online Resources

'I'll fire you on the spot': Biden tells staff to treat others with respect. CNN online 20 January 2021. https://edition.cnn.com/videos/politics/2021/01/20/joe-biden-white-house-staff-swearing-in-treat-people-with-respect-inauguration-sot-vpx.cnn

John Lewis Shop Live Look Report 2020. https://www.johnlewispartnership.co.uk/content/dam/cws/pdfs/Juniper/JohnLewis/John-Lewis-Shop-Live-Look-Report-2020.pdf

Revealed: Top UK and Ireland Employers for 2021. Phil Sproston, Regional Manager (UK & Ireland) – Top Employers Institute. 25 January 2021. https://www.thehrdirector.com/business-news/branding-communication/revealed-top-uk-and-ireland-employers-for-2021/

TUC History Online – The labour movement in World War Two. www.unionhistory.info/timeline/1939_1945.php

'Why good leaders make you feel safe.' Simon Sinek. TED Conference 2014. Vancouver, British Columbia. 21st March 2014. "The Next Chapter." www.google.com/search?q=%E2%80%9CWhy+good+leaders+make+you+feel+safe.%E2%80%9D+Simon+Sinek.&rlz=1C1GCEA_enGB893GB893&oq=%E2%80%9CWhy+good+leaders+make+you+feel+safe.%E2%80%9D+Simon+Sinek.&aqs=chrome..69i57j0i22i3014j0i10i22i30j0i22i30j0i10i22i30.3591j0j4&sourceid=chrome&ie=UTF-8

'Why we do what we do.' Tony Robbins TED Conference 2006. Monterey California. 22–25 February 2006. "The Future we Will Create." www.ted.com/talks/tony_robbins_why_we_do_what_we_do?language=en

Interviews (comments from the questionnaires and interviews occur throughout this chapter)

Craig Wilcockson. Group People and Strategy Director, Orbit Group. 13 January 2021
Louise Palese. Director of Customer Services, Orbit Group. 1 February 2021
Mark Hoyland. CEO Orbit Group. 12 January 2021
Nick Horne. CEO Wythenshawe Community Housing Group. 22 December 2020
Paul Richards. Group Director, Customer Services, Orbit Group. 6 January 2021

19 The Modern Leader

A Focus on Wellbeing

Liam Hartley and Graham Wilson

***

Crises can cause extensive disturbance within both a company and peoples' lives. Crises often turn daily life on its head, with employees largely becoming demotivated, confused and increasingly anxious about the future. The focus on wellbeing is generally exacerbated in times of crisis due to the increased strains people are under as they continue to adjust to the ever-evolving situation. This chapter aims to highlight how leaders can promote wellbeing during a crisis in order to have a sustained impact on people's lives, written from the perspective of millennials who have been led through crises in the past and aim to lead others in the future.

Global interest in wellbeing and positive psychology (which focuses on societal and individual wellbeing) has exploded in the past forty years. The wellbeing industry, which is thought to be valued at $4.5 trillion in 2018 (5.3% of all global economic output),[1] has become omnipresent in society. As the wellbeing industry has grown, so too has the cost of poor mental health (£45 billion each year in the UK, a rise of 16% since 2016).[2] Many companies and leaders are aware of these costs and have sought ways to address them, to varying degrees of success. These efforts largely revolve around training employees on how to care for their wellbeing, and then providing them the tools to do so.

Due to the multifaceted and subjective nature of wellbeing, it can be difficult to pin-point how leaders can best address employee wellbeing and measure progress in addressing it. The challenge is made even more difficult as there is no 'one size fits all' when it comes to addressing wellbeing. But certain approaches to wellbeing have been seen to work on many, and it is these that we look to focus on.

The definition of wellbeing (the state of being 'comfortable, healthy and happy') leaves it wide open for various interpretations. We will explore two main vehicles through our millennial lens that leaders can utilise when addressing their employees' wellbeing: culture and communication. In discussing culture and communication, we will touch upon three different aspects of wellbeing: hedonism, eudaimonia and social wellbeing. Hedonism is the pursuit of pleasant feelings and pleasurable actions. Eudaimonia is associated with personal growth and a sense of meaning or belonging (such as an employee's role within a team or organisation), self-actualisation and the pursuit of becoming the best version of themselves. Finally, social wellbeing is associated with positive relationships and social integration. This is the social element of employees' lives that helps everyone feel connected to and supported by others. Leaders need to be aware of these three types of wellbeing to become better equipped to support employees during a crisis through their culture and communication.

DOI: 10.4324/9781003171737-21

Culture

The culture of a company consists of the foundational written and unwritten rules that underpin all interactions between employees. Some of the key facets of culture are the values, attitudes and behaviours that define a company and its people. It could be as simple as the unspoken understanding that it's OK to start a meeting five minutes late, which could be a deadly sin in another company. One of the authors once travelled to Amazon's London office, arriving fifteen minutes late. Within their team it was generally acceptable to arrive late to meetings, however, it quickly became apparent that this was a cultural sin within the time-efficient Amazon offices.

Culture and leadership are closely intertwined, and both permeate through all levels of an organisation. Leaders set the tone from the top and are vital in shaping an organisation's culture. Getting company culture right is fundamental to success; it goes without saying that a good culture can lead to a happier and more productive workforce. Building a positive culture is not simple, and it is even more difficult to maintain in the face of mounting pressures and anxieties. It is for this reason that it is so important for leaders to reinforce their culture in times of crisis. There are three key areas of company culture that leaders can focus on in order to improve their employees' wellbeing: social support, job control and organisational architecture.

Social Support

Leaders should first look to create a positive social environment inside the office, as well as providing social support when possible. A good culture is behind a strong sense of camaraderie, with teammates being willing to go the extra mile for one another during times of crisis. When company culture and personal values are closely aligned, culture can help employees conjure tremendous levels of energy to reach a shared purpose. This is most evident when you simply want to go the extra mile for your team – not because you necessarily have to. The author and their team at the time had to migrate to new cloud computing services whilst they continued to run a lot of old systems in parallel to keep the lights on. The positive team culture empowered the author to work overtime to resolve issues when these older systems gave way at critical times. Unfortunately, this culture can be a double edged-sword – as we feel a shared sense of purpose, we may naturally work longer, which can cause burnout to occur more often.[3] Jeff Bezos, founder of Amazon, describes the dogma of work–life balance more aptly as having work–life harmony (which he suggests implies less of a strict trade-off between work and life).[4] This harmony has become a key priority for millennials, perhaps more so than any generation before them. Culture is crucial for companies to get right when addressing employees' wellbeing, and building a sense of a supportive team is invaluable to this.

Employees can quickly become disengaged without any social support. No one enjoys going to work in a toxic office environment – not even an open bar or larger paycheques can lighten the mood. Some companies even use key performance indicators (KPIs) to publicly shame you if you're underperforming relative to your colleagues, which breeds toxicity. The author has a friend who previously worked for a large recruitment company in England. At this company, there were monthly emails which clearly highlighted which individual has made enough calls to hit their target and which individuals have not. This public show of humiliation didn't create a sense of teamwork, it created rivalries. A member of his team hadn't hit their numbers for the week and the manager insisted that the entire team would have to work late one Friday evening. My friend didn't feel strongly enough about his team to stick his neck out for them, so instead left early. KPIs should encourage teamwork by setting team level objectives, whilst personal development plans should be reserved for private conversations between managers and employees. When targets are missed, conversations should be more open in understanding the cause of this, particularly during crises. This allows whole teams to self-actualise and become their best selves.

In many cases, leaders also address some of their employees' most basic social needs. Financial wellbeing is even more fundamental than our sense of belonging; we need money to obtain food and shelter in order to survive. COVID has shown how fragile and quickly this financial security can be taken away from many. It was normal to hear stories of people being furloughed, or even let go as companies struggled to pay salaries. A study of small UK companies found that more than half of employers worry about their employees' financial health, and that 90 percent of employers agree that financial concerns have an impact on employees' work performance. However, many employees also felt that their finances were a personal matter, not to be discussed at work.[5] How leaders and employers tackle their employees' financial security can vary quite significantly depending on the size and resources of the firm. Whilst employers may not always be able to raise pay universally for their employees, there are alternative solutions. Offering financial advice sessions, one-off contingency cheques or simply showing colleagues where to find further information has been commonplace. Those who utilise the services will reap the benefits and help partially relieve the burden of financial stress.

Job Control

Second, how much control and freedom an employee has in their work is closely linked to their wellbeing. Extensive research in this area has shown that job control has a statistically significant effect on the mental wellbeing of employees. One study of Swedish white-collar workers who had undergone a change in their roles found that those who had a higher level of influence and task control in the reorganisation process had lower levels of illness symptoms overall and experienced less depression. A similar study of individuals in the United States also highlighted the relationship between lack of job control and poor mental health.[6] Job control plays an integral role in an employee's wellbeing – and during a crisis, when much seems out of our control as our environment changes rapidly, this becomes ever more important.

Leaders must trust their employees in order to give them more job control. However, in times of crisis, trust can be harder to come by as many people feel safest when they have complete control. Another situation that affects trust and is rather unique to COVID is the scale and pervasiveness of working from home. As more of the world began to work from home during the COVID pandemic, sales of surveillance software used to monitor users' every action increased dramatically.[7] This is the exact opposite of what leaders must do in a time of crisis; they must trust that their employees genuinely want to do their jobs, and that is why they are there. Any reduction in productivity should be questioned with an open mind, as everyone will handle a crisis differently.

A common symptom of distrust between leaders and their employees is micro-management, which can destroy team morale and productivity very quickly.[8] One of the authors has previously worked for a team which was functioning incredibly well, independent of a formal line manager. Unfortunately, the team was assigned a new line manager who aggressively micro-managed. The team went from having to deliver daily updates to our stakeholders to updating the manager and stakeholders three times a day. It went from being a customer-focussed team to a boss-focussed team. Team morale plummeted and so too did productivity. We spend much of our lives at our jobs, and no one wants to give that much time to a job that refuses to let them think or work for themselves in any capacity. This is commonplace for when a leader takes on an environment that is rapidly changing, when things start to feel out of our control we desperately hold them tighter. As difficult as it may be, leaders should relinquish some of this control rather than harbour it so as to benefit not only the wellbeing of the employees but also the wider team.

Generally, it is the most junior employees who suffer the most from this tightening of control by leaders, crisis or not. Studies have found that junior employees feel more stressed at work than their senior counterparts, and this is largely due to the feeling of loss of control. For more junior jobs, the role is very much a 'doing' one and these junior employees largely have little control over what they do and when. A recent UK survey has shown that, on a weekly basis, 31% of 25–34-year-olds experience work-related stress, followed by 18–24-year-olds coming in a close second (27%) and lastly 18% of those 55 and older.[9] Overall, the figures for experiencing work stress on a weekly basis is common across the board. For this reason, there needs to be an emphasis not only on tone from the top by leaders, but also an understanding from middle management as to how this focus on wellbeing can be disseminated to help foster a positive culture of wellbeing.

Organisational Architecture

The third way to facilitate a culture of wellbeing is to have sound organisational architecture. Company culture is powerfully influenced by the organisational architecture and leadership behaviours. Mis-alignments between leadership roles and the overall strategy of a company can have detrimental consequences.

These consequences can clearly be seen during the Space Shuttle *Challenger* disaster. In 1986, seven astronauts boarded the *Challenger* on an unusually cold morning in Florida. Their mission was to deploy new satellites, as well as to lift the collective spirit of the United States during the Cold War. As the *Challenger* began its ascent into space, the entire vehicle burst into a giant fireball, killing all seven of the astronauts immediately. Even more shocking than the disaster itself was the revelation that engineers contracted to work on this job recommended that the managers of the programme postpone the launch because of concerns about critical components operating in such cold conditions.

The overly bureaucratic 'readiness review process' consisted of four levels of approvals; the first approval was 'level four readiness decisions' that came from the contracted engineers, and the final approval was 'level one readiness' from mission management. The contracted Thiokol engineers at the bottom of the decision tree (level four) raised concerns with US National Aeronautics and Space Administration (NASA) managers (level three) about the low temperatures the night before the launch, and recommended that the flight be postponed.

The pressure placed on NASA by the US federal government to launch (in order to secure more funding) was so intense that no one wanted to report a critical issue so early in the decision making process – NASA's managers felt more accountable to their respective centre of management than to the shuttle programme as a whole. In jobs where lives are at risk, safety is paramount and should never be sacrificed or stretched to meet the demands of a stakeholder. A commission's report mandated by then-US President Ronald Reagan after the disaster led to significant organisational restructuring to increase accountability and safety.

Research has shown that organisational structures affect employees' overall wellbeing.[10] Therefore, it is essential that leaders ensure that organisational hierarchies and decision processes are designed to improve lines of communication. Ineffective lines of communication pose the risks of inefficiencies in processes which can compromise employees' safety and wellbeing, leading to an increased risk of burnout.

Burnout

One of the authors was completely exhausted at work. They found themselves constantly checking the time and the latest BBC news headlines as they felt completely mentally drained after a very difficult quarter at work during the first British lockdown of 2021. That wasn't just a stressful day – that was the early sign of burnout.

Stress and burnout are different; the vast majority of people will face stress at work in the form of long hours or making highly pressurised decisions. However, not everyone who is stressed succumbs to burnout. The World Health Organisation (WHO) classifies burnout as an occupational phenomenon which is "a syndrome conceptualized as resulting from chronic workplace stress that has not been successfully managed."[11] It is generally thought that there are six key drivers of burnout; workload, control, reward, community, fairness and values. Burnout isn't a single-event phenomenon, but more the result of a plethora of increasing pressures that build to an intolerable level. As this experience becomes more and more uncomfortable, employees may start to experience some of the common symptoms of burnout. These symptoms can be as minor as a lack of motivation or feelings of cynicism and frustration, but severe cases of burnout can lead to complete physical exhaustion.

Several high-profile business leaders in high-pressure jobs have taken time off as a result of difficult working conditions. The inspirational Arianna Huffington (founder of the successful media platform The Huffington Post) collapsed from exhaustion within two years of founding her company. Her doctor told her that there were no obvious signs of illness, but that she was suffering from 'civilizations disease' (burnout) after attempting to look after her two children and her company. She had succumbed to the ideas spread by phrases like "I'll sleep when I'm dead" and had completely forgotten about herself during her quest for greatness. The lack of productivity brought about by burnout through excessive stress and sick days is estimated to cost the world approximately £255 billion.[12] Burnt-out employees are also 63% more likely to take a sick day, and almost three times as likely to be seeking out a different job.[13] So looking out for our team's health isn't just the morally correct thing to do; it is also the correct strategic move for businesses.

Companies have created policies in attempts to address burnout in employees, but these haven't always been successful. A study of hours worked by junior bankers pre- and post-implementation of the companies' 'protected weekend' policy revealed that although they no longer worked as long on weekends, hours worked during the week increased to compensate. This shows the difficulty in changing a culture by order, as well as the unintended consequences that can result from doing so.[14]

Like with Arianna, there was no single event that led the author to feeling burnt out during the first quarter of 2021. It was the result of feeling like he had an unmanageable workload every day for weeks at a time with unreasonable deadlines. There was nothing stopping him pushing back on these deadlines, and that's what he knows he should've done sooner. Fortunately, he had a very understanding manager who was eager to listen to his problems. As millennials, we value being able to have discussions about our own mental health in order to ensure that we can remain productive within our roles for a sustained period of time. We know that if we are stressed or overworked, the quality of our work decreases and so does our ability to make sound business decisions. In order to prevent burnout, it is imperative to keep lines of communications open so that anyone can easily raise a concern about their health or others.

Communication

Every company will have faced periods of prolonged adversity during its time, yet how the leaders of these companies choose to respond can vary drastically. A crisis can lead to daily or even hourly changes in approaches taken by a company. This uncertainty and state of flux can cause unease and feelings of anxiety among employees if communication is ineffective.

Communication is critical in everyday life, not just during crises. A solid communication plan for leaders, to be used during a crisis, helps people to be guided through and cope with the constant turmoil that is synonymous with crises. During times that employees crave safety most, people look for comfort, feelings of inclusion and a sense of being understood that their leaders should aim to provide.

Purpose and the 'Why'

When the going gets tough, leaders should seek to reinforce the 'why' that lies behind everyday operations. The 'why' was completely forgotten in the case of the *Challenger* disaster – it became a case of pleasing everyone's direct reports instead of pushing humanity to the next frontier. A more extreme case of enduring any 'how' with a powerful 'why' is the chilling account of Holocaust survival by Viktor Frankl in his bestseller *Man's Search for Meaning*.[15] Leaders and companies have to emphasise the 'why' even more during a crisis to help their employees endure any 'how.' Purpose helps act as a guiding principle for decision making and allows employees (particularly junior millennials who are often far removed from strategic discussions) to better understand leaders' decisions. Reinforcing the 'why' is also imperative in keeping teams feeling like, well, teams. A common sense of purpose and goal-orientation can help act as the social glue that binds a team together, many can feel isolated without a sense of purpose (both physically and mentally). This has unfortunately been a clear con of the potent combination of COVID lockdowns and working from home.

Millennials value the 'why' of a company very highly. They want to work for a company that aligns with their values – arguably more than any other generation prior to them. Having a lasting positive impact on the world, such as addressing climate change, is high on the majority of millennials' minds inside and outside of work. Millennials like ourselves also value open and honest communication highly, even more than older generations. A study stated that millennials strive for brutal honesty from others and expect this from their employers, too.[16] Open conversation also helps address inefficiencies. We have both worked in numerous junior positions at companies where we would complete a piece of work and then discover that another department had already solved that problem months ago. This is not only incredibly frustrating, but also demoralising due to the wasted time, and can contribute towards burnout.

Positive but Realistic

Should leaders' communications during crises focus solely on positive affirmations in an attempt to create a more reassuring environment? Studies suggest that when people focus solely on – and seek only – positive affirmation, they deceive their minds into believing that they have already reached their goal and consequently begin reducing their efforts.[17] A 'fake it until you make it' sort of approach can lead to leaders alienating employees who perceive them to have lost touch with reality as leaders seem to believe that the problem is already solved.

The Stockdale Paradox, coined by Jim Collins in his book *Good to Great*, contains wisdom as to how leaders can manage crisis communication.[18] The Stockdale Paradox states that if you retain absolute faith in completion of your task and are realistic in terms of your expectations, you can and will prevail in the end (even in the face of ever-growing difficulties). Simply put, the paradox describes the combination of confidence and realism, or "bounded optimism."[19] Both authors have worked under inspiring managers who have clearly communicated their vision and goal, but they made no illusion that the journey itself will be an easy one. This led to both of us – and the team – to rise to the challenge. Leaders with unbounded optimism, or excessive confidence, can actually deter people from bringing them the brutal facts, as well as demotivate their employees due to a perceived loss of reality and credibility of the leader.[20] As Churchill famously said upon reflection of the Second World War:

> There is no worse mistake in public leadership than to hold out false hopes soon to be swept away. The British people can face peril or misfortune with fortitude and buoyancy, but they bitterly resent being deceived or finding that those responsible for their affairs are themselves living in a fool's paradise.[21]

As the UK government's responses to the COVID crisis have shown, people begin to distrust leaders who continually fail to deliver on their rose-tinted promises, which in turn can cause confusion that exacerbates crises.[22] On the other hand, New Zealand's response to the first year of the COVID crisis has been lauded by many as exceptional, quoted in some cases as the best response of any government.[23] New Zealand's success was arguably in its ability to create a strong social identity which binds both leaders and followers in focussed efforts to tackle pressing issues, whilst being realistic about the extreme measures they felt were needed for the greater good of the collective.[24] There are many factors that played into New Zealand's favour in being able to address the crisis relative to other countries: geographical remoteness, low population size and low population density. Nonetheless, New Zealand's response is a great example of a leader showing 'bounded optimism' and successfully addressing eudemonic wellbeing. As exemplified by New Zealand's response to COVID, leaders can be more effective if they convey confidence in their ability to find a way out of the crisis and also simultaneously recognise the hardship and uncertainty that comes with crises. In times of crisis people's minds first turn to their own basic needs like their own health and the safety of their family.[25] These basic needs become more pronounced because people crave psychological safety so that they can freely discuss concerns during tumultuous times without fear of repercussions. This allows teams and companies to have healthy debates about how best to address the situation and move forward.

Before expecting employees to perform at their fullest, leaders need to understand employees' anxieties, frustrations and motivations in order to support them. Leaders must prioritise connections and meet their people where they are, rather than where they want them to be.

Communication in the New Working Environment

As mentioned earlier, the COVID pandemic has added an additional layer of complexity for leaders that few crises have presented before: the work-from-home environment. In

April 2020 in the UK, 46.6% of employed people did some work at home; 86% of those who did, did so as a result of COVID.[26] Although many leaders generally have pooh-poohed the idea of allowing employees to work from home forever, many have seen benefits in allowing greater flexibility in terms of where and when employees work. Almost half of the participants from a study in the UK believed there would be a permanent change to their employers' flexible working approach once lockdown ends.[27] However, it would be hard to argue that face-to-face meetings with clients, colleagues, shareholders and others are not of more benefit than an online meeting. Therefore COVID may not have been the catalyst for the death of the office as we know it, but it could see the normalisation of flexi-working arrangements for companies going forward.

There are generally two broad categories of home and office relationships that employees fall into, both of which will affect people's wellbeing:

- *Segmenters*: individuals who set up clear physical and non-physical barriers between their work and home lives.
- *Integrators*: individuals who allow their work life to mix with their home life, and vice versa.

Segmenters find it far easier to 'switch off' outside of work due to the clear mental and physical boundaries that they have created for themselves. By contrast, integrators are happy to let their work life mix with their home life. This can result in less negative reactions when work life conflicts with home life, and vice versa. Integrators place themselves at higher risk of burnout if they are unable to 'switch off' from their roles at the end of the day. Most are subconsciously a blend of segmenters and integrators. Research suggests that segmenters may actually cause themselves more stress than integrators due to their desire to have clear and regimented separation of their work and home lives.[28] With this new norm come both challenges and benefits, which leaders have begun to address. Stories of employees becoming increasingly overwhelmed and feeling the need to be constantly plugged in at home are disturbingly common. The expectation of being constantly contactable and responsive became the norm for many as their social lives became severely restricted through repeated national lockdowns. Having an honest conversation about this topic opens up the possibilities for individuals to clearly define where their boundaries lie. People should be mindful of their own boundaries, whilst leaders should be respectful of these boundaries. This can lead to less stress and absenteeism whilst boosting their productivity and loyalty to the team and to the company.

Wellbeing Post-Crisis

It is clear that wellbeing is – or should – be a key focus for companies in times of crisis. However, should leaders continue to enthusiastically focus on wellbeing post-crisis? Should there be a growing proactive approach to wellbeing post-crisis, rather than a reactive stance when a crisis happens?

Compassionomics, a term coined by physicians Trzeckiak and Mazzarelli, and title of their best-selling book, explores the idea that compassion ("empathy in action") is crucial in healthcare in order to reduce mortality. They note that being compassionate is not only the right thing to do, but also measurably better for employees' wellbeing, and in this case, survival rates. They describe the health sector as being in a "crisis of compassion," and that as little as forty seconds of compassion can save a life, reduce the effects of burnout and reduce costs in healthcare.[29] Other studies have also shown how helping others can help you, albeit that a person has to have a genuine desire to help rather than a forced one.[30] This is sometimes referred to as the 'helper high'. Expressing empathy produces effects that calm us in the moment and act to strengthen our long-term sustainability, reducing the likelihood of burnout. So not only do others benefit from a person's empathy, but that person benefits too.[31]

Humans are largely products of their environment, so creating the right working environment and giving the right tools to them is becoming increasingly crucial. Given the amount of time people spend at work, effective leadership will play a large role in our daily attitude. For example, studies have found that if a junior physician's mentor shows a lack of compassion in their daily work with patients, then the junior physicians will learn to do the same.[32] This is because humans are hard-wired to replicate emotional cues: when someone conveys negative or positive emotions, this is likely to be reciprocated by others. Therefore, it is of grave importance that compassion and empathy are not only shown, but are also made a priority for managers. Not only is it for the benefit of the employees, but it also can be of huge financial benefit to companies. A controlled trial conducted by the US National Institute of Mental Health offered additional telephone outreach, care management and optional psychotherapy to depressed workers in large national corporations. This trial found that after twelve months, the additional wellbeing support significantly improved depression outcomes for workers, employee retention rates and hours worked among the employed.[33] This is clearly of benefit to the workers, their companies and their leaders alike.

Compassion is tied in closely with the final component of wellbeing mentioned earlier: social wellbeing. A warm smile, a good catchup or a sincere compliment can completely re-energise people, especially when they are feeling down. Leaders affect the wellbeing of their teams, both inside and outside of the office. Inside the office leaders must strive to foster positive relationships between themselves and their teammates, as well as among team members themselves, through social events or catch ups. Leaders can also positively affect a team's social wellbeing outside of the office by encouraging them to leave on time (or early) throughout the week so that teammates can maintain their relationships outside of the office, or by sending emails on Monday morning instead of over the weekend.

Leaders need to consider if more should be done than the bare minimum to address their employees' wellbeing after a crisis. Evidence has increasingly shown that addressing employees' wellbeing has led to better business and social outcomes. The current approach to wellbeing is largely reactive rather than preventative, which we hope to see more companies push for in the future in order to better employees' wellbeing.

Summary

There are multiple components comprising an individual's wellbeing which need to be addressed by leaders in order to inspire individuals to do their best at work, regardless of whether or not there is a crisis. Creating a good culture and effectively communicating this during times of crisis can help foster an environment that is conducive to wellbeing, benefitting both leaders and their employees.

Wellbeing shouldn't just be a focus of leaders during times of crisis; it should instead be an integral part of a companies' identity. This message of wellbeing has to be effectively communicated by leaders and embodied in their companies' culture. Companies need leaders who understand this, who are emotionally intelligent, who can communicate effectively and who prioritise the wellbeing of their people. Modern leaders should prioritise conversations about mental health, help everyone's jobs be more enjoyable, create a sense of team and genuinely trust their colleagues. Prioritising people does not mean leaders have to sacrifice profits; prioritising people's wellbeing has been shown to improve profitability in the long run. It is promising to see so many leaders and companies understand and act on this due to the unfortunate circumstances brought about by the most recent crises and we hope it continues to do so long after.

We believe that the transition of companies and leaders moving from where they are today to a culture that prioritises its employees wellbeing is inevitable, and many have already begun on this journey. Those who fall behind may struggle to attract the talent that they so desperately want. Crises can often act as catalysts for long-term, fundamental change. In these unfortunate circumstances, wellbeing has hopefully been escalated up the priority list for many leaders.

Notes

1 'Wellness industry statistics and facts', *Global Wellness Institute,* https://globalwellnessinstitute.org/press-room/statistics-and-facts/
2 'Poor mental health costs UK employers up to £45 billion a year', *Deloitte,* 22 January 2020, https://www2.deloitte.com/uk/en/pages/press-releases/articles/poor-mental-health-costs-uk-employers-up-to-pound-45-billion-a-year.html
3 J. Moss (2019), 'When passion leads to burnout', *Harvard Business Review,* 1 July 2019, https://hbr.org/2019/07/when-passion-leads-to-burnout
4 Z. Bernard (2019), 'Jeff Bezos' advice to Amazon employees is to stop aiming for work-life "balance"', *Business Insider,* 9 January 2019, https://www.businessinsider.com/jeff-bezos-work-life-balance-debilitating-phrase-career-circle-2021-7?r=US&IR=T
5 'Financial Well-being in the workplace: A way forward', *Financial Advice Working Group for HM Treasury and the Financial Conduct Authority,* March 2017, www.fca.org.uk/publication/research/fawg-financial-well-being-workplace.pdf
6 J. Pfeffer (2018), 'The overlooked essentials of employee well-being' https://www.mckinsey.com/business-functions/people-and-organizational-performance/our-insights/the-overlooked-essentials-of-employee-well-being; C. Spell and T. Arnold (2007), 'An appraisal of justice, structure, and job control as antecedents of psychological distress', *Journal of Organizational Behavior,* 28(6), 729–751.
7 M. Baker (2020), '9 Future of work trends post Covid 19', *Gartner,* June 8, 2020, www.gartner.com/smarterwithgartner/9-future-of-work-trends-post-covid-19/
8 C. Leitch (2016), 'The devastating effects of micromanagement', *Career Addict,* 11 February 2016, www.careeraddict.com/the-devastating-effects-of-micromanagement
9 'The 2020 UK workplace stress survey', *Perkbox,* www.perkbox.com/uk/resources/library/2020-workplace-stress-survey
10 A. M. Zotti, G. Omarini, and P. Ragazzoni (2008), 'Can the type of organisational structure affect individual well-being in health and social welfare occupations?' *Giornale italiano di medicina del lavoro ed ergonomia,* 30(1 Suppl A), A44–A51.
11 'ICD-11 for Mortality and Morbidity Statistics', The WHO, Version: 05/2021, Chapter 24, Section QD85 https://icd.who.int/browse11/l-m/en#/http://id.who.int/icd/entity/129180281
12 S. Tottle (2016), 'It's costing the global economy £255 billion, so what can we do to stop workplace burnout?' *World Economic Forum,* 31 October 2016, www.weforum.org/agenda/2016/10/workplace-burnout-can-you-do-anything-about-it
13 B. Wigert and S. Agrawal (2018), 'Employee burnout, part 1: The 5 main causes', *Gallop,* 12 July 2018, www.gallup.com/workplace/237059/employee-burnout-part-main-causes.aspx
14 D. Okat and E. Vasudevan (2021), *Going the extra mile: What taxi rides tell us about the long-hour culture in finance,* SSRN, *https://papers.ssrn.com/sol3/papers.cfm?abstract_id=3810864*
15 V. Frankl,(1963), Man's search for meaning: An introduction to logotherapy, New York, NY: Washington Square Press.
16 'Meet the Millenials', *KPMG,* June 2017, https://home.kpmg/content/dam/kpmg/uk/pdf/2017/04/Meet-the-Millennials-Secured.pdf

17 A. Gollwitzer, G. Oettingen, T. Kirby, A. Duckworth, and D. Mayer (2011), 'Mental contrasting facilitates academic performance in school children', *Motivation and Emotion*, 35, 403–412.; G. Oettingen and T. A. Wadden (1991), 'Expectation, fantasy, and weight loss: Is the impact of positive thinking always positive?' *Cognitive Therapy and Research*, 15(2), 167–175.

18 B. Groysberg and R. Abrahams (2020), 'What the Stockdale paradox tells Us about crisis leadership', *Harvard Business School Working Knowledge*, 17 August 2020, https://hbswk.hbs.edu/item/what-the-stockdale-paradox-tells-us-about-crisis-leadership; Collins, J. (2001), *Good to Great*. London, England: Random House Business Books.

19 G. D'Auria and A. De Smet (2020), 'Leadership in a crisis: Responding to the coronavirus outbreak and future challenges', 16 March 2020, www.mckinsey.com/business-functions/organization/our-insights/leadership-in-a-crisis-responding-to-the-coronavirus-outbreak-and-future-challenges

20 Ibid.

21 W. Churchill (1986), *The hinge of fate*. Houghton Mifflin Harcourt, 125 High St, Boston, MA 02110.

22 'The UK government's handling of the coronavirus crisis: public perceptions', 6 December 2020, www.kcl.ac.uk/policy-institute/assets/the-handling-of-the-coronavirus-crisis.pdf

23 M. Farrer (2020), 'New Zealand's Covid-19 response the best in the world, say global business leaders', 8 October 2020, www.theguardian.com/world/2020/oct/08/new-zealands-covid-19-response-the-best-in-the-world-say-global-business-leaders

24 S. Haslam and S. Reicher (2016), 'Rethinking the psychology of leadership: From personal identity to social identity', *Daedalus*, 145, 21–34.

25 D'Auria and De Smet, 'Leadership in a crisis.'

26 'Coronavirus and the latest indicators for the UK economy and society', Office of National Statistics, April 2021, https://www.ons.gov.uk/employmentandlabourmarket/peopleinwork/employmentandemployeetypes/bulletins/coronavirusandhomeworkingintheuk/april2020

27 'A flexible future: Brits expected to call time on office life after lockdown', O2 the Blue, 6 May 2020, https://news.o2.co.uk/press-release/a-flexible-future-brits-expected-to-call-time-on-office-life-after-lockdown/#_ftn1

28 B. Smit, P. Maloney, C. Maertz, and T. Montag-Smit (2016), 'Out of sight, out of mind? How and when cognitive role transition episodes influence employee performance', *Human Relations*, 69(11), 2141–2168.; D. Burkus (2016), 'Research: Keeping work and life separate is more trouble than it's worth', *Harvard Business Review*, 9 August 2016, https://hbr.org/2016/08/research-keeping-work-and-life-separate-is-more-trouble-than-its-worth?registration=success

29 S. Trzeciak (2018), 'How 40 Seconds of Compassion Could Save a Life', *TEDxPen*, https://www.youtube.com/watch?v=elW69hyPUuI

30 A. McKee and K. Wein (2017), 'Prevent burnout by making compassion a habit', *Harvard Business Review*, 11 May 2017, https://hbr.org/2017/05/prevent-burnout-by-making-compassion-a-habit?ab=at_articlepage_recommendedarticles_bottom1x1

31 *Ibid.*

32 S. Trzeciak, A. Mazzarelli and C. Booker, (2019), *Compassionomics: The revolutionary scientific evidence that caring makes a difference*, Pensacola, FL: Studer Group

33 P. S. Wang, MD, DrPH, G. E. Simon, MD, MPH, and R. C. Kessler, PhD (2008), 'Making the business case for enhanced depression care: The national institute of mental health-Harvard work outcomes research and cost-effectiveness study', *Journal of Occupational and Environmental Medicine*, 50(4), 468–475.

Bibliography

'Coronavirus and the latest indicators for the UK economy and society', *Office of National Statistics*, April 2021, https://www.ons.gov.uk/employmentandlabourmarket/peopleinwork/employmentandemployeetypes/bulletins/coronavirusandhomeworkingintheuk/april2020

'A flexible future: Brits expected to call time on office life after lockdown', *O2 the Blue*, 6 May 2020, https://news.o2.co.uk/press-release/a-flexible-future-brits-expected-to-call-time-on-office-life-after-lockdown/#_ftn1

'Financial Well-being in the workplace: A way forward', *Financial Advice Working Group for HM Treasury and the Financial Conduct Authority*, March 2017, www.fca.org.uk/publication/research/fawg-financial-well-being-workplace.pdf

'Meet the Millennials', *KPMG*, June 2017, https://home.kpmg/content/dam/kpmg/uk/pdf/2017/04/Meet-the-Millennials-Secured.pdf

'Poor mental health costs UK employers up to £45 billion a year', *Deloitte*, 22 January 2020, https://www2.deloitte.com/uk/en/pages/press-releases/articles/poor-mental-health-costs-uk-employers-up-to-pound-45-billion-a-year.html

'The UK government's handling of the coronavirus crisis: Public perceptions', 6 December 2020, www.kcl.ac.uk/policy-institute/assets/the-handling-of-the-coronavirus-crisis.pdf

'The 2020 UK workplace stress survey', *Perkbox*, www.perkbox.com/uk/resources/library/2020-workplace-stress-survey

'Wellness industry statistics and facts', *Global Wellness Institute*, https://globalwellnessinstitute.org/press-room/statistics-and-facts/

Baker, M. (2020), '9 Future of work trends post Covid 19', *Gartner*, June 8, 2020, www.gartner.com/smarterwithgartner/9-future-of-work-trends-post-covid-19/

Bernard, Z. (2019), 'Jeff Bezos' advice to Amazon employees is to stop aiming for work-life "balance"', *Business Insider*, 9 January 2019, www.businessinsider.com/jeff-bezo-advice-to-amazon-employees-dont-aim-for-work-life-balance-its-a-circle-2018–4?r=US&IR=T

Burkus, D. (2016), 'Research: Keeping work and life separate is more trouble than it's worth', *Harvard Business Review*, 9 August 2016, https://hbr.org/2016/08/research-keeping-work-and-life-separate-is-more-trouble-than-its-worth?registration=success

Churchill, W. (1986), *The hinge of fate*, Houghton Mifflin Harcourt, 125 High St, Boston, MA 02110.

Collins, J. (2001), *Good to great*, Random House Business Book, England

D'Auria, G., and De Smet, A. (2020), 'Leadership in a crisis: Responding to the coronavirus outbreak and future challenges', www.mckinsey.com/business-functions/organization/our-insights/leadership-in-a-crisis-responding-to-the-coronavirus-outbreak-and-future-challenges

Farrer, M. (2020), 'New Zealand's Covid-19 response the best in the world, say global business leaders', 8 October 2020, www.theguardian.com/world/2020/oct/08/new-zealands-covid-19-response-the-best-in-the-world-say-global-business-leaders

Frankl, V. (1963), *Man's search for meaning: An introduction to logotherapy*, New York, NY: Washington Square Press.

Groysberg, B., and Abrahams, R. (2020), 'What the Stockdale paradox tells Us about crisis leadership', *Harvard Business School Working Knowledge*, 17 August 2020, https://hbswk.hbs.edu/item/what-the-stockdale-paradox-tells-us-about-crisis-leadership

Gollwitzer, A., Oettingen, G., Kirby, T., Duckworth, A., and Mayer, D. (2011), 'Mental contrasting facilitates academic performance in school children', *Motivation and Emotion*, 35, 403–412.

Haslam, S., and Reicher, S. (2016), 'Rethinking the psychology of leadership: From personal identity to social identity', *Daedalus*, 145, 21–34.

Leitch, C. (2016), 'The devastating effects of micromanagement', *Career Addict*, 11 February 2016, www.careeraddict.com/the-devastating-effects-of-micromanagement

Lyubomirsky, S., King, L., and Diener, E. (2005), 'The benefits of frequent positive affect: Does happiness lead to success?' *Psychological Bulletin*, 131(6), 803–855.

McKee, A., and Wein, K. (2017), 'Prevent burnout by making compassion a habit', *Harvard Business Review*, 11 May 2017, https://hbr.org/2017/05/prevent-burnout-by-making-compassion-a-habit?ab=at_articlepage_recommendedarticles_bottom1x1

Moss, J. (2019), 'When passion leads to burnout', *Harvard Business Review*, 1 July 2019, https://hbr.org/2019/07/when-passion-leads-to-burnout

Oettingen, G., and Wadden, T. A. (1991), 'Expectation, fantasy, and weight loss: Is the impact of positive thinking always positive?' *Cognitive Therapy and Research*, 15(2), 167–175.

Okat, D., and Vasudevan, E. (2021), *Going the extra mile: What taxi rides tell Us about the long-hour culture in finance*. SSRN, *https://papers.ssrn.com/sol3/papers.cfm?abstract_id=3810864*

Pfeffer, J. (2018), 'The overlooked essentials of employee well-being' https://www.mckinsey.com/business-functions/people-and-organizational-performance/our-insights/the-overlooked-essentials-of-employee-well-being

Smit, B., Maloney, P., Maertz, C., and Montag-Smit, T. (2016), 'Out of sight, out of mind? How and when cognitive role transition episodes influence employee performance', *Human Relations*, 69(11), 2141–2168.

Spell, C., and Arnold, T. (2007), 'An appraisal of justice, structure, and job control as antecedents of psychological distress', *Journal of Organizational Behavior*, 28(6), 729–751.

Trzeciak, S., Mazzarelli, A., and Booker, C. (2019), *Compassionomics: The revolutionary scientific evidence that caring makes a difference*. Pensacola, FL: Studer Group

Trzeciak, S. (2018), 'How 40 Seconds of Compassion Could Save a Life', *TEDxPen,* https://www. youtube.com/watch?v=elW69hyPUuI

Tottle, S. (2016), 'It's costing the global economy £255 billion, so what can we do to stop workplace burnout?' *World Economic Forum*, 31 October 2016, www.weforum.org/agenda/2016/10/workplace-burnout-can-you-do-anything-about-it

Wang, P. S. MD, DrPH., Simon, G. E. MD, MPH, and Kessler, R. C. PhD. (2008), 'Making the business case for enhanced depression care: The national institute of mental health-Harvard work outcomes research and cost-effectiveness study', *Journal of Occupational and Environmental Medicine*, 50(4), 468–475.

Wigert, B., and Agrawal, S. (2018), 'Employee burnout, part 1: The 5 main causes', *Gallop*, 12 July 2018, www.gallup.com/workplace/237059/employee-burnout-part-main-causes.aspx

Zotti, A. M., Omarini, G., and Ragazzoni, P. (2008), 'Can the type of organisational structure affect individual well-being in health and social welfare occupations?' *Giornale italiano di medicina del lavoro ed ergonomia*, 30(1 Suppl A), A44–A51.

20 Dynamic Amidst Change

Exploring the Roles of Millennials and Gen Zs

Karl Moore and Lauren Kirigin

***

Karl's parents grew up during the Depression. It left an indelible mark on them. His mother, to her dying day, would turn off every light as she left a room, not to save money at that point in her life, but as a result of having grown up during a time of need. Hopefully, we will not undergo the kind of economic recession his parents and those of countless others experienced almost a century ago. However, members of Generation Z, those born from 1997–2012, will almost certainly have their worldview shaped by this current crisis to a considerable degree.

Every generation is influenced by the unique set of circumstances of its time. Informed by historical context and endured experiences, the cohort builds a perspective different from those preceding it.

The literature suggests that the end of high school, time spent at university, and our early work years tend to shape our worldview significantly (Arnett, 2004). This period following adolescence is one of exploration and self-discovery. While our views continue to evolve after that, this time of emerging adulthood acts as a critical foundation for the remainder of much of our lives. We can look to those at the center of this pivotal point of learning to understand the shared mindsets of the younger generation.

For the last decade, Karl – and more recently with Lauren's help – has been conducting research on Generation Z. We reference insights obtained from the literature and from undergraduate college students, aged between 18 and 24, from his time at Oxford and McGill universities, to understand their perception of careers, business and leadership. In his forthcoming book, *It's OK, Boomer: How to Effectively Work With Millennials/Generation Z*, a generational distinction is made between the modern and postmodern worldviews. Modernism is the worldview of university-educated Boomers. It involved challenging many social norms surrounding religion, politics, sexuality, and art. Contrastingly, Millennials and Generation Zs have grown up with a postmodern worldview. There are multiple descriptions of what postmodernism entails. Most generally, it describes the movements which both arise from and reject trends in modernism (Heartney, 2001).

Our reaction to medical care is an excellent example of the modern and postmodern worldviews and attitudes in everyday life. For moderns, doctors are largely considered to be infallible experts whose extensive education and training support the legitimacy of diagnoses – they were not to be questioned. For post-moderns, a doctor's word is no longer taken at face value. Patients often conduct their own research, challenge their doctor's verdict, and seek additional advice from other medical practitioners in order to be satisfied. This illustrates a shift in hierarchy between the individual and established system. The apparent challenge of authority and distrust in the established system is a result of the openness of

DOI: 10.4324/9781003171737-22

information made possible by the technological advancements which have occurred over the course of the past few decades.

Boomers often shake their heads when they discuss the younger generation and their aspirations. If you have been taught at college that your ideas have as much value as those in authority, then you take this belief with you to your next step. In your career, you might be more ready to challenge your boss than those of the previous generations would have been at the same age. If you were taught in a post-truth world that truth or race is a social construct to a considerable degree, then you will have a flexible understanding of what is considered to be the truth. Although what we are taught cannot stand alone, it is supported – and often accentuated – by what we experience.

For someone who grew up during the Great Depression, this experience would have left an undeniable mark on their views and behaviors. Uneasy from the prospect of reliving another recession, they might be hardwired to focus on preservation, always saving for a time of need. Current generations have not had to undergo the severe kind of economic recession experienced by countless individuals almost a century ago. However, each will certainly have their own worldview shaped by the current health crisis to a similar degree.

Someone who graduated from post-graduate studies in the late 1970s entered the workforce into a period of prosperity across the United States, Canada, and Western Europe. Everybody in the graduating class would have multiple job offers. Companies would be desperate enough for new recruits to extend multiple offers at various divisions, needing to fuel the team to capitalize on emergent growth. Joining their company of choice, the good times rolled on. By the time there was any real financial crisis, with the next one rolling around in the early '90s, most Baby Boomers occupied reasonably safe positions. Consistent wage growth created a faith in corporate culture and an ability to build a solid adult life. Individuals believed in the application of their talent, and that the capitalist system would reward hard work. All in all, this formed a fairly sunny view of the world. While not everyone benefited from such luck, in much of the Western world, the early careers of Baby Boomers were marked by good times. This formative experience largely had an effect on the generation's shared worldview for the rest of their working lives. In spite of encountered difficulties along the road, this optimistic view of a benign world persisted from early experiences, regardless of the ups and downs.

For Millennials, the scenario is quite different. Much of the generation is entering a new life period. Still, they remain unable to satisfy the traditional milestones of adulthood (Lowrey, 2021). Affording a house in current market valuations while growing savings for retirement seems a far-off dream. While not as prominent of an issue for the Millennial top 10%, those who are not a part of this group are even further behind. Researchers of the St. Louis Fed found that the average Millennial without a college degree has almost 20% less wealth than would be expected based on trends from previous generations. The typical older Millennial with a college degree will have a 4% shortfall from expected wealth, while older Millennials without a degree will have a shortfall closer to 19% of expectations (Hernández Kent & Ricketts, 2021). This data highlights that Millennial children are in fact not financially better off than their parents, a trend largely assumed over recent generations. This generational delay has been furthered by the pandemic, as these adults postpone buying a car, getting married, or buying their first house.

Born in the post-WWII era, Baby Boomers lived the majority of their working years in a reasonably prosperous economy. Contrastingly, many Millennials started their careers in the wake of Financial Crisis of 2008. Today, Millennials and Generation Zs face an array of challenges unfamiliar to those that came before them. Among them are financial challenges.

Rising debt is prominent, with Millennials and Generation Zs taking on an average 67.2% increase in debt from 2019 to 2020 (Visual Capitalist, 2021).

The current global pandemic is almost certainly a formative moment for younger Millennials and Zs as they navigate through similar challenges. Paul Tellier, previous Clerk of the Privy Council Office of Canada and CEO of Canadian National Railways and Bombardier, acknowledges that the impact of this seismic event has been like no other. He puts it this way: "It's global, it's the best illustration of the global village that we live in, and there is no end in sight," said Tellier (interview with Prof. Karl Moore). "This is by far the biggest crisis that we have seen in our collective lifetimes."

Generation Z's grandchildren will ask them where they were and what they did during the COVID pandemic. They will want to hear stories of the lockdown and the hardships faced. Social distancing has imposed a new lifestyle, and for essential workers in situations of precarity, that lifestyle is mired in dangers. While less at risk of developing severe forms of COVID, students and young workers have suffered disproportionately more from the pandemic's economic fallout than other groups.

The pandemic has amplified previous trends including low wages, stagnant job markets, and rising student debt. Over the course of COVID, Generation Z unemployment rates were two times greater than older generations (Visual Capitalist, 2021). For those unlucky enough to enter the workforce at this moment, graduating during a recession leads to a large loss in initial earnings. These loses, on average, amount to about 9% of annual earnings (Nesvisky, 2006). Receding slowly, losses will most likely halve within five years and only disappear ten years after graduation. Graduating in a recession can also force workers to begin their careers at smaller, lower-paying firms, as graduates search for any appropriate positions. As time goes on, they may switch jobs more frequently than those who graduated in better times, with better support from their employers, leading to the feeling of constantly playing catch-up.

Economists tell us that this recent global recession has been the worst since the Great Depression. Students explain how summer jobs, internships, and full-time positions are being cancelled or at best deferred to a later date. At this point, few organizations seem ready to commit to new hires. This is a strong contrast to the war for talent identified in 1998 by Steven Hankin of McKinsey & Company. In a *McKinsey Quarterly* article, Hankin foresaw that companies were on the verge of engaging "in a war for senior executive talent that will remain a defining characteristic of their competitive landscape for decades to come." This assertion was correct. The concept continued to gain relevance and momentum since, with the only exception caused by the financial crisis of the mid 2000s.

While some progress has been made, many firms struggle to hire and retain upcoming top talent. An increasing number of emerging adults have the importance of meaningful and satisfying work as a part of their worldview. In fact, nearly 35% of Millennials plan to look for a new job with a different employer once the pandemic is no longer an issue, relative to 25% of Gen Xers, and only 10% of Boomers (Stoller, 2021). Corporate culture and role fulfillment are cited as being significant factors according to Prudential, Pulse of the American Worker Survey, conducted by Morning Consult in May 2021. Not as prominent in prior generations, organizations must be aware of the importance of these characteristics.

The urgent need to integrate the ideas and experiences of Millennials, and now Generation Zs, will continue to influence this next period. They bring technological expertise, a willingness to reinvent what has come before them, a youthful energy, and flexibility that breathes new life into organizations. Professors have seen it first-hand in their classrooms, while newly graduated students have lived it. This past year especially has highlighted the importance of recruiting diverse, new talent. The global pandemic and its aftermath call for flexibility, agility, and resilience of the younger generations.

Yet, the response to the pandemic has accentuated a distrust in leadership and established systems. Many feel that imposed measures fail to target core sources of concern and all and all, have been poorly handled. Elsa Pilichowski, leader of the Organization for Economic Cooperation and Development (OECD) Directorate of Public Governance, explains how the younger generation's confidence in public institutions and their perception of having political influence and representation in decision-making has stalled (Cocco, 2020). The OECD shows that trust in government among young people has been declining across the developed world since 2016. According to Naumi Haque, senior vice-president of research at Ipsos, "Gen Z and millennials are more likely to feel like things in their country are out of control right now than older generations" (Cocco, 2020). This deepened political disenchantment further solidifies the growing distrust in leadership.

It is expected that the mental health impact of the pandemic will outlast the virus itself. Studies conducted by public health specialists in the United States and UK show that those aged 18–29 experienced higher levels of distress compared to other age groups during this period (Cocco, 2020). Not only significant, but the rise in depression and anxiety related to pandemic uncertainty has proven to be consistently worse than expected. Since April 2020, in any given month, young adults have been experiencing the lowest levels of mental health (Kwok, 2021). A report from the US Centers for Disease Control and Prevention found that anxiety symptoms have tripled while those of depression have quadrupled relative to a representative 2019 sample (Wallis, 2020). These CDC findings show that 62.9% of the young adult group report symptoms of the aforementioned. The gravity of these findings creates a need to examine the impact of pandemic-related stressors. In order to create targeted resources, we must look to understand the influences creating such responses. Roxane Cohen Silver, a psychologist at the University of California, Irvine, explains how this demographic in particular has seen significant disruption in life milestones (Wallis, 2020). The interruption of key transitional periods such as graduation, senior year, and entering the workforce – coupled with a lack of much needed social connection – has fueled this experienced sentiment.

The *Financial Times* conducted a global survey regarding the lives and expectations for those younger than the age of 35 in the aftermath of the pandemic. For respondent Killian Mangan, who graduated during the pandemic and struggled to find a job, it feels as though "we are drowning in insecurity with no help in sight" (O'Connor, 2021).

Young professionals are required to position themselves in a fast-evolving landscape. With intense competition, there is a strong need to differentiate among an increasingly skilled workforce. Job insecurity remains high and many are on edge. This sense of unease, combined with housing and education becoming more expensive, jobs being more competitive, pensions being less adequate and the environment being at risk, is disheartening. Around the world, individuals feel insecure about their future, believing they will be worse off than their parents across professional and financial dimensions (O'Connor, 2021). Responses show that these challenges have translated into growing resentment toward older generations, which are both better off – holding more economic power than Millennials and Generation Zs combined – and continue to hold more political sway.

In another light, the pandemic has brought new social elements into the mix. Younger generations hold disproportionately more cultural power than their counterparts. Fueled by digital platforms, technology has allowed anyone to speak their truth directly to billions of people. It has changed who controls the narrative shared by the media, and brought attention to critical issues in our society. In the chaos of the pandemic emerged opportunity. We can consider it a chance to explore what we want out of life and re-evaluate the directions we are taking to create the future we want to see. In the simplification of the values that will really matter for this next chapter, Generation Z is the focus on this change and will be driving it to become the new normal in organizations. This disruption is the democratization of voices needed to build inclusive and resilient societies.

The world is faced by huge challenges beyond the current global pandemic, including climate change, growing inequality, and an economic recession. The burden of addressing these challenges will fall on everyone, but particularly Generation Z. The next couple of years will be the time for older generations, the Baby Boomers and established Millennials to lean in to support, help, and promote Generation Z, so that they can come out of this crisis with an inspired worldview – one that will provide them the courage and the wisdom to take on these global challenges and create a better world for their children. Now is the time for sacrifice and community, and to understand the context and influences which have shaped generational experiences. Otherwise, throughout all these pressures, it is possible that the younger generation will end up with a negative view of the world with a desire to just get by and not to courageously confront the problems the world needs them to face. Older generations will soon not have the energy, strength, or ability to tackle the problems of a modern world.

Preparing for the future will require leadership to reflect the upcoming generations. Organizations must acknowledge the most pressing issues and empower those who understand them most. By integrating ideas and learning from the insights of the emerging generations, firms will be closer to the underlying changes and more comfortable with adapting. Comfortable with pivoting, these organizations will be ready to navigate inevitable uncertainties. Mintzberg's idea of emergent strategy vs. Porter's more deliberate strategy is a debate that both resonates with the turbulent times we live in and the expectations of Generation Zs to be listened to and respected for their insights. Deliberate strategy tends to be more top-down. Hierarchical in nature, the CEO and their senior team informs the rest of the organization of the newest developments from their three-day strategy getaway with BCG or McKinsey. In a highly uncertain, turbulent, and volatile world, deliberate strategy seems to be preeminent. This is where leadership must still decide the final strategy based on considerable input from those who are boundary spanners, those with one foot in the organization and one foot in the ever-changing world – young people. Not only do they provide feedback, but they are also encouraged to frugally innovate and see what works, not only in theory, but in practice with today's – not yesterday's – stakeholders. Listening to Generation Z and younger Millennials becomes central to how the C-suite can find the winning strategy for the way forward.

Now is the time to think long term.

References

Arnett, J. J. (2004). *Emerging Adulthood: The Winding Road from the Late Teens though the Twenties*. Oxford: Oxford University Press.

Cocco, F. (2020, November 17). The Kids Aren't Alright: How Generation Covid is Losing Out. *The Financial Times*. Retrieved from www.ft.com/content/0dec0291-2f72-4ce9-bd9f-ae2356bd869e

Hankin, S. (1998). The War for Talent. *The McKinsey Quarterly*, 3(46).

Heartney, E. (2001). *Postmodernism*. Cambridge: Cambridge University Press.

Hernández Kent, A., & Ricketts, L. R. (2021, April 1). Disparities by Race, Ethnicity and Education Underlie Millennials' Comeback in Wealth. *Federal Reserve Bank of St. Louis*. Retrieved from www.stlouisfed.org/on-the-economy/2021/april/disparities-race-education-millennials-comeback-wealth

Kwok, N. (2021, June 15). Who Suffers the Most When it Comes to Pandemic-Related Stress? Look Closely at the Data. *The Globe and Mail*. Retrieved from www.theglobeandmail.com/business/careers/leadership/article-who-suffers-the-most-when-it-comes-to-pandemic-related-stress-look/

Lowrey, A. (2021, May 13). Why Millennials Can't Grow Up. *The Atlantic*. Retrieved from www.theatlantic.com/ideas/archive/2021/05/millennial-grandparents-unequal-generation/618859/

Mintzberg, H. (1994, January–February). The Fall and Rise of Strategic Planning. *Harvard Business Review*. Retrieved from https://hbr.org/1994/01/the-fall-and-rise-of-strategic-planning

Nesvisky, M. (2006, November 11). The Career Effects of Graduating in a Recession. *National Bureau of Economic Research*. Retrieved from www.nber.org/digest/nov06/career-effects-graduating-recession

O'Connor, S. (2021, April 25). 'We Are Drowning in Insecurity': Young People and Life after the Pandemic. *The Financial Times*. Retrieved from www.ft.com/content/77d586cc-4f3f-4701-a104-d09136c93d44

Porter, M. E. (1980). Industry Structure and Competitive Strategy: Keys to Profitability. *Financial Analysts Journal*, *36*(4).

Stoller, K. (2021, April 6). One Third of Millennials Plan to Quit Their Jobs After the Pandemic – Here's Why, and What Employers Can Do. *Forbes*. Retrieved from www.forbes.com/sites/kristinstoller/2021/04/06/one-third-of-millennials-plan-to-quit-their-jobs-after-the-pandemic-heres-why-and-what-employers-can-do/?sh=247cf0e85803

Visual Capitalist. (2021). *The Generational Power Index Report 2021*. Canada: Visual Capitalist.

Wallis, C. (2020, December 1). Who Suffers the Most When it Comes to Pandemic-Related Stress? Look Closely at the Data. *Scientific American*. Retrieved from www.scientificamerican.com/article/the-surprising-mental-toll-of-covid/

Index

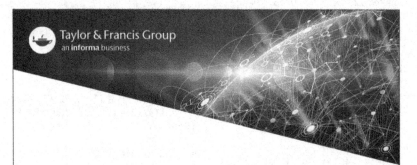